How Fibber McGee AND Molly Won World War II

To Neil White
Fellow author + a
credit to the field.
Good luck
Mickey Smith
2010

BY MICKEY C. SMITH

HOW FIBBER MCGEE AND MOLLY WON WORLD WAR II
©2010 MICKEY C. SMITH

Published in the USA by:

BEARMANOR MEDIA
P.O. BOX 71426
ALBANY, GEORGIA 31708
www.BearManorMedia.com

ISBN-10: 1-59393-516-1 (alk. paper)
ISBN-13: 978-1-59393-516-0 (alk. paper)

EDITED BY LON DAVIS.

BOOK DESIGN AND LAYOUT BY VALERIE THOMPSON.

TABLE OF CONTENTS

IN WHICH I INTRODUCE A NEW PERSPECTIVE ON FIBBER MCGEE AND MOLLY FOR REGULAR FANS OF OLD-TIME RADIO, INTRODUCE THE CONCEPT OF THE BOOK TO THOSE WHO MAY HAVE HEARD OF, BUT NOT EVER HEARD THE SHOW.

IN WHICH JIM AND MARIAN JORDAN ARE INTRODUCED AS "FIBBER AND MOLLY." THE FORMAT OF THE SHOW IS DESCRIBED AND THE REGULAR CHARACTERS AND THEIR CHARACTERIZATION DESCRIBED. A PEEK OF THE SHOW IS ALSO PROVIDED.

CHAPTER 3 — THE RADIO BROADCAST ENVIRONMENT BEFORE AND DURING THE WAR . . . 46

In which I describe how the government responded to the Pearl Harbor attack in terms of use and regulations of Radio, and how Radio reacted and cooperated.

CHAPTER 4 — THE MEN BEHIND THE WORDS . . . 74

In which I provide the reader with a profile of one of Radio's great (greatest?) comedy writers, as well as that of his writing partner.

CHAPTER 5 — THE JOHNSON'S WAX PROGRAM® — THE PERFECT SPONSOR . . . **91**

IN WHICH THE EXTRAORDINARY ROLE OF THE JOHNSON'S WAX COMPANY IN SUPPORT OF THE WAR EFFORT VIA THE PROGRAM IS DESCRIBED.

PHOTOGRAPHS . . . 101

PART II — WORDS THAT WON THE WAR

CHAPTER 6 — WORDS THAT WON THE WAR . . . 117

A CHRONICLE OF THE WARTIME BROADCASTS WITH EXTENSIVE VERBATIM EXCERPTS PRESENTED ALONG WITH MY COMMENTS. OCCASIONAL CONNECTIONS WITH ACTUAL WAR EVENTS ARE INCLUDED.

EPILOGUE . . . 240

In which I comment on the changes that have occurred since World War II in the way in which Americans, the broadcast industry and commercial sponsors have come to view the country's involvement in armed conflict from Korea to Iraq.

WARTIME IMAGES:

UPPER LEFT: Author and parents.

LOWER LEFT: Author's wife and father.

ABOVE: Author ready for battle.

Dedication

To Victor V. and Lucille Smith,
Edward A. and Dorothy Hopkins.
They, too, won World War II.

PREFACE AND ACKNOWLEDGMENTS

I was just a little kid when Pearl Harbor was attacked (My third birthday was December 9, 1941). One of my first memories is of my father stopping by on his beer truck delivery route to tell us he had joined the Air Force. Of course, I had no idea of the significance at the time. Nor could I have predicted in my wildest, childish dreams that in the summer of 1945 my father would be a mechanic on a little island called Tinian working on a B-29 named *Enola Gay*.

My wife is five days younger than I. Her memories are similar, but different. Her father was in Europe with the illustrious General George S. Patton. His role in the Engineer's Corp included, among other things, both building and blowing up bridges. He got to know many German civilians and told poignant stories of sharing food with them.

I listened to a lot of radio during the War. Everyone did. My tastes ran to *Superman* and *Tom Mix*. The signal was too weak for us to hear *The Lone Ranger*. I was aware of *Fibber McGee and Molly*, but their humor and their serious messages were a little over my head.

In the two years following the War, my tastes and the programming changed, but I was still an avid fan until such classics as *Gunsmoke* finally were served up with pictures.

My interest in Old-Time Radio (OTR) as a hobby probably started when I found a phonograph record titled, *Themes Like Old Times*. It was like finding a lost friend. Then I read an article in *Time* about an organization called North American Radio Archives. I joined immediately and OTR became a full-fledged hobby. That's about all the reader needs to know about how I came to have a relatively modest collection of a couple of thousand programs.

I was able to find in my hobby applications to my "daytime job," a pharmacy professor at the University of Mississippi. That resulted in one book, *Pharmacy and Medicine on the Air*, a few "scholarly" articles in our journal, *Pharmacy in History*, and a couple in OTR publications.

So why this book? No single reason, surely, but my age and experiences of the past seventy-plus years in the United States were certainly the foundation. I strongly believe in the heritage and future of this great country and saw this book as a way to preserve one of those often-overlooked phenomena that continue to make us great.

For some readers, there should be sufficient nostalgic to justify a reading. I hope, as well, that there is enough historical content and context to provide interest to those with a broad interest in U.S. history. In any case, I sincerely hope the readers enjoy it.

It is rather a tradition in an acknowledgements statement to note that someone or something will probably have been missed. I'm sure that applies here and for omissions I am truly sorry.

Personal thanks are due to such fine people as:

- **DAVE SIEGEL**, telephone friend, cheerleader, and supplier of missing programs.

- **CHARLES STUMPF**, who provided photographs, suggestions, and some otherwise-unavailable printed matter.

- **CLAIR SCHULZ**, who also provided advice and missing programs, and without whose book, *Fibber McGee and Molly On the Air, 1935-1959*, my book would not have been possible in its present form.

- **TOM PRICE**, whom I have never met, but whose two-volume, *Fibber McGee's Closet*, was similarly indispensable to my work.

- **STEVE KREMER**, for photos and background on the *real* Kremer's Drug Store.

Help or efforts to help were also received from the following:

- **KELLY M. SEMRAU**, Vice-President — Global Public Affairs and Communication, S.C. Johnson and Sons, Inc.

- **WILLIAM D. PEREZ**, President and CEO, Wm. Wrigley Jr. Company

- **JEANNETTE BERARD**, Thousand Oaks Library

- **BLAIR VEDDER**, Glenview, Il

- **STEVE DARNELL**, *Nostalgia Digest*

- **KEITH REINHARD**, DDB

North American Radio Archives (N.A.R.A.) and SPERDVAC (Society for the Preservation and Encouragement of Radio Drama, Variety, and Comedy) have both provided hours of nostalgic pleasure, information, and publishing opportunities.

Dr. Barbara Wells, Dean of the School of Pharmacy and Dr. Donna West-Strum, Chair of the Department of Pharmacy Administration at the University of Mississippi provided much-needed assistance on a project definitely out of field.

Sheree Jones brought first apprehension (I suspect) to the task of preparing the manuscript. That was quickly replaced by enthusiasm as draft after draft appeared on her desk. Ashley Rather assisted greatly in bibliographic work.

Finally, and most important, my wife of nearly 50 years who somehow accepted my continued work on the book in spite of my repeated earlier promises that I would *not* do another book. Mary, for your patience, love, and forgiveness during this and the other twenty-seven books, I am eternally grateful as I am for all the other things you do to make our life together *wonderful.*

A word on the Reference style: For more than 30 years, I wielded a tyrannical red pencil on mistakes in form made by my graduate students on references in theses and dissertations. With myself, I have been much more lenient. In fact, I believe this method is just as effective and a lot more user friendly. I hope you agree.

And a few words of regret: Someone has written that "a book is never finished; it is only abandoned." In addition to any other shortcomings, this book would have been closer to a finish had I been able to contact members of the Quinn family for more insights into his personal views on the war. The same goes for Phil Leslie. I had an opportunity to explore this with him in a telephone conversation a number of years ago. I didn't know about this book then, and missed a wonderful opportunity. Similarly, there appear to be extant no written records concerning the decisions made by the sponsor to commit the show so thoroughly to the war effort. Without such information, I am left with the conclusion that these were all patriotic Americans, just like millions of others, who had the opportunity and the will to make an extraordinary difference.

FOREWORD
A PRESCRIPTION FOR GOOD READING AND LISTENING

The year was 1935. The entire world was in a state of turmoil. The Japanese had surprised most western nations by defeating Russia earlier in the century and were in the process of developing plans for a takeover of China, Korea, and Manchuria. In India, Hindus and Muslims alike were increasingly demanding independence from England. In Europe, the German people were becoming accustomed to the consequences of having delivered their country into the hands of the Nazi party. Crowds cheered enthusiastically when the Fuhrer, who in 1933 had became chancellor, gave speeches denouncing the Versailles Treaty, blamed the Jews and Communists for the loss of jobs which at one point left half of Germany's labor force unemployed, and said that what Germany needed was *Lebensraum*, or room for expansion. Events were not much better in the United States. The stock market crash of 1929 caused banks to fail and businesses to go under. The loss of savings, jobs, and hope left little time for most people to think about what was happening elsewhere in the world; paying the rent and providing food for families came first. Millions of Americans were counting on President Franklin D. Roosevelt to turn things around. They listened attentively whenever the president addressed the nation via his innovative fireside chats; hearing the president on the radio made it seem as if he were right there in one's own living room, speaking directly to them.

At a time when Americans could hardly afford the price of the ticket to the local movie theater, let alone a live musical or play, the radio (which added only pennies to the electric bill) was the major source of amusement and information. Radio provided millions of Americans with an array of comedy, music, drama, and variety programs that could take their minds off the troubles of the day. They could laugh along with Eddie Cantor, Jack Benny and Fred Allen, listen to Kate Smith or the Metropolitan Opera Company, hear a radio version of a popular movie on the *Lux Radio Theater*, or get the latest news and gossip from Walter Winchell.

Listeners who happened to have their radio tuned in to the NBC network at 10 p.m. on Tuesday evening, April 16 of 1935 heard two voices that may have sounded familiar. Jim and Marian Jordan, already known to many radio listeners for their roles on *Kaltenmeyer's Kindergarten* as well as the *Smackout*, heard the popular couple in a new program: *Fibber McGee and Molly*. Sponsored by the Johnson Wax® Company, the program offered listeners a new kind of comedy, one that in many ways was the forerunner of what today we call a "situation comedy." Unlike other comedy shows of the day that were based on telling a series of jokes and relied on weekly guests, *Fibber McGee and Molly* was different. The program was designed to make listeners laugh, but the laughter came from each week's story line and the dialogue between an array of funny friends and neighbors who populated Wistful Vista. Week after week, for more than 20 years, the show's writers, Don Quinn and Phil Leslie, together with a cast that included some of radio's leading actors, kept Americans laughing. Even today, more than 50 years after the program went off the air, the laughs keep coming.

Fast forward to December 7, 1941, the day that changed the lives of every American. While our young men enlisted and went off to battle, at home the media was enlisted by the government to build support for the war effort. It was a time of unbridled patriotism that enlisted all Americans, from coast to coast, the rich and the poor, the young and the old. Everyone, in real life and in popular culture, chipped in and did what they could to help the boys on the battlefront. While Superman fought the Nazis on the pages of comic books, popular radio programs like *Fibber McGee* exhorted listeners to plant victory gardens, donate to paper and scrap iron drives, and buy war bonds. Off and on the airwaves, people everywhere were heard singing patriotic songs like "Let's Remember Pearl Harbor" and "Praise the Lord and Pass the Ammunition."

Memories tend to fade, however, and as our population has aged there are fewer and fewer folks who recall that sense of patriotism that was imbued in all Americans between 1941-1945. We've forgotten how patriotism was so inextricably intertwined into the popular culture of the day. Today, we think more in terms of anti-war protests and preventing government intervention in the media.

Yes, times have changed. But there are lessons to be learned by revisiting the past. And that's what Dr. Mickey Smith has done for us in this, his second book dealing with radio. Dr. Smith, who was only a small boy during World War II, takes us back to another time in American history. A perilous time when, as a country, we weren't sure we would survive. And what may sound corny today was very, very real 65 years ago. A scientist and respected university professor by training, Dr. Smith combines his academic skills with his love of radio to shed light on an important chapter in the history of American popular culture.

DAVID S. SIEGEL
JUNE 2009

PROLOGUE

JUNE 6, 1944
THE FIBBER MCGEE AND MOLLY D-DAY SHOW

"Dedicated to those men who look through their bombsights for a glimpse of the victory to come."

That is how Molly McGee (Marian Jordan) introduced "The Bombardier's Song."

What would you do if you had worked all week planning and writing a 30-minute live comedy radio show only to learn that less than 24 hours before air time the long-awaited Allied invasion of Europe had begun? If you were the people at Fibber McGee and Molly, you would have prepared for this day, weeks, maybe months, in advance. And they did!

The broadcast begins with a network announcement that the news will take precedence over all other programs. The program proper begins with a statement by Fibber (Jim Jordan): "Ladies and Gentlemen, Molly and I are mighty proud to be associated with the radio industry, which at this moment is fulfilling its promise of instant communication in time of world crisis."

"The next half hour will be devoted to bringing you information immediately as received by NBC's News Bureau!" Molly adds.

The program consists of patriotic musical selections by Billy Mills' orchestra and the King's Men, interspersed with comments by the McGees.

The musical selections range from such standards as George M. Cohan's, "It's a Grand Old Flag," to such lesser-known numbers as "The Bombardier's Song."

Harlow Wilcox is next to speak, but not with a commercial. The Johnson people have donated this time for the broadcast, a gesture made many times during the war. Instead of a commercial, he will introduce most of the musical selections.

Fibber comes on to introduce a song, "The Time is Now." He notes that this is particularly appropriate because if there ever was a time that is "Now, it is now." He also introduces a song that "puts into words what is in all our hearts . . . This is Worth Fighting For."

The program is interrupted once by a report from the NBC Newsroom: "Here's the latest version of the invasion coming from the enemy. Swedish correspondents in Berlin said the German High Command expects new and larger landings before Wednesday dawn and declare that several divisions now are fighting on the big beachhead, in some places hand-to-hand. These correspondents quoted Hitler's command as saying the invasion front stretches two hundred and forty miles . . . In a broadcast statement the German High Command described the fighting . . . in the Le Havre area as being in full swing and declares that everywhere along the invasion front British and American troops are putting up a most tenacious resistance."

When Fibber next speaks, it's to note that: "It's comforting to note that [the military] has the finest equipment and the best leadership of any army in the world. And that no military operation in history has had the careful planning and preparation that preceded this operation."

"In addition, our men have a weapon which our enemies cannot have: The knowledge that God is on our side," Molly says. "To us, D-Day means Divine help and each hour the hopes of all of us for a speedy victory."

The program ended with a reminder that it would be followed by an address from President Roosevelt.

Throughout, and even after the war, for nearly 150 broadcasts, *Fibber McGee and Molly* provided entertainment interlaced with important wartime messages. Many times an entire program would be devoted to a war issue, and virtually every program had some mention of a war need or duty. Often the sponsor, Johnson's Wax®, donated commercial time to those messages.

In a later chapter, I note that in time of war a democratic

government needs to inform, inspire, console, cajole, and exhort. Jim and Marian Jordan and their writers, Don Quinn and Phil Leslie, did all of these things. They also educated and sometimes even shamed. In the latter case, shame was always directed at the hapless hero, Fibber. Notably, he always got the right message in the end, especially with the help of his devoted wife, Molly. All of this was made possible by one of the most cooperative, flexible and patriotic sponsors imaginable: Johnson's Wax®.

In a time of four years of national crisis, the *Fibber McGee and Molly* program was an AMERICAN TREASURE.

PART I
THE LITTLE ARMY THAT WON THE WAR

CHAPTER ONE: INTRODUCTION

Between December 7, 1941 and V-J Day (officially declared as September 2, 1945), there were 144 Fibber McGee and Molly shows broadcast on radio. In virtually every one of these broadcasts, some reference to the war then raging throughout the world was mentioned either explicitly or by implication.

Sometimes an entire show was dedicated to a war-related issue — shortages, military service, home front support for the war effort. Somehow these vital and serious messages were delivered with great humor, warmth, and wholesome patriotism. How this happened is the subject of this book.

An early word to the reader. If you have never listened to a Fibber McGee and Molly broadcast, be advised that the messages of this book will be greatly enhanced if you do so. The audio images which you will create in your mind will be very real. The printed word cannot possibly capture the inflections, the timing, the reaction of a live studio audience (no laugh tracks here), and the genuine good humor brought to the air by the cast.

For fans of Old-Time Radio (OTR throughout the book), there is much that will be familiar. I have tried to give OTR aficionados an ample supply of insights to assure that you will not be bored. As I conducted the research, I was continuously both surprised and certainly stimulated to learn more about the remarkable combination of coincidences, talent, and motivation which made Fibber McGee and Molly not only a very funny and successful radio program but also (I hope to demonstrate) an important morale booster and aid in mobilizing home front efforts in support of the war effort.

In Chapter Two, we introduce Jim and Marian Jordan, best known as Fibber McGee and Molly, although in their early days they had other identities. We will see how they "paid their dues" in the field of entertainment and how a very fortunate set of coincidences resulted in one of radio's all-time favorite comedies. The format of the show (which one writer has described, not in a pejorative sense, as a "comic strip") will be elaborated. The extraordinary talents which created the characters who appeared regularly or only briefly will be identified, and some characters that were never heard will also be described.

The character of the show is also limned. The running gags (Fibber McGee's incredibly messy closet), the metaphors, the puns, the surprise endings, the sound effects — all of the things which went together to make the show popular with the radio audience and the live studio audience (itself a contributor to the show's success).

The chapter concludes with a glimpse of the wartime humor through a review of one show. Note to the readers who want to know more. Three sources are especially suggested, *Heavenly Days*, by Charles Stumpf and Tom Price, provides an engaging and considerably detailed history of the careers of the Jordans and the show. The two-volume *Fibber McGee's Closet* (by Tom Price) offers a truly encyclopedic collection of information. Every person who ever appeared on the show, a program-by-program list of subjects of the show, the frequency of use of the "closet gag" — and much, much more. Both of the first two are out of print, but copies can sometimes be found on the Web. This author owes a considerable debt to each. The latest addition to the literature, *Fibber McGee and Molly, On the Air 1935-1959*, published in 2008 by Clair Schulz, is a true treasure containing brief, individual summaries of every single show.

Before we move to the next chapter, perhaps we should pay a visit to 79 Wistful Vista. We chose the V-E (Victory in Europe) broadcast as an introduction to the program because it captures the wartime problems and the way in which the writers and actors could make them entertaining and meaningful.

The show opens with the redoubtable Harlow Wilcox intoning, "It's *The Johnson's Wax® Show, with Fibber McGee and Molly*." (Note, that in the same way that The Tonight Show was not officially "The

Johnny Carson Show," the Johnson Wax® Company was keeping its options open. Most listeners, I am sure, did not see a distinction. Instead, the Johnson Company and Fibber and Molly were wedded in the listeners' minds).

FIBBER MCGEE AND MOLLY ON V-E DAY

The first voice you hear is that of Harlow Wilcox, serious but optimistic, tempered with caution: "Ladies and gentlemen, this is Harlow Wilcox. The curtain has fallen on the first act of the greatest drama the world has ever seen. The second and, we hope, the last World War. Act two is going on in the Pacific Theater. In expressing our tremendous admiration and gratitude to our fighting forces, we feel that it is best to support their efforts until we complete the final victory by carrying on with our own jobs the best we can. In this case our job is to bring a few smiles to the home front and to do our best to relieve the tension and anxiety in the homes of the men whom are not here to laugh with us. So tonight, we present the regular Johnson's Wax® Program as our stars go on the air in a tribute to the stars in your windows." (Windows usually displayed small flags representing family members in the military. Gold stars meant a mortal casualty.)

After the theme music, we hear the familiar voice of that same Harlow Wilcox who has been selling Johnson's Wax® on the program for 10 years: "The makers of Johnson's Wax® products for home and industry present Fibber McGee and Molly, written by Don Quinn and Phil Leslie, with music by Billy Mills and his Orchestra and the King's Men."

The theme of tonight's show on V-E Day itself is the Wartime Housing Shortage. Fibber offers to perform a housing survey of Wistful Vista for the City Council for a mere $50. He arrives home at 1:45 to inform Molly of his good fortune. The survey must be completed by 5:30 the same day. Fibber is not concerned; he has a plan! (He *always* does).

The rest of the show deals with the skepticism of all the other characters about his ability to do the job. The first skeptic is Alice Darling, a roomer with the McGees, and very popular with the boys. She also works in an aircraft factory. She thinks McGee has taken on an important but difficult job. Molly asks Alice if V-E Day will make any difference in her work at the airplane factory. Alice responds: "Well, not until the other half of the war is over, Mrs. McGee. I figure if Europe is morning and Japan the afternoon, V-E Day is just the whistle blowing for lunch."

"You're absolutely right Alice," McGee says. "It ain't fair for the players to go home after the first game of a double header."

Both Molly and Alice find it hard to believe that McGee can do the job by 5:30. The same is true for the local newspaper editor, as well as the mayor himself. McGee uses one of his patented tales to illustrate his quick thinking — how he stopped a train at midnight when a warning light went out. When Alice inquires of McGee, "How did you stop the train in the dark?" he replies: "I just have a flare for that sort of thing."

To Molly's chagrin, McGee is busy with a crossword puzzle instead of doing a "survey." A visit by the wealthy Mrs. Carstairs is next. She invites Molly to appear in a local stage play: "*The Importance of Being Earnest*," as Molly notes — "By Hemingway."

Harlow Wilcox turns up in his role as a cast member. He, too, is skeptical about McGee's ability to do the job in the limited time remaining. He invites McGee to go bowling, but McGee believes the bowling alley won't be open on V-E Day. Wilcox puts him straight on that. The alley is run by Wilcox's cousin, Big Frankie Wilson, who says he'd close every other day of the year, but not on V-E Day because "there are a lot of soldiers and sailors in town who need inexpensive recreation. He says he'd feel like a rat slamming the door in the faces of those who made this day possible — some of them on the way to the Pacific to do some more fighting. Today they can all bowl free."

Next to knock on the door was "Doc" Gamble, Fibber's favorite friendly antagonist. After an exchange of their patented insults, the doctor leaves and leaves behind more skepticism about McGee's project.

Then Molly — "*Oh, Beulah!*" The standard response: "Somebody bawlin' for Beulah?" A black maid/cook Beulah is played by a white man and his appearance and voice get an immediate laugh from the live studio audience. When McGee asks how she celebrated

V-E Day, she had gone to church. "I say a little prayer for the boys who did such a good job over there in Europe. I wasn't in no mood for no whoop-de-do. If you got a brother in the Navy like I does in the Pacific, you is prone to save your confetti for another day." When McGee notes that is still good news, Beulah agrees: "I ain't denyin' that but, I can't help thinkin' there ain't no dancing in the streets of Manila." After a little talk about the post-war plans of Beulah and her intended, Beulah notes that they plan to raise cows and ducks on the truck farm. When McGee says that represents the perfect midnight snack, "milk and quackers," Beulah responds in her usual way: a riotous laugh and the comment, *"Love that man."*

Well, what about the survey? Exactly at 5:30 there is a knock on the door. Looking out the window, Molly sees the street crowded with people. "Start counting them," says McGee. "What have you done?" asks Molly. "I took out an ad in the paper saying Room for Rent; apply 79 Wistful Vista at 5:30. Keep counting!" When they get the total, McGee calls the mayor's office with the news that there are 450 people looking for housing. He and Molly leave by the back door to pick up the 50 dollars.

The show closes with a patriotic song, followed by Jim and a Marian Jordan in a most serious vein.

JIM: Ladies and Gentlemen, this is one of the days we've been looking forward to for so long. This is one of the days for which men left their wives and children and their profession and put on uniforms to give their lives to end tyranny and aggression forever.

MARIAN: But this is just one of the days. There is another day coming and may it be coming soon, when we can celebrate complete victory. To leave our jobs now and quit before the job is finished would be false to the wives and children they left behind.

JIM: Perhaps you know that radio programs like this one are recorded and sent to our forces everywhere overseas for their entertainment and to bring them a smile or two from home. That's our job.

MARIAN: So, let's all keep going and keep working and keep faith with the ones who are still doing battle for the things we believe in.

JIM: Good night.

MARIAN: Good night, all.

This broadcast, on a very special day was in many ways typical of the programs throughout the war. Although the government had issued guidelines concerning messages to be broadcast to the public about war issues, Fibber McGee and Molly far exceeded them. Nearly every program contained some war-related message. Sometimes it only amounted to a wisecrack about Hitler; at other times, it was the entire theme of a program.

The ability to blend humor with such serious subjects as black market meat, gasoline, rubber and doctor shortages and, in the case of the program highlighted here, the housing shortage, can be attributed to the genius of Don Quinn, head writer throughout the war, and his partner, Phil Leslie, who joined the program in 1943 and worked seamlessly with Quinn.

Not fully acknowledged was the role played by the sponsor, Johnson's Wax®, who gave the writers free rein in developing story lines and subjects. It is doubtful that any commercial radio sponsor contributed more of the contents of a program to the war effort. The Wilcox introduction explained why, and Wilcox as a character in the series made the commercials painless. (There were no commercials on this broadcast.) The character of Alice Darling is a good example of how other players contributed to the message. She was renting a room during this housing shortage, working in production in an aircraft factory, and performing as a real (but always chaste) morale booster for the service men. Her war message was typical of others delivered by various characters in a very natural contextual way.

And there's also Beulah, delivering her patriotic message in the stereotypical 1940s black vernacular. Her devotion to the war effort is unmistakable, and the contribution of African Americans is also established. The serious, out-of-character message at the end by Jim and Marian Jordan was also typical. The only atypical aspect of the program was that a Fibber McGee scheme actually worked!

Fred MacDonald (MD1,p.2) has noted: "The culture of the populace must reflect the commercial and democratic populace . . . [Radio] never escaped the commercialism [that critics] felt hampered its sophistication." *Fibber McGee and Molly* made no pretense at sophistication. Rather, as MacDonald observed, they sought to please an audience of Americans and reflect the democratic environment in which Americans lived. It played to their tastes and "mirrored their values."

Nachman (GN,p.9) noted eloquently, "Old radio shows are not nostalgia pills; they're time capsules." I hope the reader will agree, as I do. John Dunning, in his fine book, *Two O'clock, Eastern War Time*, has one of his characters say "[Radio] is the most intimate medium that will ever be devised. It pulls people together, draws them into each other, makes them one." (D., p. 239.) He was not referring specifically to *Fibber McGee and Molly*, but, in wartime, he could have been.

CHAPTER TWO:
THE JOHNSON'S WAX® PROGRAM
WITH *FIBBER McGEE AND MOLLY*

Jim Jordan (A.K.A. Mickey Donovan, Luke Gray, and [finally] Fibber McGee) was born November 16, 1896 in Peoria, Illinois. Marian Jordan (A.K.A. Gertie Gump, Nora Smith, Teeny, several other names, and [finally] Molly McGee) was born April 15, 1898, also in Peoria. They were to be married in August 1918.

The couple could not have guessed that they would someday star in the most popular radio show in the United States, because in 1918, a career in radio entertainment was not then an option. Nevertheless, both were committed to a future in "show business." Here is a brief version of the steps along the way to their unimagined destiny.

THE ROAD TO WISTFUL VISTA

SEPTEMBER 1918: Jim Jordan is drafted and goes to France where he is taken ill, but later starts an Army show. It is not known if the experience shaped his feelings about war and the Army.

1921: After Jim works at a variety of jobs, he and Marian form a little concert company in Chicago.

1921: The Jordans get their first job for pay on radio on Chicago's WIBO for $10 a week.

1926:   After virtually starving on radio pay, the Jordans go (back) into vaudeville for a year.

1927:   They sign with WENR and appear on a popular program called *The Smith Family*. The show was a kind of situation comedy where Jim was an Irish prizefighter and Marian was Nora Smith, the distaff member of the Smiths.

1931:   WENR is sold to NBC. The Jordans were doing another little show, *Luke and Mirandy*, as well as a show called, *Smackout*. In the latter, Jordan runs a grocery store and no matter the customer's request, he is always "smackout" of it. By his own account (SP, P.4) there were 11 people in the cast, all of them with Jim or Marian.

1930:   One of the most fortuitous accidents in radio history occurred. There are several versions of the story, but according to Jim Jordan, it went this way: Thora Martin, an actress on *The Smith Family*, had a girlfriend who was dating a guy named Don Quinn and she introduced him to the Jordans. Quinn was an unsuccessful cartoonist. His writing was well-received, but not his art. In a wonderful bit of perspicacity, the Jordans spotted talent that would help make them famous. The network wanted the stars to write their own material, as did Charles Correll and Freeman Gosden of *Amos 'n' Andy*. So, the Jordans used Quinn, paid him, but did not identify him. The rest, as they say, is history.

At one point, the Jordans were simultaneously doing *Smackout*, parts on *Kaltenmeyers Kindergarten*, and Fibber McGee and Molly.

1935:   Another major coincidence, Henrietta Johnson

(sister of the CEO of Johnson's Wax®) was the wife of Jack Louis, an advertising executive. She, it just so happens, was also a big fan of *Smackout*. She finally got her husband to listen, and the audition was a success. Johnson's Wax® would be the sponsor for the next 15 years.

In some of the planning strategy meetings that followed, the prevarication proclivities of the former *Smackout* owner were kicked around. At one of these, Don Quinn walked in with a good-sized paper on which he had printed FIBBER McGEE (CS, P. 8). (There are, as was stated earlier, other versions of this story in print.)

The McGees started traveling by road around the country (and simultaneously selling their sponsor's car wax) but they quickly settled into their home at 79 Wistful Vista, which was to become one of America's most famous addresses. They won the place in a raffle!

THE FORMAT

The majority of the shows took place at 79 Wistful Vista where "drop in" company was the rule. The mayor somehow found time for a weekly visit as did "Doc Gamble." A variety of others could be counted on for regular visits most of which were fairly predictable. The mayor would be apoplectic after the McGees purposely misunderstood something he had said. The doctor would have engaged in an insult — trading session — McGee called him variously "Tummy Thumper" or "Tonsil Snatcher." The doctor gave as good, or better, than he got. When McGee complained of a pain in the small of his back, Doc responded, "I have seen your back and it has no small."

The listeners anticipated and loved the predictability. There was comfort in it. The McGees did move about town too — Kremer's

Drug Store, the bank, the Bon Ton Department Store. Everything in town was located at 14th and Oak, an inside joke for a long time. Running gags were a staple.

Regardless of the location, most regular characters eventually appeared. More about them a little later. But first, let's take a closer look at the stars. What was it about these two that kept America next to the radio for a certain thirty minutes every week?

Wolters (LW) has noted that Fibber and Molly were "too real, too human to be passed off as mere radio characters." McGee does dumb things with great confidence. He delivers non-sequiturs with pride. As one of the TV anchors recently said, McGee is "often wrong but never in doubt." As Wolters pointed out: "Garrulous and gullible, he sticks his neck out and Molly carefully and patiently helps him pull it back."

There is never anything even hinting at vulgarity in a script, but the absence isn't noticeable, nor its presence missed. The show is simply very funny without it. Fibber never so much as mentions another female, but why should he? Molly is the most amiable wife imaginable. If Fibber hopes to mystify, she is mystified. If he hopes to impress, she is impressed, while cleverly suppressing a pragmatic giggle. She accepts his crazy schemes while carefully and invisibly keeping him from making a complete fool of himself. She is a diplomatic pragmatist with a velvet disposition.

THE MUSIC

Live music was a feature at the beginning, during, and at the end of each show. Billy Mills and his orchestra provided a big-band sound mostly with the standards. Incongruously, Billy Mills sometimes appeared in character as a part of the story, a fact that nobody seemed to mind.

The orchestra also provided backup for the vocal group, the King's Men. They sang close harmony with some often unusual arrangements of standards, and an occasional patriotic song ("Wing and a Prayer," "This Little Bond Went to Battle," "You Can't Say No to a Soldier"). A few of their numbers were probably never heard anywhere else: e.g. "Don't Tetch It" and "The Enchilada Man."

THE WRITERS

At this point, it is probably a good idea to give a nod to the "Eisenhower" of the McGee war, Don Quinn, even though he will be the subject of most of a full chapter later. His approach to humor is one of the most important of many reasons for the show's success.

A real "belly laugh" has often been the goal of a radio comedy show. Not for Quinn and the McGees! They believed that their audiences preferred a "chuckle show." That is what Quinn's scripts and the Jordans' performances set out to deliver. Each week they worked to devise a story putting five to eight characters on stage and requiring 60 to 100 funny lines. A "continuous ripple of amusement" is what they hoped for (and achieved). At times they clocked as many as ninety laughs in a half hour (RMY). Lightly struck but telling notes were in Quinn's specialty. As Robert Yoder (rmy) wrote eloquently wrote in 1949:

> Principally it is life with Fibber, and Fibber has become pretty much the ordinary tough-minded, wise-crackin', loving, average citizen — who would punch your nose for calling him "average." Fibber is a hopeful over-confident guy who will tackle anything, with a brisk propensity for stepping on his own necktie. But he is nobody's fool except his own.

The Jordans and Quinn didn't do all this alone. Not by any means! The ever-changing ensemble of characters worked together with the precision of a Swiss watch.

THE ACTORS AND CHARACTERS

In approximate, alphabetical order, here are the actors/characters who were "regulars" during World War II.

- **BEULAH.** If the reader found it bizarre that the popular radio program, *Amos 'n' Andy*, starred two white men as the characters, the idea of a white guy playing the part of a black maid, must be surprising indeed. Marlin Hurt, who played the part on radio (the only medium possible), was fantastic! He didn't arrive at 79 Wistful Vista until January 25, 1944. So well did his characterization succeed that, by the summer of 1945, the first McGee "spin off," *The Marlin Hurt and Beulah Show*, was on the air.

Beulah provided one of the running gags, her answer to Molly's call, "Oh, Beulah!" The usual response, "Somebody bawlin' for Beulah," always drew a laugh.

Beulah came to the McGees from her work at the house of Mort Toops, a neighbor often heard *of* but not heard *from*. How the McGees paid her salary, when McGee had no visible means of support, remains a mystery.

Beulah was an extremely important character in this story and it is unfortunate that she had such a short run during the war. Was the character a racial stereotype? Yes, but not in the sense of some of the criticism of *Amos 'n' Andy*. She did fracture some grammar and often used "big" words that she had obviously heard and understood, although they were similarly obviously not a part of her normal conversational vocabulary. She treated the McGees with respect but not necessarily deference.

The important point is that Beulah was a wise voice of patriotism on behalf of the black population of the times. All the words of course, came from the visionary pens of Don Quinn and Phil Leslie. Hurt died in 1945, shortly after getting his own show.

- **HORATIO K. BOOMER.** Sounding and behaving like the great comedian W.C. Fields, Boomer was the source of many running gags. His bit usually ended with a search in his pockets for some item. As he itemized his findings he always ended by finding "a check for a short beer." That, and the frequent reference to the tippling habits of Uncle Dennis (seldom actually heard but living for a while with the McGees), were initially the only times alcoholic beverages were acknowledged. Fibber favored "hot buttered root beer."

The character of Boomer was played by Bill Thompson, a genius at voice characterizations and a versatile player of other parts on the show. Boomer was not his best character, although it was well executed. He had been with the show since 1936, until 1943 when he joined the Navy. He was assigned to special duty in entertainment and received a medal for selling more than two million dollars in Liberty Bonds. Boomer had little to say about the war.

- **MRS. CARSTAIRS** was played by the well-known character actress, Bea Benaderet (*Burns and Allen, The Beverly Hillbillies, Petticoat Junction*). She became Mrs. Carstairs late in the war, in March 1945. This uppity character avoided vulgarity at all costs (navel oranges were "citrus umbilicus"), barely tolerated Fibber (who called her "Carsty") but she respected Molly. In spite of her wealth, she did contribute in various ways to the war effort.

- **ALICE DARLING**, played by the popular radio actress, Shirley Mitchell, was especially important to the war stories. She had rented a room from the McGees because of the wartime housing shortage and was a model for the females who had taken jobs in defense factories — in her case an airplane factory. She used all the current slang ("creepers"), loved the McGees, and *really* loved the boys, who reciprocated. Her seeming denseness never got in the way of her ability to verbally exemplify the war effort.

- **"DOC" GAMBLE** was played by Arthur Q. Bryan, the voice actor best known as Elmer Fudd in the Warner Bros. Bugs Bunny cartoons. A local physician devoted to his patients and to a major case of cynicism, Doc Gamble's exchanges with McGee were classics. Fibber called him by a variety of mildly insulting nicknames, most often a sarcastic "Arrowsmith." Gamble usually gave better than he got. Examples are provided later in the book.

Arthur Q. Bryan had become "Doc" Gamble in April 1943 after Gale Gordon (see below) entered the Coast Guard. He had been playing the role of Major Hoople on the radio as scripted by Phil Leslie, who was now writing for the McGees and who recommended him.

"Doc" Gamble delivered some of the most serious talk about the war of anyone on the program. His remarks were usually directed at McGee who, like many thousands of Americans, was completely patriotic but who just couldn't quite believe that the wartime rules and regulations applied to *them*. In fact, McGee and Gamble had great affection for each another, but it was just more fun to trade harmless, and often hilarious, jibes.

- **THROCKMORTON P. GILDERSLEEVE** was played by Hal Peary on the show. In an almost seamless transition, the Gildersleeve role was assumed later by Willard Waterman after the "Great Gildersleeve" became a "spin off" of the Fibber show.

- **ED KREMER** was the pharmacist at Kremer's Drug Store. Kremer was never a very likable character on the show. It is not clear whether this was a result of his constant harassment by McGee or whether it was intended that he be dour. Kremer was not always played by the same actor, although Ken Christie appeared in the part most often. Also appearing in the role was well-known character actor, Ed Begley. Others for whom documentation is available in the part of Kremer are: Will Wright, Bob Easton, William Conrad (Matt Dillon on radio's *Gunsmoke*, and later *Cannon* on television), Howard McNear (who later appeared as Floyd the Barber on *The Andy Griffith Show*), and John McIntyre.

As it happens, the Kremer character as created by the show's writer, Don Quinn, was based on real life! Don Quinn grew up in

Grand Rapids, Michigan. As a young man he had a paper route that included homes as well as businesses. One business was Kremer's Rexall Drugstore. The store was owned by Edward Kremer. He was the pharmacist and ran the store. Back in those days a pharmacist was often referred to as "Doc" so his nickname was "Doc" Kremer. His store included an old-fashioned soda fountain and Don Quinn used to stop by on his route for a soda. He and Doc Kremer became friends. After he moved on to Chicago to create *Fibber McGee and Molly*, he added Kremer's Drugstore and Doc Kremer made appearances during the complete run of the show. Kremer's Drugstore and Doc Kremer were also were referenced on *Petticoat Junction*, a television program that was created and written by former "Fibber" writer Paul Henning.

In 1944 Fibber McGee and Molly was one of the most-listened-to shows on radio. The country was in the midst of World War II and rationing was in full swing. The show found humor in cigarette rationing and also gave a little compliment to Kremer (perhaps because the fictional character had received some rough treatment). An excerpt follows:

MOLLY: Have you found out yet where you can get the Doctor some cigarettes, McGee?

FIBBER: No, and I've called every drugstore and tobacco shop in town. One guy was laughing so hard he could hardly talk.

MOLLY: Is it such a laughing matter?

MCGEE: This guy was a cigar salesman.

MOLLY: Did you try Kremer's Drug Store? Mr. Kremer is always very accommodating.

The local Grand Rapids newspaper did an article about the show, and they featured "Doc" Kremer as he sold a carton of cigarettes to customers (See photographs).

It is generally agreed that Don Quinn was one of the finest

comedy writers of radio's Golden Age, and his friendship with Kremer made that pharmacist nationally famous.

- **Mayor LaTrivia** was played by the unmistakable and justifiably well-known Gale Gordon. His visits to 79 Wistful Vista (why the mayor visited every week is a mystery) were always a highlight. Both McGees delighted in pretending to misunderstand some comment or term used by the mayor. In another running gag, LaTrivia would become increasingly agitated, garbling his terms until, after a brief silence, he would intone "McGeeee," and exit on a one liner. Here's an example of how the mayor responded to how the McGees appeared to misconstrue the meaning of his remark that he was "playing possum."

> I don't want to balk a stossum? Squawk a blossom! Look — when I said I was playing posse — possum, I merely meant I was lowing lye! Er, lying low . . . I never said I was — you're the one that always miscon- words my strues . . . strue remarks my words! . . . Every time I stake a simple matement — make a staple mintment — stinkel statement — minkel statement . . . You were the one . . . I . . . You . . . .

- **Old-Timer.** Another of Bill Thompson's hallmark portrayals. He greeted Molly with "Hello, there, daughter," and referred to McGee as "Johnny." Thanks to Thompson's vocal characterization, the Old-Timer genuinely sounded old. The running gag here would find McGee telling an anecdote. Mr. Old-Timer would listen quietly then say, "Well, that's pretty good, Johnny. But that ain't the way I heared it . . . The way I heard it, one fellow says t'other fellow — S-a-ay, he says" and then launch into a story of his own.

- **Teeny** was played by Marian Jordan herself. She always (or nearly always) appeared when Molly had left the room followed by McGee's remarks, "Ah, there goes a good kid."

Teeny was a paradox who drove Fibber to distraction with remarks such as "Don't you like lit-tle kids?" Her outlandish stories often resulted in McGee giving her money. Sometimes, after listening to one of his simplistic explanations of various phenomena, she responded with a true account using appropriate scientific terms, to his chagrin and the delight of the audience.

Teeny was enchanting without being saccharine. She was world-wise beyond her years (Fibber said often, "I know that kid is a midget.") She schemed but was never truly dishonest. She just allowed Fibber to reach the wrong conclusions, with very funny results.

Teeny was, in fact, a most unusual creation. Here was a married couple (the Jordans) facing each other across a room on live radio. One played a rather gullible middle-aged man, the other a child by whom he was being flummoxed. Somehow they carried this off with panache. Each year Teeny led a group of her little cronies in a special version of Clement Moore's "A Visit from St. Nicholas" (AKA "T'was the Night Before Christmas"), backed by Billy Mills and the King's Men, and the writers even managed on occasion to put words in Teeny's mouth to support the war effort.

- **UNCLE DENNIS** was Molly's uncle. He must have been based on his frequent use of Irish phrases. He was played by Ransom Sherman, a radio veteran. Uncle Dennis lived with the McGees (as did Alice Darling), apparently on the second floor. Simply put: he drank — *a lot*. He was, therefore, one of only two characters with whom alcohol was ever associated. He had nothing to say about the war, and was, indeed, rarely heard at all.

- **NICK DEPOPOLOUS.** This was Bill Thompson with a Greek accent, a longtime favorite on the program. His malapropisms were very popular, but his character changed with the decline of ethnic stereotypes on radio. He would call Fibber, "Feezer," and Molly, "Kewpie."

- **ABIGAIL UPPINGTON** was played by Isabel Randolph, another veteran of many radio programs, who left the show in 1943 to become active in TV (*The Abbott and Costello Show, Our Miss Brooks, The Dick Van Dyke Show*). Her character was definitely upper crust and later followed by Mrs. Carstairs. McGee, of course, called her "Uppy," and defined upper crust as "a bunch of crumbs — held together by dough." Before the war she had a brief engagement to "Boomer," and on the February 9, 1943 broadcast she tried to join the WACS.

- **SIGMUND WELLINGTON** was also played by Ransom Sherman and was manager of the Bijou Theatre. His speech was strange, but pretentious, punctuated by inappropriate pauses. He had nothing to say about the war.

- **HARLOW WILCOX** was played by Harlow Wilcox. Like a few other announcers (Don Wilson on *The Jack Benny Show*, for example) he not only sold Johnson's Wax® products, but was a regular character in the program stories. The Johnson Company allowed his mid-program appearances to become humorous battles between him trying to get in his pitch and the McGees trying to disrupt these efforts. He called McGee "Pal" and McGee called him either "Waxy" or "Junior."

Wilcox's efforts, blessed by the sponsor, delivered some of the most painless commercials on radio with humor, but persuasion. He could turn the most innocuous remark into a reason for extolling the value of a Johnson's product. In addition, he often delivered war messages as part of his serious commercials at the beginning and end of the show. Certainly, he often found a way to build a small commercial into the message. But why not? Johnson was paying for the air time.

- **WALLACE WIMPLE** was, in my opinion, Bill Thompson's triumph. It is impossible to describe Wimple's voice in words. (One writer called it an "effeminate whimper.") One simply has to hear it to appreciate it. If a voice, regardless of his words used, can convey shyness, humility, and, on occasion, slyness, while at the same time portraying a man who is not just "henpecked" but physically brutalized by his wife, Bill Thompson did it. He and the writers even made it hilariously funny.

Among other things Wimple was a sometime poet and a number of his poems related to the war effort, especially buying War Bonds. For her part, his wife taught martial arts to police and military. One other contribution of this character — McGee's nickname for him — "Wimp" — has entered the American lexicon.

OTHER CHARACTERS

In addition to the "regulars" described above, there were appearances by many "bit parts," such as salespeople, stunt car drivers, and the like. Often the same actor played several parts over the years. In addition, there were a few characters, essential to the program's success, who were seldom, if ever, actually heard. One of these was "Myrt." Myrt was a telephone operator — no direct dial in those days. She was also an integral part of another running gag. It went this way.

McGEE: Operator, give me the BonTon at 14th and Oak. Oh, is that you Myrt? (Groan here from Molly) How's every little thing, Myrt? 'Tis, huh? You say you found him on the doorstep with a rattle in one hand and a bottle in the other?

MOLLY: (Interrupting) The poor little thing, how terrible! Is she taking him to someplace to get care for the baby?

McGEE: It's not a baby. It's Uncle Dennis.

This device with Molly reaching a wrong conclusion based on half of a conversation always brought a laugh. Myrt was actually heard only once, on June 22, 1943.

Other characters included Fred Nitney, McGee's former vaudeville partner, from Starved Rock, Illinois. He figured in scores of stories and especially one in which McGee planned to use his "influence" to wangle a commission for Nitney's niece in the military immediately upon enlistment. This idea was strongly discouraged by Molly and others.

MORT TOOPS was a neighbor frequently mentioned but never heard. The same was true for his boy, Willie, who was Teeny's main accomplice in various schemes. Bessie was the Old-Timer's girlfriend. She referred to him as "O.T." and was heard a few times and played by Cliff Arquette, who later became the Old-Timer.

Finally, there was **SWEETIE FACE**, Wimple's "Big Old Wife." She was never heard, but was an essential part of his characterization.

SOUND EFFECTS

Phil Leslie's daughter, Susan Leslie Peters (SLP), once wrote about sound effects on the Fibber McGee and Molly program:

> Another important cast member . . . was Monty Frazier, the sound man. Pop used to say that if he and Don [Quinn] had wanted Fibber and Molly to go to Paris, Fibber could merely have said, "Well, Molly, here we are in Paris." And Monty would have supplied the rest, taxi horns and everything.

She only told the half of it. This was RADIO, after all. Sound was virtually everything. The only visuals were those provided by the imagination. The sounds were actors' voices, music, and sound *effects*. The longest-lasting memory of the show — the hall closet — was entirely the work of the sound effects man. Judging from the reaction of the studio audience as he produced his closet avalanches, his work was pure genius.

Besides Frazier, other known members of the sound effects magic team during the war included Howard Tollefson and Jack Wormser.

Running Gags and Similes

In addition to running gags associated with the various characters described above was of course, the "Hall Closet." Indeed so popular was this sound-effects-man dream that it has become a part of American folklore. People who never heard the program still refer to many places as being as full as Fibber McGee's Closet. It was, according to one writer, "the best-known junk pile in American entertainment." According to Tom Price, it was used 128 times on the show. (PT)

Another line that has withstood the test of a long time after the show disappeared was, "*Tain't funny, McGee*," used by Molly to bring down McGee after one of his witticisms. The cigar routine was also popular.

FIBBER: Have a cigar?

OTHER PERSON: No thanks, I have one.

FIBBER: You got *two*?

There were also regular tongue twisters from McGee and exchanges between him and Molly and the meaning of words.

The writers also used hundreds of similes. Some were simple, some were elaborate. Something made by McGee would look like it was made by "a blindfolded Potawatomi with the hiccups while riding full gallop on a railroad trestle on a lame camel in the dark of the moon."

Recognition

The Jordans received many awards for their wartime work, especially in War Bond drives. There was other recognition as well. Consider the citation read on the occasion of their receipt of honorary Doctor of Law degrees from St. Joseph's College in Collegeville, Indiana.

For Doctors James and Marian Jordan: Saint Joseph's College sends cordial greetings to all who shall read these presents. What we have enacted in the name of St. Joseph's College we now hereby make known. As folklore is treasured and as folksong is loved; so too is that kindly humor that springs from homely atmosphere and experience esteemed as a precious jewel of the human spirit. For 'Humor' implies a sure conception of the beautiful, the majestic and the true, by whose light it surveys and shapes their opposites. It is a humane influence softening with mirth, the rugged inequalities of existence, prompting tolerant views of life, bridging over the spaces which separate the lofty from the lowly; the great from the humble. Mirth and merriment bars a thousand harms and lengthens life, and brings a quickening of zest and a glow of well-being.

It is fitting indeed to pay tribute to those who by their extraordinary talents contribute to the well-being of society and who strive to promote good feeling among their fellow men. More particularly is it proper to honor those whose contribution to the art of entertainment has been so wholesome, so full-hearted, so appealing as to merit the praises of millions. "The manner of jesting," says Cicero, "ought not to be extravagant or immoderate, but refined and witty. There are, generally speaking, two sorts of jests: the one, coarse, rude, vicious, indecent; the other, polite, refined, clever, witty. The second, if well-timed, is becoming to the most dignified person; the other is unfit for any gentleman." And Quintillian has said: "That laughter costs too much which is purchased by the sacrifice of decency and propriety."

We declare that those whom we honor this day are true exponents of the Law of Charity in that the coarse and the rude find no place in their entertainment; of the Law of Good Taste, in that the vicious, the improper, and the indecent are likewise absent; of the Law of Morality in the decency, cleanliness, wholesomeness, propriety, refinement characterize their offerings.

Wherefore, Saint Joseph's College, wishing to express approval of the simple and natural artistry of JAMES JORDAN AND MARIAN JORDAN, his esteemed spouse, and at the same time to honor them for the high ideals of which they give evidence in their public life as well as in their private kingdom; and wishing to serve as spokesman for the forty millions of people for whom their kindly humor is a weekly surcease from toil and worriment; as well as desiring to commend them for their truly Christian Philosophy of Life and for the acceptability of their public performances, on both state and radio, to all classes and ages of persons, confers upon them the highest honor within its power to grant, the degree: DOCTOR OF LAWS, *honoris causa.*

And we beg the Giver of all good gifts to continue to bless them with Christian courage and with those homely virtues which have endeared them to such a multitude of their fellowmen.

ANOTHER SAMPLE

At this point, it seems appropriate to give the reader another sample of the show. Much more will be provided in a later chapter and the reader is again urged to obtain one or more recordings of the show in order to truly to appreciate Fibber McGee and Molly.

SEPTEMBER 29, 1942
EPISODE TITLE: "A LOST CAMERA"

HARLOW WILCOX, ANNOUNCER: It's *The Johnson's Wax® Program with Fibber McGee and Molly*, brought to you by the makers of Johnson's Wax® products for home and industry. Written by Don Quinn with music by the King's Men and Billy Mills and his orchestra.
(Musical Interlude — "Of Thee I Sing")

WILCOX: Most of us have already experienced in our buying the effects of material shortages caused by the war. But it seems perfectly obvious that we've seen only the beginning, that in the months to come we will feel the effects of these shortages much more than we have. And that means that we need a plan of looking ahead, a plan of taking better care of the things we have. So, I make the suggestion again, a suggestion that I've made many times before, that you protect your floor, furniture, and woodwork, your linoleum and enamel surfaces, the finish of your automobile and countless other things in your home with Johnson's Wax® Polishes. I know of no other way to give your possessions protection so easily, so inexpensively, so simply and at the same time make things beautiful and save yourselves work than with Johnson's Wax® Projects.

(Musical bridge; applause)

WILCOX: As the poet said, "Home is the hunter, home from the hill." Only those hunters weren't hunting. They were fishing and they weren't in the hills, they were sitting in a rowboat. Anyway, they're home. Yes, activity has returned to 79 Wistful Vista in the well-rounded forms of Fibber McGee and Molly.

(Applause)

MOLLY: Oh my goodness, McGee, am I glad to be home!

FIBBER: Yeah, me too. You unpack while I take all the film down to the drugstore. I think these are gonna be the best snapshots I ever took.

MOLLY: *You* ever took? You made me take all of them.

FIBBER: *All*, Molly?

MOLLY: Now listen, if there's a picture of me in that lot, it's because I was reflected in your wet bathing suit.

FIBBER: Gee whiz, Molly. You know I'm no good with a camera.

MOLLY: You're no good behind it but, brother, you're a regular glamour boy in front of it.

FIBBER: Am I really? You aren't just saying that 'cause you admire me?

MOLLY:: Look, sweetie, I'm a busy woman. Now go away. Get outta my hair. What more is left of it. After thirteen weeks away from a beauty parlor [*the show had been on summer break*].

FIBBER: Okay. I'll move along. Hey did you take that last roll out of the camera?

MOLLY: No, I didn't have the camera. You were carrying it.

FIBBER: I *was?* Why I laid it on that little shelf over the seat when . . . Oh, my gosh. I left the doggone camera on the train.

[*Author note: This is a typical program set up. The listener now knows that the next twenty minutes will be spent trying to retrieve the camera.*]

The next few lines are spent in light recriminations (from Molly), followed by lame excuses (from Fibber). Molly finally states that they should forget about the camera entirely. Fibber disagrees.

FIBBER: No, sir. I sold twenty-seven subscriptions to *Master Confession* to win that camera.

MOLLY: Forget it. Buy a new one.

FIBBER: No, sir, you said we're not supposed to buy anything we don't really need. You said no government . . .

MOLLY: All right. You win, dearie. Call the railroad and see if the camera has been turned in.

FIBBER: Ok, what was our booth number again?

MOLLY: Lower eight, and if everybody sleeps as badly as I did, there should be a lower rate! Which reminds me, I want to get to bed early tonight and see how that nightmare turns out.

(There is more byplay, followed by the doorbell. Molly is concerned that they just get home and the house isn't ready for company.)

FIBBER: Oh, don't be so fussy. You've been using Johnson's Wax® so long a speck of dust looks like a sandstorm.

A visitor is the "Old-Timer."

OLD-TIMER: Hello there, kids, welcome home!

FIBBER: I'm afraid you've got the advantage of me, Bud. Who are you?

OLD-TIMER: What'cha mean, Johnny? You remember *me*?

FIBBER: No, I don't think so. Your voice is familiar, but your face is strange.

OLD-TIMER: You're Fibber McGee, ain't ya?

FIBBER: No.

OLD-TIMER AND MOLLY: (*together*) *What?*

FIBBER: No, somebody says that since my vacation I'm a different person. I don't know who I am.

OLD-TIMER: (*cackles*) That's pretty good, Johnny, but that ain't the way I heared it. Way I heard it, one fella says 'other fellow, saaay . . .'" he says.

(*Audience laughter at this running gag.*)

OLD-TIMER: Why don't somebody get that fellow, Hitler? Don't worry, says t'other fellow. Sooner or later every housepainter's bound to kick the bucket.

There follows a discussion of their summer activities. Asked how it was on the lake . . .

MOLLY: Simply humming — with mosquitoes. What about you, Mister Old-Timer?

OLD-TIMER: I was working in a defense plant, daughter.

FIBBER: How'd you get *that* job?

OLD-TIMER: Well, sir, I answered an ad, Johnny. Seems they wanted a man with vision. A man people could look up to and who could still keep a down to earth attitude. And I got the job.

MOLLY: Doing *what?*

OLD-TIMER: Testing parachutes. I'll drop in here someday and tell you about it.

When the Old-Timer leaves, it's back to the camera. McGee picks up the phone.

FIBBER: Hello, operator. Give me the Atlantic and Frantic Railroad . . . Oh is that you, Myrt?"

MOLLY: *Ah, me!*

FIBBER: How's every little thing, Myrt? 'Tis huh? Yeah, nice vacation. What say, Myrt? Your brother from Montana? Working in a government garage. Does he still have that collie?"

MOLLY: "What's he doing in a government garage with a collie dog?"

FIBBER: Jeep herding. (*Weak laughter from audience*)

FIBBER: (*ad-libbing*) Oh, well, first show, we're trying.

FIBBER: What say, Myrt? Okay, put him on. Atlantic and Frantic Railroad. Look, there was a camera on my seat . . . Yeah, I know I should carry it over my shoulder . . . (trails off).

(*Musical interlude*)

The McGees go to the train station.

FIBBER: I wonder where the Lost and Found department *is*?

MOLLY: We just want the *lost* department. We haven't found anything.

FIBBER: They just call it that because you go there when you've found you lost something. (shouts) Hey bud! Hey you, 4-F! (A WWII military draft classification exempting one from serving).

There follows some rather silly conversation with the "information officer" who is so garrulous, McGee says he'd "Go around Robin Hood's barn for a short cut."

As usually happens when they are away from home, the McGees encounter one of their regular guests.

MOLLY: Well, if it ain't Abigail Uppington.

ABIGAIL: (*Falsetto*) Well, Mrs. McGee, how nice to see you again, and Mr. McGee.

FIBBER: Hi, Uppy!

There follows some more, rather silly dialogue about Mrs. U. carrying a book on her head to improve her "carriage." McGee in response to a question about the summer says he "really got tanned."

ABIGAIL: *Really?* I always said you should be.

("Uppy" says she made a short tour with a group selling War Bonds.)

ABIGAIL: Something must be done to stimulate people into buying more bonds. She is disturbed that some men in her neighborhood spent time sunning themselves on the roof.

FIBBER: Are they still doing it?

ABIGAIL: I don't know. I gave my binoculars to the Navy.

(She departs)

MOLLY: Come on, McGee, I have a lot of housecleaning to do.

HARLOW WILCOX: *(arriving)* Who said "housecleaning"?

MOLLY: *Oh, oh*—here's that man again.

HARLOW: How are you, Molly? Look at old man McGee here. Why you're looking swell, Pop.

FIBBER: Don't "Pop" me, you big hulk. If you feel so young why ain't you in school? Duckin' a truant officer?

HARLOW: That's how I feel all right: *Young*. Had a wonderful summer.

MOLLY: Where'd you go?

HARLOW: Didn't go anywhere. Why do people go away? For relaxation, sunshine, sports. Why I had all those things right here.

FIBBER: Take it easy, Junior. You'll burn yourself out before you're ninety.

MOLLY: How'd you get all those things without leaving town?

HARLOW: Just by working a little harder selling self polishing GloCoat®, Molly.

FIBBER: *(laughs)* Subtle, ain't he folks? Like a bull in ballet slippers.

HARLOW: Yeah, to me there's no greater sport than battling lint and dust and damp using Johnson's GloCoat®. And I get a good rest because it's so easy to apply. Just to know that kitchen linoleum can be so easily protected against dust and dirt calms my nerves and I am so contented, I sleep like a log.

MOLLY: Well, how about that, Sunshine?

HARLOW: Baby, you haven't seen sunshine until you've seen the smile on a housewife's face when she takes a look at that gleaming, sparkling GloCoated linoleum.

FIBBER: Harlow, you're so full of pep. Can you put your hands flat on the floor without bending your knees?

HARLOW: Certainly.

FIBBER: And hold that position?

HARLOW: Yeah. Why?" (*Distant*) You mean *like this?*

FIBBER: C'mon Molly let's go.

MOLLY: Look back, McGee, he's still doing it.

FIBBER: That's okay. I'll send a boy down Thursday morning to tell him he can straighten up. He don't mind. He's in his favorite position, bending over looking at a floor.

The McGees retrieve the camera and when Fibber suggests us taxi home, Molly says no as the cab cost a dollar and a quarter: "We can buy five war stamps with that. We'll take the street car."

Next, they meet Mayor LaTrivia, who's been very busy with War Bond rallies, salvage programs, and the like. McGee offers a slogan (over Molly's objection) for the salvage program. "We want all kinds of scrap metal, so get the lead out."

The McGees drive the mayor to his usual state of distraction by pretending to believe that his being incensed means he uses scent. He leaves in his usual state of barely controlled rage.

At this point, the King's Men sing "Praise the Lord and Pass the Ammunition," one of the most popular songs of the war. The rendition included sound effects of machine guns and cannons.

On their return home, McGee is visited by Teeny. Molly is upstairs as the part of Teeny is also played by Marian Jordan.

Teeny tells McGee that she and Willie Toops got real "savage" over the summer.

FIBBER: What did you get savage about?

TEENY: About two tons, I betcha.

FIBBER: What made you savage? (*She means to say "salvage"*)

TEENY: We didn't make it; we just collected it in Wilie Toops' coaster wagon.

(And, yes, were they were glad to get the radiator off daddy's car.)

FIBBER: Well, that was pretty generous of your old man . . . your father. To give them his car radiator.

TEENY: Oh, he didn't know we took it. We know the government needs metal, so we took it.

Teeny's departure is followed immediately by the arrival of Wallace Wimple, who has just had a tattoo — a rabbit — because Sweetie Face (his "big old wife") always wanted him to have hair (hare) on his chest.

Wimple leaves because he has promised Sweetie's face to practice "maneuvers" for the Army. She straps him in a baby carriage and pushes him off the porch, so that he will be ready to drive a jeep, if he ever gets in the Army. (Very unlikely, but *she* might get in)

McGee says, "Wimp has all the sparkling personality of a torn sock."

The program ends with the patented surprise — Fibber left the camera on the streetcar.

The broadcast ends with this exchange, directed at the listening audience:

MOLLY: Folks, I'm not a financier. I'm just a housewife. But I think I know when to turn the roast if we have a roast. And where the Army needs the roast more than we do, we'll have macaroni.

FIBBER: I don't care for macaroni.

MOLLY: McGee, if the government needs meat, you'll eat macaroni and like it.

FIBBER: With tomatoes? All right, then.

MOLLY: I just wanted to say to your other housewives and your men who sit in the living room and read the paper while us girls do the dishes that if we put our minds to it, we can strangle a post-war depression with our own apron strings. We can avoid most of the mess we had after the last war by backing up our government right now. We've got to pay our bills and don't buy anything we don't need. We've got to pay no more for things than the price Uncle Sam has set for them. And ask our merchants to post those prices where we can see them. And in order to help pay for this war and provide a cushion for after the war. There's no better investment than WAR BONDS. Remember "V" for Victory, and if you know your alphabet, you know the only way to reach "V" is through "U."

FIBBER AND MOLLY: Good night.

The statement by Molly took time normally given over to a Johnson's commercial, another example of the company's support for the war effort.

Chapter Three:
The Radio Broadcast Environment Before and During the War

In a time of war the democratic government needs to inform, inspire, console, cajole, and exhort. For totalitarian states like Japan and Germany, during the war, one may add "inflame, threaten, and misinform." In radio, for the first time in history, both kinds of government possessed a medium of communication which allowed them to do these things almost instantaneously—and on a broad scale. The difference between the two political ideologies was that Japan and Germany owned/controlled radio, while the United States did not.

It seems reasonably clear that in the months before Pearl Harbor, the government was anticipating and preparing for war; the broadcast industry expected war as well, but had an unclear vision of what to expect from the government; and the commercial sponsors of radio shows were *not* ready.

For the reader interested in the details of the interaction of these three parties, two books are highly recommended. The first is *Radio in Wartime* by Sherman Dreyer (SHD). This extraordinary book was written and published within a year of Pearl Harbor! It is remarkable in its prescience. The second book, *Radio Goes to War* by Gerd Horten (GS), has the advantage of the author knowing history and sharing this knowledge with the reader.

In this chapter, I have tried to distill the essence of the wartime environment and the reaction to it in order to put the actions of the stars, writers, and sponsors into perspective.

The portents of war were predicted by some, embraced by some and denied by others in the United States. In any event, the government was not *well* prepared for what would be expected, nor was the broadcasting industry. Certainly neither knew what to expect of the other. World War II was the first war in which world-wide broadcasting facilities were available. No precedents were available as models.

Siepman (CS4, p.27) observed that "In peace, we listeners used radio for our pleasure, as a toy. War forces us to recognize it as a tool, indispensable to the prosecution of war and to the preparation for peace." His implication is so eloquent it would be wrong to paraphrase, as we quote verbatim:

> Our enemies have here forestalled us. Exploiting our childlike use of it, they long ago converted radio into a tool with a destructive purpose. They have used it, like a demented dentist, as a drill to work on the decay in our wisdom teeth and drive through to the nerve ends of our morale. Belatedly we recognize that we must "put away childish things." The challenge of war, to radio and to radio's listeners is challenge to adult responsibility. By this criterion, we must define its purpose and judge the value of its services on the home front. Both the matter and the manner of radio's communication are being crucially affected by the war. Its uses on the home front fall into three main categories, none of them wholly new, but each affected by the war, by the country's need of us, and, equally, by our own needs, as we emerge from the first dazed bewilderment that war induces and grope towards the self-discovery and the new clarity of mind and purpose that is asked of us. (CS4, p.27)

The three categories referred to by Siepman are as follows:

1. News, where authenticity is more important than immediacy (where perspective is important), and where tone and "meticulous discretion is necessary to reduce the sensitivity to the incongruous." (e.g. crude advertising alongside fearful news)

2. Relief from care. Relaxation. As Siepman put it: "We need a tonic, not a laxative."

3. Building and sustaining morale. The military was off guard and unprepared for Pearl Harbor. So, too, was the populace generally, mentally, and emotionally unprepared. It was necessary, in this regard that the collaboration between the government and the broadcast industry (just getting started when this was written) was a necessity.

Siepman's description of the state of radio at the time, its need to adapt to the wartime environment, and its challenges for the future was articulate and compelling. A thorough reading of the complete 1942 pamphlet which served as the source of this brief and incomplete excerpt is highly recommended.

OWI, NAP, and other Letters of the Alphabet

The government began to develop an organization to energize public opinion in 1941. There was no shortage of civilian groups eager to participate. The effects came together in 1942 with the formation of the Office of War Information (OWI).

Other agencies also contributed in overlapping and ultimately restricting ways to the government-information effort. One was the Office of Emergency Management, which proved to be ineffective. The Office of Government Reports (OGR), directed by a close friend of the president, was charged with the propagandizing on behalf of the administration. In May 1941, (before Pearl Harbor of course), the president created the Office of Civil Defense (OCD) under the direction of New York City's Mayor La Guardia. The mission of OCD was to build morale toward defense efforts and improve public relations with the media. Within a short time, FDR established a branch of OCD, the Office of Facts and Figures (OFF) to "provide public opinion samplings and give Americans an accurate and coherent account of government policy." No propaganda! It is important to realize that at this point, the U.S. was not yet at war and that FDR had won the 1940 election for an unprecedented third term on a platform of neutrality.

Yet another agency, the Office of the Coordinator of Information (OCI), was created in 1941 (July) to be an information collection bureau concerned with issues of national security. OCI would eventually become the CIA and in August of the same year produced yet another offshoot, the Foreign Information Service (FIS), to direct U.S. propaganda to the rest of a world already at war. This agency eventually became known as "The Voice of America."

Is the reader confused? No wonder others were.

Pearl Harbor forced a quick end to the confusion over who should do what about war — related communication. The result of comparatively quick action was the establishment of the Office of War Information (OWI) in June 1943. The mission, under Elmer Davis, was to formulate and carry out, through the use of press, radio, motion pictures and other facilities, information programs designed to facilitate the development of an informed and intelligent understanding, at home and abroad, of the status and progress of the war effort and of the war policies, activities, and aims of the government; review, clear, and approve all proposed radio and motion picture programs sponsored by federal departments and agencies, and serve as the central point of clearance and contact for the radio broadcasting and motion picture industries respectively in their relationships with federal departments and agencies concerning such government programs.

OWI consisted of a number of bureaus. It was the Bureau of Campaigns which became the seat of advertising-sponsored patriotic promotion in all media. The Bureau of Campaigns worked closely with the War Advertising Council.

The Radio Bureau, directed by William B. Lewis, had primarily a function of coordination and was launched in October 1942, with the following dictum:

> All plans or proposals for new or continuing series or for individual radio programs developed by or for the national headquarters of the several Government Agencies for local stations or networks will be submitted to the Chief of the Radio Bureau, OWI, for clearance . . . At the discretion of the Radio

Bureau, this material will be channeled to the proper outlets.

The result was the development of the Network Allocation Plan (NAP), which circulated "an average of three messages a week" on more than one hundred of the highest-rated sustaining and commercial programs, through submission of timely themes and campaigns to the advertising agencies and networks that produced them. The ways in which specific messages were to be incorporated into programs were left to the discretion of the producers; anything from a few lines of dialogue to a spot announcement at some point in the program, to a dramatic enactment within the show's plot served to advance wartime messages, or, in the case of Fibber McGee, a comedic treatment.

NAP

The Network Allocation Plan began in April 1942, and was applied only to sponsored shows carried over the three networks. It *asked*, but did not *require*, the advertiser to feature a war message on every fourth show if they were a weekly program, and on a biweekly basis if they aired more often (such as news broadcasts and soap operas).

The OWI drew up plans on a four-week basis, including three or four war topics which were matched with the show's ratings. The most important topic was assigned to the highest-rated show. Horten (GH, p.126) provides an example of Tuesday night programming in Table 1.

TABLE I

RADIO NETWORK ALLOCATION PLAN FOR TUESDAY NIGHTS
(APRIL 27 – MAY 24, 1942)

FIRST WEEK: (APRIL 27 – MAY 3, 1942)

7:30 NBC – RED	8:00 CBS	9:00 BLUE	10:00 CBS
BURNS & ALLEN	MISSING HEIRS	JURY TRIALS	GLENN MILLER
22.1 RATING*	13.0	7.1	3.4
WAR BONDS	MARINES	NEED FOR NURSES	SCRAP METAL

SECOND WEEK (MAY 4 – MAY 10, 1942)

8:00 BLUE	8:30 NBC	9:00 CBS	9:30 NBC
CUGAT	TREASURE CHEST	DUFFY'S TAVERN	FIBBER MCGEE
3.3	14.4	6.4	40.8
SUGAR RATIONING	WAR BONDS	PRICE CONTROL	SUGAR RATIONING

THIRD WEEK (MAY 11 – MAY 17, 1942)

7:00 BLUE	7:30 CBS	9:00 NBC	10:30 NBC
EASY ACES	SECOND HUSBAND	BATTLE OF SEXES	RED SKELTON
6.1	8.5	15.3	22.6
PRICE CONTROL	NEED FOR NURSES	WAR BONDS	USO

FOURTH WEEK (MAY 18 – MAY 24, 1942

6:15 CBS	8:00 NBC	8:30 CBS	10:00 NBC
VOICE OF BROADWAY	JOHNNY PRESENTS	BOB BURNS	BOB HOPE
3.7	12.9	16.7	34.3
CAR POOLING	WAR BONDS	WAR BONDS	USO

*CAB ratings of April 1942, as given in the OWI outline; obviously these ratings changed over time, but they presented general estimates of a program's popularity. The themes reflect the priorities of the OWI for the first four weeks after the inauguration of the Allocation Plan on April 27, 1942. (Source: GH, p.126)

The president was enthusiastic about the plan, calling it "the most powerful weapon of communication on government information ever designed in any country." (GH, p.125) Indeed, the messages reached 90 million Americans daily. The editor of *Variety* praised "radio's showmanship" in integrating OWI message into plots rather than simply making announcements. From the outset, *Fibber McGee and Molly* provided a model for other shows in this respect and also set a pattern for this wartime effort. The first element was the "theme show." One example can be found in a show dated May 5, 1942. The subject was the effort to register the public for sugar rationing. Fibber decided to help the government by preparing a sugar substitute. The entire show focused on the issue of sugar rationing. In fact, Fibber's development was the simple practice of roughing the bottom of coffee cups. The hoax was so successful that some of the show's "regular" visitors even complained that Fibber had given them too *much* sugar.

The second element, used throughout the war by the show, was the use of short exchanges usually between Fibber and Molly, or one-liners. Fibber explained his sugar substitute plan to Molly adding, "Hitler's got a substitute for everything!" Molly, who frequently got to deliver the laugh line, retorted, "And do you know they'll soon need a substitute for Hitler."

One observer described the NAP as being as close to a "master morale plan" as the United States ever developed. (GH, p.126)

In 1942 Dreyer (SHD, pp.66-71) brilliantly described the future as it needed to be: "The secret of radio as a weapon can be cracked if radio is able to effectively inform people and clarify issues . . . it must be understood that information without clarification, or attempts at clarification without adequate information [will fail]." He set about to assist in the "digestion" of news by "news-hungry" Americans.

In 1945 Dreyer (SHD, pp.5-19) called the Office of War Information "the most important of all government agencies to radio in wartime." The OWI, shortly after Pearl Harbor, issued a list of government messages and war themes to be emphasized on the air. At the national level the Priority Rankings, for use by all stations was as shown in Table 2.

Table 2
Priority after War Messages

A: This material is "rush" and should be allotted about 50 per cent of the total "program units" you can use for war messages (a spot announcement or a 15-minute show are each considered one "program unit").	This material is of a major importance and should be allotted about 30 per cent of your available "Program units."
Recruiting for Naval Services: Navy, Marines, Merchant Marine, Coast Guard.	Automobile and truck pooling (WPB and Department of Agriculture).
Recruiting for Army Production Drive information (WPB) Price Control (WPB-OPA) Salvage of rubber (WPB) Sale of War Bonds and Stamps (Treasure) USO (until July 4)	Gasoline rationing (WPB-OPA), Labor recruitment and training for war industries (state and local offices of the U.S.E.S.). Need for nurses (Federal Security Agency), Civilian enrollment for voluntary service (Office of Civilian Defense). Recruiting of shipyard workers (Maritime Commission, and state and local offices of the U.S.E.S.).
B: This is supplementary material and should be allotted no more than 20 per cent of your available "program units."	C: This material should be used only if material in the preceding classifications has been adequately presented.
Salvage of scrap metal, rags (WPB-OPA) National nutrition drive (Federal Security Agency) First aid information (Office of Civilian Defense) Child welfare in wartime (Department of Labor) Information on the other Americas	Conserve electric power (WPB-OPA) Conservation of household equipment — refrigerators, stoves, etc. (Office of Civilian Defense and Department of Agriculture) WPA concerns (Federal Works Agency) Civil service war jobs.

Dreyer listed six areas of necessary public understanding if the general public was to be enlisted in a concerted war effort. In addition, he carefully (and, again, brilliantly) identified the problems associated with each area. These problems were elucidated based on public opinion polls, and confirmed by leaders and specialists.

1. THE ISSUES
We are fighting to defeat our enemies and crush predatory militarism. We don't want to be pushed around by international gangsters. We were attacked and had to fight ready to give up our standards of comfort as the need arises.

2. SACRIFICE
We know that war is expensive in blood and treasure and we say we are

PROBLEMS
BUT we are not agreed on what the peace should be. We are divided on post-war international cooperation. We are not clear on just what constitutes the justice and morality of our cause. We think the *leader* of our enemies and not the *peoples* are at fault. We cannot agree on the basic causes of the war.

BUT we toy with the idea that the war will last only a year or two longer and that we won't have to give up *too much*. We are confused about rationing, shortages, civilian production, man-power control. Congress plays politics with Selective Service. On a voluntary basis we are not cooperating sufficiently on bond purchases. We do not really understand the powerful economic forces at work which will ultimately cut our living standards greatly. We hope against hope that the pinch will somehow never come.

3. THE UNITED NATIONS
We admire and applaud the heroic defense of the

Russians and the raids of the British Commandos and air forces. We praise China's five-year war against Japan. We take pride and hope in the fact that most of the world's population is on our side.

BUT there is widespread dissatisfaction with the British, whom we suspect of trying to muddle through instead of fighting through. We applaud Russia with crossed fingers, and are suspicious of the Kremlin and Communism. We have faith that China will fight on and that we don't need to help her too much. We are race-conscious, and in the same breath castigate the "yellow bastards" of Japan and embrace our Chinese allies. We are confused as to the global implications of the war.

4. THE ENEMY

We are sorry for the Italians and make them the butt of our jokes. We respect the German military machine and power and realize that the Japanese are a shrewd and unscrupulous foe. We know that victory over the Axis won't be too easy. We are shocked by the regimentation and cruelty of the Axis. We are determined to crush the enemy.

BUT we will still believe that when we can lay our hands on the Japanese we'll take 'em good and proper. We clutch at the idea their lines are over-extended. We think a small military clique is leading the nation and that a few tough defeats will cause trouble at home. We believe the Japanese are cowards when they meet real opposition, and that their low standard of living will ultimately trip them up. We believe to a large extent that Nazi Europe is seething with revolt and that the peoples of Europe may yet overthrow Hitler for us. We believe Hitler is responsible for the trouble, and if Hitler dies, maybe peace can be made. We do not really understand the forces and issues of fascism except on the naïve level that they are brutal and regimented.

5. WORK AND PRODUCTION.

We understand that in a total war (a phrase we are fond of using) everyone probably has a job to do. We understand that America is the United Nations' arsenal and that our factories hold a key to victory. We know that our production can outstrip Axis production. There is widespread belief that our equipment is the best in the world.

BUT we are suspicious of high wages for labor and distrustful of unions. We know that profiteering by management is going on. We do not understand fully the importance, the place or role of agriculture in the total effort. Millions of us fail to see how our jobs help the war. We are not aware of the very serious problems in transportation and believe unwisely that production alone may win for us. But we have a better understanding of the need for work and production than we have of any of the other five points.

6. THE FIGHTING FORCES

We admire our sailors and soldiers and are cocky about their ability to win victory. We believe they are the best-equipped in the world. We trust our military leaders, and have made heroes of several of them — MacArthur, for example. We understand that all elements of the military must be coordinated as a fighting unit.

BUT we are largely ignorant of the elements of strategy, tactics, and logistics. We believe our military forces are the best — but we do not know why. We are sharply divided on the question of air power — its place and management. We temper our trust in

our military leaders with transient suspicions of their
judgment and competency. We do not understand
the reasons for a large army or the extent to which it
will disrupt civilian life. We suspect that the military
aren't always putting the best abilities of soldiers to
the best use.
(Source: SHD pgs. 67-70)

Dreyer noted that the "need for information and clarification is
clear," and that the responsibility did not rest solely with radio, "but
radio probably offers the best single means of reaching the public."
It is not known whether the writers and performers on *Fibber
McGee and Molly* ever read these words, but it is not hyperbolic to
say that at one time or another in their broadcasts virtually all were
addressed.

CENSORSHIP

Censorship was viewed as a necessary evil by the broadcast industry.
It was not seen in the pejorative sense that is usually embraced by
writers and artists. Even before the U.S. entered the war, there were
self-imposed restrictions. As MacDonald notes (MD1, p.63), on a
single day, (September 3, 1939) Americans heard live transmission
of the following:

1. The declaration of war against Germany issued
   by the British and French governments.

2. An address to the British Empire by King George
   VI of England.

3. A speech by the British Prime Minister, Neville
   Chamberlain.

4. A speech by President Roosevelt.

5. A speech by the Canadian prime minister,
   Mackenzie King.

6. News reports about the torpedoing of a transatlantic liner.

Over the next two years radio broadcasters struggled to stay neutral. Without government suggestions they instituted the following:

1. That avoidance of horror, suspense, and undue excitement in reporting the news and the plight of refugees.

2. Scrupulous checking of news sources before broadcasting.

3. Careful labeling of propaganda when used in broadcasting.

The network policy of neutrality also extended to entertainment programming. Dramatic shows could not involve sabotage, subversion, or spying within the United States. Heroes could not be involved for one side or another in the war. Broadcasters could not openly side with any of the combatants. Yet programs skirted prescriptions by concentrating upon patriotic topics. By lauding American society and its institutions, radio effectively proclaimed the principles of democracy, equality, freedom, individualism, and the rule of law. It was not difficult to link such values with the anti-Fascist cause.

Once the war began, the National Association of Broadcasters (NAB) issued its own, voluntary rules:

• DO NOT broadcast rumors, "hot tips" or "unconfirmed reports," no matter what their source. "Hot tips" and rumors may burn your fingers. If you have the slightest doubt on any story, check with your press association. It is better to have no news than to broadcast false or harmful news.

• In this connection, a word of caution on news flashes. A good practice is to wait a few minutes after the first flash until you are perfectly satisfied from the following story that the flash is borne out.

- Radio's speed of light is cause for caution.

- DO NOT broadcast news which concerns war production figures unless such news is *officially* released by the government.

- DO NOT broadcast the movement of naval or any other vessels.

- DO NOT broadcast news about the movement of troops or personnel either outside or within the continental limits, unless it has been released *officially* by the War or Navy Departments.

- DO NOT broadcast the location of vessels, either under construction or about to be launched.

- DO NOT broadcast figures of Selective Service enrollments and inductions.

- DO NOT broadcast personal observations on weather conditions. Watch sports broadcasts for this. A late night or early morning comment that "it's a fine, clear night (or morning)" might be invaluable information to the enemy. Stick to official weather reports your station receives from your local weather bureau.

- DO NOT broadcast such imperatives as "Attention all men! Report to your local Civilian Defense headquarters tonight at eight." Reserve such "attention compellers" for important war purposes.

- DO NOT overestimate American power nor underestimate the enemy strength and thereby tend to create complacent confidence. Stick to the facts as presented in official releases.

- DO NOT allow sponsors to use the news as a springboard for commercials. Such practices as starting commercials with "Now some good news, etc." should *never* be permitted. Also it is important that such news-phrases as "bulletin," "flash," "news" and the like be used only in their legitimate functions. Do not permit, "here's good news! The Bargain Basement announces drastic reductions, etc."

- DO NOT use any sound-effects on dramatic programs, commercial announcements or otherwise which might be confused by the listener as air raid alarms, alert signals, etc.

- DO NOT try to second-guess or master-mind our military officials. Leave this for established military analysts and experts, who are experienced enough to await the facts before drawing conclusions.

- DO NOT broadcast any long lists of casualties. This has been specifically forbidden.

- DO NOT permit speakers, in discussions of controversial public issues, to say anything of aid to the enemy.

- DO NOT broadcast location of the plants engaged in the manufacture of war materials unless approved by the government. This applies to emergencies such as explosions, sabotage, etc., unless such reports have been approved by the government or cleared at the source by press associations.

- DO NOT take chances with ad-lib broadcasts, on the street or in the studio. An open microphone accessible to the general public constitutes a very real hazard in times of war. Questions should be prepared and approved in advance and extreme care should be exercised to avoid the asking of questions which would draw out any information or answer which would disclose matters or information of value to the enemy.

Dreyer (SHD, 21-22) was critical of these efforts.

The real opportunities for radio lie in what other categories of programs *might* and *should* do. Here censorship offers no guidance. In the area of positive action the responsibility is radios exclusively. And here the industry's thinking is conditioned by two things. First, in wartime it is preoccupied with "don'ts." Censorship and caution have so impressed them that most program ideas are *first* scrutinized from the angle of what they should not do or say. Second, radio is still wedded to the peacetime idea that entertainment is its prime function. Hence, it next scrutinizes programs from the angle of likely audience response. Now both of these predispositions delimit sharply the likelihood of effective positive policies emerging, for they are restrictive, not creative, influences. As a consequence, programs are increasingly serving the war effort in one of these ways: by simply inserting war plugs in the body of a program; by weaving occasional war references into dialogue; by originating programs at military camps or training posts, thereby providing an opportunity for passing comment on "our armed forces"; by setting dramatic programs against a background of war or sabotage, but in no other way changing the cops-and-robbers formula; or by producing special "morale" programs which generally garnish known events and information with music, sound effects and large casts.

All of these techniques are radio costuming. With a few notable exceptions they are peacetime radio fare dressed up in khaki. They make us aware of the existence of war, but they seldom inform us about the facts and issues of the war. Information and clarification are the chief areas in which positive and creative contributions might be made by radio.

The producers of *Fibber McGee and Molly* took *all* of Dreyer's observations seriously and applied them vigorously.

Morale

Dreyer (SHD, pp.107-127), in quoting the Office of Public Opinion Research, listed seven components of morale.

1. A good morale in a democracy requires that public opinion be informed. This means more than keeping pace with the headlines; it means understanding fully the issues and principles at stake in the war.

2. Morale depends upon the extent to which the people agree on objectives. Objectives can be defined only on the basis on information and an understanding of events and issues. An uninformed or confused people cannot readily agree on objectives; hence, communication is the thread which gives integration to opinion.

3. Morale depends upon the faith men have that their objectives can be obtained, and on their determination to achieve the objectives at whatever cost is necessary. There seems little doubt that the American people are confident of ultimate victory and seem more than willing to pay whatever cost is necessary to achieve victory; hence, in this regard their morale may be considered good.

4. It is important that the citizen have a realistic picture of the job ahead to attain objectives. Methods of indirection and sugar-coating are grim reminders of a former war and are recognized today as methods of totalitarian states. In other words, the people must receive more than exhortations to victory and more than facts about progress toward victory. They must receive frank clarification and in short they must be prepared for reverses.

5. Morale depends upon confidence in leadership. In war, people may agree upon objectives without having the capacity or opportunity to decide how those objectives may best be achieved. As a result, there is great reliance on leadership.

6. Morale depends also on the extent to which people feel their allies in distant lands are carrying on, too. The first requisite, of course, is complete information about one's allies.

7. Morale depends upon the extent to which the country is unified for a common effort, and the extent to which the individual feels himself a functioning part of that effort. In total war, every citizen has a role to perform.

Again, Don Quinn and the Jordan's, using Quinn's words, continued to be on target!

PROPAGANDA

"It is a terrible weapon "the hands of those who know how to make use of it."

— Adolf Hitler commenting on the medium
of radio in his book, *Mein Kampf*

Hitler, not only *believed* this, he put his words to work appointing a minister of propaganda, Joseph Goebbels, who shared his views. As early as 1933 at the Berlin Radio Exhibition, he declared that "in the twentieth century, radio" would take over the role that the press had played in the nineteenth (see JH for an elaboration of the "Nazi Model," including the role of "Lord Hawhaw" in broadcasts to Great Britain).

The term "propaganda" — even more than "censorship" — is generally viewed as pejorative. Again, Dreyer (SHD, p.123) puts a more positive "spin" on the concept.

> The American people are elusive as the target of propagandists. They have morale of great potential; the propagandist's job is to help them realize their potential more speedily than they probably would without his help. Whatever strategy may be determined upon for the technician to follow, it cannot ignore the fact that much of its effectiveness will depend on how that policy is packaged.

An example of that packaging is the use of humor.

> Humor is valuable for two reasons — humor accompanies self-insight and, like it, makes for a sense of proportion having a marked signifying effect. Second, humor pricks what is pompous, reducing it to dust. A sense of humor is necessary to the attainment of a maturely integrated personality wherein knowledge, values and a sense of proportion are well blended. (SHD, p.122)

> Hitler, and to a lesser extend the Japanese, were easy and frequent targets of humor. American radio had no plans for war. We had no blueprints, no spare antennae, no passwords, and no sealed orders. Above all, we had no corps of propaganda master-minds standing by complete with directives for psychological blitzkriegs. To have possessed these things would have been in a very subtle sense, profoundly un-American.

American radio did, however, offer an abundance of humor and entertainment. Dreyer (SHD45) admonished that

> radio must abandon the belief that entertainment in itself is a primary contribution to the war, if it is to maximize its effectiveness as a weapon. Entertainment has its place even in wartime broadcasting, and the problem is to put it in its place. Wartime broadcasting is most successful when it stimulates interest, resolve, and *active response*.

William B. Lewis of the Office of War Information recognized the foregoing: "Let's not forget that radio is primarily an entertainment medium and must continue to be if it is . . . to deliver the large audience we want to reach [with wartime messages]." Then, compellingly, "Radio propaganda must be painless." (GH, p.117)

In his insightful review, Horton (GH, p.118) put this in perspective:

Radio comedy was in the vanguard of radio's efforts to supply propaganda through entertainment. It was the most popular radio genre and thus reached the greatest number of Americans on a regular basis. Even during the war, it maintained its transgressive and carnivalesque function by turning accepted norms upside down and pushing against the boundaries of what was deemed acceptable. Most important, these comedy shows simultaneously informed and inspired their listeners through a steady stream of well-dosed and well-orchestrated propaganda campaigns.

A notable exception to the view that humor was an effective propaganda tool was that of the celebrated radio writer Arch Oboler, who, while (*not* according to his own words) urging that we *hate* our enemies, was at least all for calling specific and graphic attention to the evil they represented.

Yet another point of view was expressed by Siepman (CS, p.28) in 1942:

The wartime listener looks to radio, secondly, for relief from care, for relaxation. Laughter and entertainment are more than ever necessary. But again war qualifies the nature of the need. We need a tonic, not a laxative. We need, if we do not yet clamor for, an end to all invitation to cheap, vicarious experience. The morbid indulgence in escapism, for which peacetime radio sometimes catered, always a doubtful luxury, is in war a dangerous liability. Webster calls (propaganda) "any organized or concerted group effort, or movement to spread particular doctrines, information, etc." In this sense, propaganda is the influencing of people's ideas so that they will think or act in a certain manner . . .

In this sense was the *Fibber McGee and Molly* show "propaganda"?

Something for the Children

MacDonald (MD, p.68-69) made no bones about his view that ". . . nowhere was the propagandizing more obvious than in children's programs." "Impressionable minds," MacDonald asserted, "how became targets of plots that were as brutalizing as anything intended for adult listeners. American children fought World War II in front of their radio sets."

For *real* heroes there were *Don Winslow of the Navy* and *Hop Harrigan.* Winslow, a naval aviator, bombed ships attacked Nazi's and hated the Japanese. Harrigan, ostensibly an eighteen-year freelance aviator, also bombed ships, engaged in dog fights, rescued a buddy while dodging German machine-gun bullets.

Enemies were fought throughout the world by such unlikely heroes as *Captain Midnight, Terry and the Pirates,* and even *Jungle Jim* (who did so in the movies as well). Back in America, children had such fighting heroes as *Superman, The Green Hornet, Jack Armstrong (The All-American Boy),* and (although a little out of his cowboy era) *Tom Mix.*

Nachman (GN, p.209) explained the ease with which Tom Mix made the transition for children, who were more interested in action than in logic.

> Routine cattle-rustlers and stagecoach bandits were replaced by such polecats as spies and saboteurs. In May 1945, Tom mounted the soapbox and vowed "We've shown Hitler and his gang that we know how to lick bullies and racketeers, but we've still got a big job to do for our brothers, and our cousins, and our uncles, and our dads who are still fighting the Japs." It was easy to spot the bad guys on westerns in the 1940s because in lieu of black hats they sported Asian or German accents.

As MacDonald put it, "Never had a war been taken so directly to American youngsters."

It should be remembered that children also comprised a substantial part of the audience of "adult" shows such as *Fibber McGee and Molly.*

SOMETHING FOR THE LADIES

Lichty and Topping (LT, 380) judged that "radio" drama fell far short of its potential to inform, inspire, and motivate. Not that the war was ignored. Here are some examples.

- On *The Story of Mary Marlin*, the leading character's missing husband turned up in Tunisia with bandages over his eyes.

- Portia (*Portia Faces Life*) found her husband falsely accused of Nazi spying; when, in fact, he was working for American Intelligence in Germany.

- *Young Widder Brown* was, for the war, affianced to a doctor in the Medical Corps.

- *Young Dr. Malone* went to England in 1942 and accepted a commission in the British armed forces. (This story of star-crossed lovers brought on many tears.)

- *Ma Perkins'* son was killed as a infantryman.

- The husband of the heroine of *The Right to Happiness*, returned from being wounded in action just as she, mistakenly believing him dead, was just about to marry another.

- *Front-Page Farrell* found his wife a job in an ammunitions factory.

- *Stella Dallas* took a job in a war plant and soon became involved in foiling a plot by enemy agents.

For many more examples as well as an enlightening discussion of how OWI worked with writers and producers, the reader is referred to Lichty and Topping (LT).

SOMETHING FOR THE BOYS

(This section draws heavily on MH, pp.259-260.)

As domestic radio struggled to redefine American identity on the home front, the increasing number of troops abroad soon brought about an extension of the OWI's mission to include broadcasting overseas. The shortwave rebroadcast of sports results to troops stationed in Iceland in 1941 expanded to the formation of the Armed Forces Radio Service.

THE INDUSTRY AND ITS SPONSORS

The radio broadcasting industry, essentially the three major networks, was perpetually between the proverbial rock and hard place. The "rock" was the government, which controlled the licensure and which had (at least theoretically) the power to take over radio or, in these circumstances, to initiate the "C" word, Censorship. The "hard place" was, of course, the commercial sponsors, who provided the revenue necessary to keep the networks in business.

Both had, of course, enormous resources of talent. Rex Stout (creator of *Nero Wolfe*), was a strong anti-Nazi voice, serving as chairman of the War Writer's Board and moderated the CBS series, *Our Secret Weapon*.

The Office of War Information was meanwhile tangled in a wilderness of problems. Since Pearl Harbor, every government agency had bombarded sponsors, advertising agencies, directors, and performers with requests for the insertion of announcements in popular network series. Each such announcement was represented as crucial to the war effort. Americans *must* be persuaded to save cans, buy War Bonds (they were no longer "Defense" Bonds), learn nursing skills, black out windows, eat properly, avoid rumors, become air raid wardens, write letters to soldiers, and curb travel. The advertising agencies requested that the government determine priorities in some organized way. OWI acquired this function. Before long, the message-distribution system was in operation as described above.

While some government groups were pressing an argument against war advertising, others were playing into the hands of the advertisers. The government units besieging sponsored radio for help with war announcements were providing it with a potent argument. Advertising began to call itself "the information industry," and to dramatize its role in the relaying of war messages. The War Advertising Council could cite the pleas of government agencies and the subsequent letters of praise and gratitude. The war, it seemed, could hardly be won without advertising. By mid-1942 the battle was over. After a conference with U.S. Treasury officials, advertising leaders announced triumphantly that agreement had been reached. Advertising, including institutional advertising, would be deductible, if "reasonable."

The result was this: although advertising had dropped during World War I, it increased steadily in World War II — especially in radio. The victory of the advertisers made the radio boom secure. (This section relies heavily on reference EWB, pp. 165–169.) The challenge was to use the tremendous power of radio while keeping the audience which made radio so valuable, as Horten put it, "skillfully superimposing the war effort on the existing structure." (GH, p.124.) The broadcasting industry was eager to cooperate.

The advertisers were relatively early in finding ways and reasons to lend their talents to the war effort. In some ways it was a case of enlightened self interest. No matter!

> With little to sell or to advertise, advertising should sell itself, as well as American business and free enterprise. As James W. Young, Senior Consultant of the J. Walter Thompson Company, reassured his colleagues, advertisers did not have to fold up their tents during a wartime crisis: Let us ask ourselves whether we, as an industry, do not have a great contribution to make in this effort to regain for business the leadership of our economy. We have within our hands the greatest aggregate means of mass education and persuasion the world has ever seen — namely, the channels. Why do we not use it?

In (GH, p.92) . . .

> The representatives of two trade associations did
> agree, however, to begin making plans to establish
> the Advertising Council, an umbrella organization
> for advertisers to fend off criticism of the industry
> and to deal with the challenges of a likely wartime
> crisis. A little more than two weeks later, in early
> December 1941, America was at war, and, after
> meetings with government officials, advertising
> executives began operations of the council.
>
> The War Advertising Council (WAC) brought together
> advertisers from all media. Its board of directors was
> composed of an equal number of representatives
> from each of three groups: commercial clients
> (companies with large advertising budgets), advertising
> agencies, and the advertising media. The WAC proved
> its effectiveness in the very first campaign in which
> it collaborated with the government in February
> 1942. This was the Treasury Department's payroll
> deduction plan, which asked all working Americans
> to have 10 percent of their monthly pay automatically
> deducted from their payroll and applied toward buying
> war bonds. Through extensive advertising of the payroll
> deduction plan, twenty-four million workers had
> enrolled by the end of 1942, funneling $365 million
> into the Treasury each month.
>
> A new tax law provided the single-most important
> boost to wartime advertising. Even if companies had
> nothing to sell, how could they pass up a chance to
> use practically free advertising paid for by the American
> taxpayer for institutional and goodwill copy? America's
> entry into the war had forced government and business
> to work in ever-closer collaboration. Advertising, as
> an extension of the free enterprise system, was part
> of this confluence.

Emil Schram argued in *Printer's Ink*: "In a certain sense American business is now being submitted to an acid test. If American business . . . proves once and for all its capabilities, it will occupy an unassailable position when the difficult period of post-war readjustment sets in." In an article entitled "Opportunity!," Walter Weir of the Lord and Thomas Agency echoed the same sentiment for advertisers: "Here we sit with the greatest force for moving mass psychology that the world has ever seen . . . We can demonstrate the power of advertising as it has never been demonstrated before. We can justify its existence as it has never been justified before . . . And if we make advertising fight today, we'll never again have to defend its place in our economy."

Radio entertainment played a crucial part in this wartime process. Like no other medium, radio entertainment merged the various layers of wartime culture into one: advertising as the selling of the product; advertising as selfless wartime service, with official government sanction no less; and, finally, advertising fused with radio entertainment and closely connected with the favorite radio stars of the American people. Despite persistent criticisms and controversy over specific radio advertisements or the amount of advertising on the air, and despite Americans' continued skepticism toward advertising and propaganda, it was a winning combination for business.

Something should be said here about the special contribution of commercial sponsors to programs broadcast on the Armed Forces Radio Service. Though at first existing network programs were recorded in their entirety, it soon became apparent that listening to familiar plugs for products singularly lacking overseas actually had a detrimental effect on morale. The AFRS instituted a policy of deleting commercial announcements from programs — a process called, interestingly, denaturing — but the often integrated nature of commercial content in radio programming made for broadcasts with large and gaping holes, such as those left by the deletion of introductions in which product names were inextricable woven into the narration or of transitions performed in interior commercial spots. AFRS personnel tried various methods to compensate for the lack of commercials by substituting "gag" announcements or extended musical interludes, but for some programs complete reworking was necessary.

Obviously, those in the military were hungry for news (and entertainment) from home. Finding enough receivers was a problem early on, but the difficulties and delays were, at last, offset by the qualities of the broadcasts. The soldiers got the pick of the best programs from the home networks, minus only the advertising. Strangely enough, not a few of the men professed to miss the commercials! They yearned nostalgically for the programs just as they had heard them in the States. Yet the commercials were omitted to save the G.I. the irritation of hearing about things that were not available to him. A marine on Iwo Jima would get no lift from a spiel recommending ice-cold Coca-Cola. In the malaria-infested jungles of the Pacific the men might see only bitter irony in the warning to guard against "the dangers of the common cold." The most depressing commercials, heard via shortwave early in the war by the survivors on Bataan, had been descriptions of the feasts planned at home for Christmas dinners.

To the credit of the advertisers, it must be set down that not a single objection was raised to the Army request that they make their programs available for troops overseas *without commercials*. However, the true "commercials" of AFRS programs consisted of morale messages. Someone described the AFRS's basic sales pitch: "Morale, Americanism, security, things are going 'OK' at home, we are sending you the needed materials, we are doing all we can to help you, this is your country — America, you are the best soldier there is, the "why" of things and finally you will win!"

Despite all the trials and delays and missteps, broadcasting to the troops brought its own rewards in the enthusiastic reactions of the G.I.'s. They loved it.

CONCLUSION

As Dreyer observed less than a year after the Japanese attack on Pearl Harbor, "like the legendary steed, radio is riding off furiously in all directions." Yet World War II was a radio war from Roosevelt's "Day of Infamy" speech to the surrender ceremonies on September 5, 1945.

Clearly, the radio industry and the government would be compelled to work together. Radio was patriotic and willing but, as one executive put it: "We want to be regulated, but not run." (SHD, p.51.) Censorship, propaganda, programming, and advertising were all issues addressed.

Dreyer was able to state in 1942, "radio, which had been principally a medium of entertainment in peacetime, became in war one of the great lifelines of the nation. It became a vital nerve center of communications as well as a morale-builder. The challenge had been accepted, and the responsibility had been shouldered. Overnight American radio had grown up." (SHD, p.52.)

Radio quickly began to experiment with three approaches to public service with regard to the war, exclusive of brief announcements:

(1) utilizing big stars in special mass audience appeals;

(2) insertion of appropriate material within existing programs;

(3) development of new program series . . . *Fibber McGee and Molly* took the second of these to the highest level.

Under the Local Station's Allocation Plan, described above, eventually each major network radio station would carry 15 government messages a day. More specifically, a broadcaster who sponsored a once-a-week program obligated himself to the equivalent of one full program's commercials to a government message each month (NM, p.326). It is not known how the "Fibber" show factors into this calculation, but we will demonstrate that they did far more than their share.

I have described the environment of commercial radio broadcasting during World War II. In the chapters which follow, I will relate how the writers and the sponsor, Johnson's Wax®, not only adapted to the environment but exceeded its requirements.

CHAPTER FOUR:
The Men Behind the Words

How could an out-of-work cartoonist become the highest-paid and most popular comedy writer in radio? All it took was:

- A magnificent command of the English language combined with . . .

- an irrepressible sense of whimsy (On one broadcast he even had Fibber convinced that his lack of "pep" was due to a clinical case of "whims"), leading to some of the most intellectual (and some of the worst) puns on radio;

- a deep understanding of all levels of the American population as represented by his characterization of the "upper crust" and an immigrant janitor, Ole the janitor of the Elks Club. This same understanding allowed writing that appealed to all levels;

- a personal philosophy that was quietly evident in his wartime writing and which was allowed free rein in his next radio effort, *The Halls of Ivy.*

- an ability to work closely with and win the respect of entertainment professionals and business executives; and

- abiding patriotism.

The writer was, of course, Don Quinn.

Quinn and his soon-to-be partner, Phil Leslie, were the second part of a three-part symbiosis consisting of the stars and other cast, the writers, and an unusually accommodating sponsor. The listening audience and America were the fortunate beneficiaries of this union.

In this chapter, I will provide at least a snapshot of the remarkable men who wrote the words that made *Fibber McGee and Molly* a weapon of war.

HOW IT HAPPENED

There are a number of versions of how he and the Jordans hooked up. According to Jim Jordan, Quinn was introduced to him by a "friend of a friend." Jordan went on to say that Quinn had never written for radio; he was a commercial artist: "It was 1930, after the crash, and he went *Kaplop* with the agency that he had. He was a very clever artist. He wanted to write and he started writing stuff for us and it just evolved from there." (CS, p. 4.)

According to Stumpf and Price (SP, p.28), Quinn (who was born in Grand Rapids, Michigan, in 1900), began his association with the Jordans writing for their show, *Smackout*. Quinn had quit high school (RMY: p. not known) and joined the Navy in 1918. He did go back to school after leaving the Navy. At the time, radio was "just a funny noise from Pittsburgh," according to Quinn.

Another account had Quinn "hanging around Chicago radio stations in hope of landing some script work." One day at Station WENR, he noticed a certain preoccupied gent with a harassed look. According to Yoder (RMY) "he was the glummest-looking man Quinn had seen in a long time."

"Who's the sourpuss?" Quinn asked.

"That's Jim Jordan," somebody answered. "He's a comedian."

In fact, the Jordans had not intended to be comedians any more than Quinn had intended to be a radio writer. Somewhere in the heavens an angel with an eye for show business must have taken a hand.

THE BIRTH OF FIBBER AND MOLLY

Why the names "Fibber McGee and Molly"? It is not clear exactly, but it seems that the monikers had their origin in a Lion's Club Award won by Jim Jordan. One version says the name was the brainchild of Jack Lewis of the ad agency. More likely is the version told by Jordan himself. In that version, Lewis only suggested the name should be something synonymous with a liar. According to Jordan, ". . . at the next meeting Don Quinn came in with a slip of paper. I'll never forget this; it was about an inch high and eight inches wide. He had it all decorated up like a commercial artist would do. On it, it said 'FIBBER McGEE' . . . and that was it!" The Jordans had already agreed that if Marian ever got to play an Irish character again, her name would be Molly (SP, p.45).

Then came the challenge of coming up with a suitable title for the show, one that would stay in the public's awareness for what all hoped would be years to come. "The Fibber McGee Show" was not inclusive enough; Jim and Marian had, after all, been partners from the beginning. How about "The Fibber and Molly McGee Show"? Too long. They finally settled on "Fibber McGee and Molly," with great results and, in fact the program was always introduced as "The Johnson Wax® Program with Fibber McGee and Molly."

HOW IT WORKED

The *Fibber McGee and Molly* format and characters obviously did not spring from the womb in its finely honed, fully developed form. Some serious tinkering was required. In its earliest form, the McGees roamed the country in a well-worn car. (Their sponsor did, after all, sell car wax.) Soon, however, they won a house in a raffle, settled into America's best-known radio address at 79 Wistful Vista, and the quintessential situation radio comedy was born.

The mechanics of putting together each week's live show were remarkably simple. The genius and mutual participation necessary to make it work are almost incomprehensible. Once a regular Tuesday night time slot had been secured, the following work pattern was followed.

THURSDAY: Quinn meets with the Jordans with ideas for the next week's program. The Jordans (very actively) make suggestions/ changes. Quinn then goes back to his office to begin work. According to Yoder (RMY, p. unknown) and others, the three were totally in tune; disagreements were productive, never acrimonious. "[Quinn] wants it simple, and often makes it so timely it seems to continue the listeners' dinner table conversation." Thursday was the earliest that this process began as Jordan insisted that Wednesday be a day of rest.

FRIDAY: Quinn meets with the cast to talk about the upcoming broadcast.

SATURDAY: Taking all suggestions into account, Quinn outlines the plot.

SUNDAY: Quinn does the actual writing, often typing until dawn. According to one account, he had not slept on a Sunday night for years. (*Advertising and selling*, May 1945, p. 70) The same account relates that he wrote one script while suffering from pneumonia. Another time he alternated standing and lying down while writing because of a broken coccyx.

MONDAY: Several rehearsals, during which Quinn revised the script, often cutting lines that failed to elicit laughter. The performers were a big help here, having a kind of sixth sense of what would work.

TUESDAY: Broadcast day. Early on, the orchestra and vocal quartet rehearse. Then the cast returns for a final, "table reading." The dress rehearsal begins in the early afternoon and by six p.m. the studio audience begins to arrive. Those 350 individuals are, in fact, an important part of the show since they help the folks at home spot the laughs. Of course, sometimes the reason for their laughter was not obvious to the radio listeners. Beulah, for example, has a funny opening line, but only the studio audience sees it delivered by a white man. Similarly, the radio audience never gets to see the sound effects man producing an erupting hall closet.

It has been written that during the early years, everyone involved tinkered with ways to make the program better. The tinkering extended even to the theme music. The original theme, "Save Your Sorrow for Tomorrow," served through most of the time until 1940, when an original piece, "Wing to Wing," was written and introduced by Billy Mills (SP, p.59).

JORDAN ON QUINN

Obviously, the Jordans respected Don Quinn's importance. They agreed, with only a handshake, to share the wealth equally, one-third for each. Responding to a question by Schader (CS, p. 14) about the genius behind the show being Don Quinn, "Fibber" responded:

> That's right. All the story lines came out of a meeting. Not that Don didn't bring them in, but we would hash them over. Sometimes other people would bring in an idea that would become a story. We always had a couple of them ahead, more or less. He would develop them. It seems to me people are beginning to realize what a great writer he was. I was over at Walt Disney Studios yesterday, talking with some people, and one of these fellows said to me, "Don Quinn, he was one of the great writers, wasn't he?" We hear that now more than we did 20 years ago, which is as it should be. Several times we would give up on a show on Monday noon. It's all on paper, ready to go and it wasn't just coming off. I can remember him saying, "Well, I'll start here, and I'll take it home and rewrite it tonight." Monday night!

And we'd do it Tuesday. We had a lot of things that
were pat that we could do, that would take time.
Sure-fire, like the closet, and this, and that, and the
other thing. But *very few* writers can do that.

During that same interview, Jordan confirmed that Quinn was
the one who conceived and implemented the integration of the
commercial into the show itself (with Harlow Wilcox making the
pitch). "I think that was the thing that made the show as much as
anything," Jim Jordan stated.

In a short article dated May 25, 1943 (no more information on
the source is available), Jordan said, "Not many listeners realize that
there are three of us: add Don Quinn to Molly and me when you
listen to our program. . . . Don's greatest talent lies in his amazing
facility for creating likeable characters. And that's because he's such
a likable guy himself. McGee's a mighty gabby guy, and Molly's no
slouch either. Don Quinn, our writer, is the fellow who makes all
that phenomenal word mileage possible. It mounds up to a lot of
vocabulary."

CRITICS, PEERS, AND COLLABORATORS ON QUINN

In a review of the show in the December 2, 1945 *New York
Times*, Diana Gibbings, remembered the oft-quoted NBC page
who stated that "Fibber" was "just another of those shows that
won't last." In addition, variety could only give the show a
"deadly blast." Gibbings notes the early shows were "in the best
vaudeville tradition" with the action in silly costumes, and the
humor relying on painfully delivered dialects before evolving
into the "suave and simple performance that it has assumed in
the last few years."

In an issue of *Advertising and Selling* (May, 1945), an anonymous
reviewer noted that "Jim and Marian Jordan and their little company
of associates are experts in character delineation. They have developed
an infallible sense of timing, phrasing, and modulation. They are
pretty slick actors. But the Jordans give most credit to the writing
genius of [Don] Quinn."

Not that it was always easy. In a column called "Listen Here," an unidentified writer describes some of the writing action regarding the characters.

> Don Quinn . . . must have devoured a dozen pencils when he lost the services of Bill Thompson . . . In (Doc) Gamble, Don Quinn is on Terra Firma . . . Harlow Wilcox, the plug from Racine, Wisconsin, always can be counted on to deliver a nifty commercial job; however, I hope Harlow will forgive me if I give the lion's share of the credit to the person (Quinn) who so deftly weaves the material into the comedy pattern.

After a brief criticism of Quinn's handling of the Alice Darling character, and noting that Uncle Dennis was funnier when *not* heard, the writer concludes with what may be the ultimate compliment:

> If my appraisal is worth the paper it's written on, how does one account for the fact that the show as a whole hasn't slipped a notch in the radio ratings? That's a tough question but I am forced to the conclusion that if *all* the supporting characters were suddenly jerked out from under the McGees, they would, single handed, lift the show by its very boot straps to its usual Alpine level. No other line of reasoning makes any sense. . . . You're either a Fibber and Molly fan or a neurotic.

One of Don Quinn's early collaborators was Paul Henning, a major radio and television writer in his own right. Henning, who worked with Quinn for a while starting in 1937, called his collaborator "the most brilliant man I've ever met." But Quinn was used to working alone. As Henning recalled, "I would make contributions, and Don would put my name on the script. Then when I took the script down to be — whatever they did in those days, it wasn't mimeograph but some process — I'd scratch my name off, because I felt like I shouldn't have it on the script. Later

I wish I'd left my name on a few scripts." (JY, p.26.) "He'd say, 'Do whatever you like on this particular scene.' It was fun; I enjoyed it. And I learned a lot from Don. And some of it was good and some of it was bad. Staying up all night with the cigarettes and coffee was bad — but he had an absolutely fabulous sense of humor. His favorite expression was, "Idiots delete." (JY, p.28.)

Elsewhere, Henning is quoted as saying that Quinn "committed suicide, really; he killed himself by his work habits . . . And I admired him so much that I began to think that that was the way to write, so I tried it, but I couldn't." Quinn also had a hard time delegating any of the writing to someone else. He hired young Henning but couldn't relinquish control of his "baby." Still, Henning describes his mentor as a "wonderful, brilliant man; never went beyond high school, he just read constantly, widely." (LM, p. 145.)

Horton, in his brilliant exposition, *Radio Goes to War*, describes how Quinn brought *Fibber McGee and Molly* into the war effort.

> The show's writer, Don Quinn, usually left it to Fibber to bring up all the self-serving criticisms against government rationing measures — "They should have foreseen this"; "What in the case of an emergency?"; "It's an infringement of civil liberties" — only to have each of his charges deflated by the show's more respectable and socially responsible characters. Yet Fibber echoed many of the sentiments of actual citizens, who were as dissatisfied as he was about the measure. Like Fibber, these citizens were told through both subtle and more direct means to lighten up and put their petty self-interest aside and focus more on the national interest and the war effort. (GH, p.122.)

During the war, Don Quinn was one of the acknowledged masters of the integrated (Office of War Information) war messages.

> When asked about the success of his "propaganda shows," Quinn argued that he was simply following established rules for comedy writing. Listeners were

already interested in these war-related topics, which made it easier for the writer: "We have better audience reaction, we get more fan mail, our Crossley (Listener rating) goes up." In fact, to test the effectiveness of popular radio programs, the OWI agreed to give *Fibber McGee and Molly* the exclusive rights to one OWI plug, an appeal for merchant seamen. On the day after the program was aired, according to the War Shipping Administration, the number of people who signed up to be merchant seamen doubled. (GH, p. 122.)

Quinn on Quinn

By his own account, Don Quinn had a simple set of rules for writing the program: "Be fair in all things; don't offend people; don't hurt their feelings, keep it clean — and keep it friendly — and it will keep you." (SP, p.59.) In the interview for Diana Gibbings (*New York Times*, December 2, 1945), Quinn recalled the program changes from its earliest days, slowly jettisoning what Quinn called the "falderals" such as costumes and the painful dialects.

> [These outdated comic devices] have given place to more or less plausible characters whose chief charm is that they would fit into anyone's household — or at least into one of the neighbors.

> "We don't have grandfathers coming out of the grandfather clock anymore," Mr. Quinn explains it. "Fibber's lapses into a lunacy are sufficiently toned down these days to be easily identified with those of your Uncle Ed. Over the years we have acquired a sense of values, and Jim, in particular, has a very sure instinct for what will go over best. The most important thing . . . is to build up an affection for the characters among the audience and then to put them in very uncomplicated situations."

Quinn wrote in a 1949 column (under the title, "Hollywood," although the publication is unknown) details how the popular show was constructed.

> Everyone on the show . . . has contributed to these situation ideas in one way or another, but they generally evolve at a "bull session" at the Jordan's home. There's nothing as formal as a conference about it. Jim and Marian Jordan have been playing Fibber and Molly for so many years that they know the mental processes of the characters they portray almost as well as they do their own. And Phil Leslie, who helped me write the show, is generally there. We just sit around the house and chin, maybe have a sandwich and a cup of coffee, and try to recall little things that have happened to us during the week that might give us a lead on our themes.

> Once the theme of the program is decided upon, Leslie and I go to work. We don't visualize the characters. They exist in our subconscious, and we know how each character will react in any situation. We just sit down and type and the characters do the rest.

His views on what makes a program a success were often reported. In a publication called *Off Mike*, he observed:

> Many radio programs have tremendous audiences, week after week. But they are audiences who would feel no slightest pang of regret, experience no sense of personal loss, if said program were never broadcast again. Conversely, the shows which live and build over the years are those for which the listener feels an abiding love and friendship. If you're a star on one of these happy productions, you are, by acclamation, a paid-up life member in good standing of millions of American families.

They will stay home from bridge parties and movies to tune you in. They will agonize over your misfortunes and gloat over your triumphs. And, what is a far more important thing, they will buy your sponsor's product, whether they need it or not. You'd better mind your p's and q's, too, because you're in their homes on sufferance, though you may stay for years and years if you remain nice. (LT, p.146.)

He even went so far as to suggest that the popular Fred Allen could do even better in a situation comedy. "This gratuitous suggestion is made," he wrote, "in the belief that an idea, a gag, a message or a theme gets a warmer reception when delivered by an established fictional character than by a comedian working as a mere comedian. May God forgive me for the 'mere'!"

In 1965 — just three years before his death — Quinn appeared on a panel comprised of America's top comedy writers. He waxed philosophical in his comments.

To me, a sense of humor is a sense of proportion and when things are out of place you get humor. This is the basis for 75 percent of our comedy — things out of time and place, a distortion, an anachronism. I disagree that much, comes from cruelty or malice. . . . Humor can't be slide-ruled. It isn't cerebral; it's visceral. You feel it in your belly. I spent a great deal of time, or wasted a great deal of time, trying to figure out what people laugh at and why. And I think I've come to some conclusions. For instance, people love a tricky piece of wordage or a pun. They love the switches.

Someday I hope to write the definitive work on comics, comedians, and humorists . . . A comic is a strange and fascinating breed; almost always from the wrong side of the tracks; no education — anything for a laugh. . . . A cut above him, the comedian, who's a little more literate, a little more

educated . . . And above the comedian is the humorist.
They fall pretty well into categories.

I could find no written evidence of Quinn's personal views on the war and its combatants. *Time* (June 4, 1945) called him "the first radio scripter to see profit in building an entire comedy show around (one of the Office of War Information topics). Most programs written confine themselves to a sly line or two or else beat the listeners' ears back with earnest messages."

Quinn put the "bromidic complaints of a disgruntled civilian" into Fibber's mouth and then showed the "vulgar errors in Fibber's thinking." Some listeners complained, but the large majority just laughed (at Fibber's foolishness and, I suspect, their own)

One bit of WWII irony. According to the same *Time* article, Quinn was quoted as saying that he "does not mind driving 30 miles into Hollywood three days a week to work free for OWI. One night after a Fibber and Molly show about gasoline rationing, Quinn got home to find himself in a quandary: There was a telegram from William Jeffers, then national rubber director, complimenting him on the program; there was also a letter from his ration board, denying him supplemental gasoline."

Quinn's views on the relationship to the sponsor have been recorded. On the *Fibber McGee and Molly* program, announcer Harlow Wilcox would suddenly (and peremptorily) appear in the midst of the week's story, and Fibber or Molly would engage him in conversation that would lead to a message for Johnson's Wax®. Obviously, writer-director Don Quinn felt the audience would accept the banter between the fictitious Fibber and Molly and the very real Wilcox, understanding full well that it was simply a device to make a commercial as painless as possible.

That very device even became fodder for jokes. When the announcer turned up one night, Fibber queried impatiently, "What do you want, Wilcox? Though as the guy said when he sat on the bee, I have a deep seated suspicion." Quinn had no compunction about kidding his sponsor, but he felt there were definite limits. "Whatever is being sold must never, never be held up to ridicule," he wrote in 1944. "The circumstances under which the subject is introduced, the person who introduces it, everything surrounding it may be made the butt of devastating wit if available, but the product — ahhh, the product! It's our bread and butter, kids; let's keep it right side up."

QUINN AND *THE HALLS OF IVY*

Sometime during the 1949 season, Don Quinn made it known that he would be leaving the McGee show. (Interestingly, Johnson Wax® left the show shortly thereafter, at the end of the 1950 season.) Although this was well after the war, a few words about Quinn's next venture will help to establish the legitimacy of his negotiation as a genius of comedy writing.

The Halls of Ivy, written by Quinn, first aired in January 1950. It starred Ronald Colman and his wife, Benita. The show was set in the college town of Ivy, where Colman played the part of Todhunter Hall, president of Ivy College. Although the show had a comparatively short run, it was uniformly acclaimed. Some of that was due to the talents of the Colmans, but Quinn's talents were again widely recognized and praised.

Halls, although a comedy, was a major departure from *Fibber*. Thomas Brady, writing in the *New York Times* (June 11, 1950) called it "the most literate continuing drama on the air." The program's genesis is revealing. Brady reports that Quinn had been complaining to his manager of "world sickness and nameless frustration, even when "the manager, not Wolff, who had a deep affection for the 'Fibber' show, challenged him sarcastically: 'Why don't you write a program about a college president?'" *Halls of Ivy* was the result.

After the first broadcast, noted critic John Crosby gave it high marks. While praising the Colmans, he also had plenty to say about Quinn: "Like all good radio comedians, Mr. Quinn has come up with a simple, solid format and then carefully refrained from cluttering it up with too many other ideas (*New York Herald Tribune*, January 12, 1950). Noting one phrase used on the show: "The test of manners is to meet bad manners with good ones." Crosby searched *Bartlett's*, which he notes "lists far less witty epigrams." Failing to find this particular quotation, he suggests "admitting Mr. Quinn, one of radio's great sages."

In a separate review (*New York Herald Tribune*, February 16, 1951), Crosby focuses on some of Quinn's epigrammatic skills, which he calls "an almost vanished literary form." Examples: "While some folks have no enemies, none of their friends like them either," or "When people say, 'Let's be realistic,' it means that a price tag has been tied to an ideal," or "When it comes to business, his head rules, not his heart. He finds that you can't read the fine print with tears in your eyes." There is plenty of that kind of writing — "But," as Crosby notes, "you mustn't get the idea that [the program] is just a long philosophical discussion. It is fundamentally a comedy, and a very funny one, matchlessly played, brilliantly produced and — above all — meticulously written."

Finally, Crosby pointed out that, in the scripts for *Halls of Ivy* there are occasional flashes of "a not unhealthy bitterness noting the low pay of teachers and $20 million spent on bubble gum in a year." As Quinn explained, "you begin to wonder how much the American people care what goes into their children's heads."

Another well-known critic, Leo Mishkin, (*New York Morning Telegraph*, May 26, 1952), called it "Remarkable" that Quinn never went to college and observed that he "has a much more comprehensive understanding and a much keener perception of what kind of people do go to college than many thousands of *cum laudes*, B.A.'s, and Phi Beta Kappas." Mishkin noted one line in particular: "the trouble with fighting with prejudiced people, you get so taken up with the battle you forget what it's for."

In the *Halls of Ivy*, Quinn obviously had the chance to deliver personal messages such as those on Fibber in a mature, intelligent, cultured and sophisticated manner."

In his *New York Times* obituary (January 1, 1968), Don Quinn was remembered by one of his earliest collaborators, Leonard Levinson, who said, "Nobody ever got as much fun out of words as Don Quinn did."

I might add that few *gave* as much fun with words as Don Quinn did.

Phil Leslie Joins the Team

No one, especially Phil Leslie himself, would have suggested that anyone could quite equal the extraordinary talents of Don Quinn. Leslie was, however, a superior writer in his own right. Warm, humble, witty (of course), Leslie's transition onto the writing team was as smooth as the transition from Hal Peary to Willard Waterman on the "Great Gildersleeve", i.e., the listener couldn't tell the difference. Phil Leslie did not receive the written coverage as did his colleague (and mentor) Don Quinn. He nevertheless contributed both talent and continuity to the work and the message of the program after joining the team in 1943.

Leslie became head writer on "Fibber" after Quinn left to do *The Halls of Ivy*. He later wrote for *Beulah* and other shows on radio. For television he had many credits as well including *The Beverly Hillbillies, Petticoat Junction, The Brady Bunch*, and the pilot script for *The Donna Reed Show*. Another happy coincidence: Phil Leslie had written for a show called *Major Hoople*. The Major was played by Arthur Q. Bryan. With the departure of Gale Gordon and Bill Thompson, several characters were lost. Leslie recommended Bryan, who brilliantly played the part of Doc Gamble, and whose acerbic, sometimes cynical, wit was an immediate hit.

It was my good fortune to interview Phil Leslie before his death. My agenda was to determine the origins of Kremer's Drug Store. He was rather sure that the store was not an invention of Don Quinn, but rather based on a real experience. As we saw in Chapter 3, there was indeed, a *real* Kremer's Drug Store.

Commenting on his time as a writer for Fibber McGee and Molly, Phil Leslie told me, "It was a wonderful way to make a living." He repeated these very words in a talk before a group of OTR fans in 1986, with Jim Jordan was in the audience. Leslie, who was born in Missouri in 1909, traveled to California in 1938. He was out of work in his chosen field — writing — for two years during which time he worked at Lockheed to put food on the table. By his own account, he "kept hounding the agencies with sample scripts, writing jokes for Victor Borge (who was a one summer replacement for *Fibber and Molly*) and writing the show *Major Hoople* (where he met Arthur Q. Bryan). This gave him the boost he needed to land a job in 1943 as assistant to Don Quinn.

Here, in his own words, is how the work developed.

> It was my responsibility to write the first draft and I'd go up to Marian and Jim's house on Saturday with a first draft of the show and maybe three copies. I'd give Don [Quinn] one and Jim one and I'd sit there and sweat while they read it. We'd take it from there. Saturday night we'd have a rewrite and Sunday we'd have another reading. Monday and Tuesday we'd have cast meetings. After a while Don felt I was writing enough like him that we divided the show. I'd write one half of the show and Don would write the other half. We'd stitch it together and sometimes we had even used the same joke. And that was it. Sunday night [we would] relax, and more and more toward the end . . . Eventually, I took on more and more responsibility.

Leslie was interviewed in 1973 by Charles Schaden in his book, *Speaking of Radio*. He talked a lot about Don Quinn and how it happened that he fit in with Quinn's writing style: "Don liked the fact that I could do stories, which he always had trouble with . . . [*Fibber*] didn't require much of a plot, but it needed a story to finish of some kind to hang the door knocks on." (In most shows each character appeared after knocking on the McGees' door.)

Leslie described his collaboration with Quinn as "a fine chemistry." True to his own character, he was lavish in his praise of his boss: "Don was a wonderful, wonderful man . . . Comedy dialogue just flowed out of him, just a beautiful, quick, comedy mind . . . he liked me and I was just as eager to please . . . It just worked out that I began to write enough like him." He described his experience as "just wonderful." As he put it: "Radio was a charmed life for me . . . I had the best years of radio."

That is vintage Leslie, self-effacing, genuinely enjoying his associations, his career and life.

Susan Leslie Peters, his daughter, wrote in a "Collector's Edition" of *Reminisce* that her father especially enjoyed the incredible sound effects produced by the sound effects man when

the "hall closet" door was opened, but his favorite "sound effects" were "the laughter and applause of the studio audience."

After Quinn left (he continued to be a consultant), Leslie's scripts continued to be funny, clever, and warmly human. He proved to be another "natural" in the amazingly long line-up of cast and staff who had been associated with the highly successful program throughout its many years on the air.

Phil Leslie died in 1988.

CONCLUSION

Was there something special that led Don Quinn and Phil Leslie to focus so much of their respective comedic talents on weaving war messages into their shows? There is nothing to indicate so (although Quinn had served in World War I.) More likely, they were two patriots using their unique and special skills (not unlike the B17 pilot or even Alice Darling in a war plant) in the service of their country.

CHAPTER FIVE:
THE JOHNSON'S WAX® SHOW – THE PERFECT SPONSOR

As mentioned in the previous chapter, the McGees got off to a rocky start, blasted by critics including an NBC employee. Diana Gibbings (*New York Times*, December 2, 1945) noted: "A patient and no doubt clairvoyant sponsor did not take fright at this distressing opening gun and the skit was allowed to outgrow the strange extortions of its infancy into the suave and simple performance that it has assumed in the last few years."

Outgrow them they did, and the McGees enjoyed a wonderful fifteen years with that clairvoyant sponsor, Johnson's Wax® — now the S.C. Johnson (A Family Company) Company.

The Jordans, their writers, and their sponsor enjoyed a relationship that can accurately be described as unique (in the dictionary sense, not the cavalier misuse of the word when "unusual" would be more correct). In this chapter, I will describe some of the happy coincidences and decisions that led to fifteen years of enjoyment by the listening public.

THE JOHNSON'S WAX® COMPANY — A SHORT HISTORY

Anyone who watches American television will have seen the ads with the small note in the lower right hand corner, "The S.C. Johnson Company — A Family Company." And indeed it has been and was until very recently. The list of the company's current products includes brands that are almost generic they are so well-known and popular. They include, but are not limited to: Ziploc®, Raid®, Glade®, Pledge®, and Windex®.

When the Johnson's Wax® Company began its sponsorship of *Fibber* (two years after the company first sponsored a radio program) the company had only two products. It all began in 1886 when Samuel C. Johnson, a parquet flooring salesman in Racine, Wisconsin (still the company headquarters), bought the flooring business from his employer, The Racine Hardware Company. In the first year, there were 40 employees and a profit of $300. When his flooring customers asked for help in protecting them, Johnson began with shellac but later expanded into the "prepared paste wax" business. By 1898, he was selling more wax than flooring. A few years earlier, his son Herbert was already experimenting with car wax! Obviously the Johnsons had vision. In 1906 that son became the "Son" in the company's new name, S.C. Johnson and Son.

In 1919 on the death of its founder, Herbert became president. He was succeeded in 1928 by Herbert Fisk Johnson, Jr., who had "paid his dues" in various company positions. In 1932 Herbert introduced a new product "GloCoat®" at the height of the Depression. The company survived the Depression without a single layoff and, indeed, was the first U.S. company to provide paid vacations to employees.

In 1939 the company headquarters was constructed. The architect was the famous Frank Lloyd Wright. The building is considered to be an exceptional design and still serves as headquarters.

It was Herbert Johnson, who (in 1935) made the decision to sponsor *Fibber McGee and Molly*. Here's how it happened.

COMMERCIAL SPONSORSHIP DURING THE WAR

The war brought to commercial sponsors both dilemmas and opportunities. Let's start with the latter.

Advertising on radio nearly doubled during the war (LT, p. 201). An important reason for the growth was tax-related. Radio was exempt from the excess profits tax of 90 percent, which was placed on newspapers and magazines because of the paper shortage. In effect, the radio advertisers could buy advertising for ten cents on the dollar as the government had decided (only recently) that advertising was a legitimate business expense. Many firms who had little or no actual product to sell because of war shortages nevertheless used institutional ads to create good will anticipating post-war sales. (It is notable that the industry sponsored War Advertising Council was responsible for millions of dollars of "free" spot advertising on behalf of government programs and agencies.)

It is probably risky to observe, as have others, that the war was one of the best things to happen to radio advertising. Local radio stations increased their return on investment by 800 per cent from 1939 to 1945 (K, p.211-212).

It had taken a while for this "opportunity" to present itself. Money was necessary for radio to prosper, but in the early years, there was wariness toward investing in radio advertising. Perhaps the most important step toward making radio an attractive advertising medium was the establishment of an effective network of stations, the National Broadcasting Company. NBC could reach listeners across the country (JG DS, p. 11). This was in 1926. The "magazine of the air" was on its way. Early on many shows were named after the sponsor — *The Eveready Hour, The Ipana Troubadours, The Goodrich Zipper.* And later, of course, there was *The Johnson's Wax® Program.*

(Then) Senator Harry Truman had objected to allowing advertising to be deducted as a legitimate business expense for taxation purposes. This was before the war, which changed things drastically. As (Bernauw) noted:

> Government agencies were coping with a tangled forest of problems. Americans *had* to be persuaded to save cans, buy war bonds, learn nursing, black out windows, change eating habits, avoid rumors, become air raid wardens, write letters to soldiers, curb travel. How to achieve all this? "Advertisers saw the barrage (of requests for help) as a burden, a duty — and an opportunity." (EWB, p. 39)

The advertisers responded by establishing their War Advertising Council to allocate messages according to preorders. The messages could be dramatic, musical, or "straight." Johnson's Wax® used all of these and added comedy.

Within weeks the system was in operation, and a stream of messages poured forth from the air. Advertising leaders began to speak of their industry as the "information industry." They issued release after release detailing its war services. A 1943 brochure proclaimed that it had already contributed "$100,000,000 worth of talent and time" to the war effort. The brochure was titled, *This is an Army Hitler Forgot!* and carried photos of dozens of stars. Secretary of Commerce Jesse H. Jones was persuaded to issue a statement on "the many values of advertising to a free nation fighting to maintain its freedom." On behalf of the Commerce Department, he praised the war work of the "great information industry . . . essential ingredient of a free society." (EWB, p.39)

Again, Dreyer, in his extraordinary views just after the beginning of the War, warned radio of the dangers inherent in their new-found opportunities. His words are too eloquent to paraphrase.

> Prosperity nurtures complacency and self-satisfaction, and this is no time for radio to beget either. Income is no adequate criterion of public service rendered. War demands of radio more than traditional functions. This is a period in the growth of radio when, if it is to stay free, it must prove its right to freedom. It must prove its value in the emergency — a value which cannot be measured in dollar-volume nor in the number of news, entertainment and "morale" programs broadcast. Programs, not radio time, are the new basis of value. Radio must prove itself — in a period when non-essentials have no value at all — an essential to the preservation of our way of life. In short, radio must demonstrate its effectiveness as a medium of *education* far more convincingly than ever before. (SHD, p. 29)

Whether or not the people in Racine ever read these words is unknown, but they certainly put them into practice.

THE JORDAN-JOHNSON MARRIAGE

There are a number of written accounts of how Johnson's Wax® came to sponsor *Fibber McGee and Molly*. The facts, according to my source — a former employee of the agency, Needham, Louis and Brorby, (NLB) — are these. In 1935 the Jordans were doing the radio show *Smackout*, which, by another happy coincidence, was a favorite of Henrietta Johnson Louis, the sister of Herbert Johnson. She was also the wife of John "Jack" Louis, an executive with NLB. With her encouragement and that of a Henry Selinger — a producer for *Sam 'n' Henry* (Later *Amos 'n' Andy*) — Louis asked for sample scripts (Quinn was already writing) and gave them an audition. The Jordans were hired at $250 a week (W, p.217).

Early on, the agency decided to keep the tenor of *Smackout*, but change the premise. The main characters would be a middle-aged couple touring the country in a car — again, this premise offered plenty of opportunities to for the characters to plug Johnson's car wax products. At one time the agency toyed with a program name, "Free Air." Fortunately, as noted earlier, Quinn intervened with the name, "Fibber McGee" (Another happy coincidence — according to Yoder "Free Air" had already been used by Sinclair Lewis in a *Saturday Evening Post* article. The title was for sale at $50,000.

A note on the role of Jack Louis from my source: In the 1920s Maurice Needham, founder and chairman of the agency, was approached with a proposition — if Needham would hire Jack Louis and put his name on the door, Louis would capture the Johnson's Wax® account. Needham reminded Louis that there was a Depression raging. Louis proposed that his salary be based on a fixed percentage of Johnson billings. A deal was struck. (In fact, Louis already had an agreement with Johnson.) Because of the original deal, more or less on speculation, and the success of the show, Jack Louis became a very wealthy man. (Author's note: in one show Quinn named three policemen, Needham, Louis, and Brorby)

As Yoder and others have noted:

> To get the No. 1 Hooper Rating took thirteen years, but long before that the show was a success. It was good business, that is, producing a high listening

score per dollar of cost. One of the most remarkable factors in its success has been a lucky break in sponsors. Instead of getting the axe if they didn't score in the first thirteen weeks, the Jordans hit a sponsor willing to hire relative unknowns and let them grow, if they could, with a minimum of interference. If the McGees have stuck to one sponsor all these years, a *laissez-faire* attitude almost phenomenal in radio helps explain it. (RMY, p. 13)

In 1924 Secretary of Commerce Herbert Hoover said in an address to the National Association of Broadcasters, "I believe the quickest way to kill broadcasting would be to use it for direct advertising. The reader of a newspaper has an option whether he will read an ad or not, but if a speech by the president is to be used as the meat in a sandwich of two patent medicine advertisements, there will be no radio left. To what extent it may be employed for what we now call indirect advertising I do not know, and only experience with the reactions of listeners can tell. The listeners will finally decide in any event."

They certainly did.

THE JOHNSON FAMILY AND THE JORDAN FAMILY

There are few entertainment programs that have been so closely identified with their sponsor and vice versa as Johnson's Wax® and Fibber McGee and Molly. The Johnsons and the Jordans obviously valued one another: The mutual respect began almost immediately.

Just a year or so after the beginning of the Johnson's Wax® sponsorship, in December 1936, *Broadcasting Magazine* reported:

Dealers everywhere report sales increases of 30 to 50% on Johnson's polishes and an impartial "pantry shelf survey" in a city of 150,000 shows an increase of nearly 20% for wax in 1936 over 1935. In the same survey, Johnson's auto cleaner and auto wax products were found in twice as many homes as in

1935. A big reason for the increase is Johnson's radio program on NBC, *Fibber McGee and Molly.*

The popularity of the program had hardly had a choice to grow, but the Johnson people obviously felt they were backing a winner.

The program's success so pleased the sponsor that the Jordans were given a new contract, upping their salary to $2,650 per program putting them among the best-paid performers on radio. NBC, also, showed confidence by changing the broadcast day and time making it air directly opposite the very popular *Lux Radio Theatre* (another program directly identified with a sponsor). The Johnson people, with their ad agency, also launched an advertising campaign in print media featuring the performers in character. This type of promotion would continue for years to come.

The Jordans, for their part, were always careful (with the help of writer Don Quinn) to remind the listeners who was paying the freight. There were frequent references to Racine by both Fibber and Molly. One occasionally used artifice would have Fibber and/or Molly delivering the middle commercial to show that they knew what was coming from Harlow Wilcox.

Herbert Johnson, Jr. appeared on the program one time, in 1935, and told of his forthcoming three-month expedition by air to the northeastern part of Brazil to obtain carnauba wax for the company's products. Later, in November 1946, the program was broadcast from Memorial Hall in Racine, the occasion being S.C. Johnson's sixtieth anniversary. The audience included some 1,800 Johnson Wax® Company employees and guests. It was on that occasion that they met the Herbert Johnson, Sr. for the first time.

In 1972 Jim Jordan returned to the air waves to do television commercials for his family of friends at Johnson's Wax®. All in all, this was a model of amiability between sponsor and stars. That amiability transcended the ultimate commercial decision by Johnson to discontinue their sponsorship of the show.

Making the Marriage Work

The Johnson's Wax® commercials and sponsorship were unusual, if not unique, in a number of ways. One was their continued sponsorship over fifteen years, at a time when most shows changed sponsors often.

A second difference was the way in which the Johnson people allowed/encouraged the program's writers and producers to do much more than was necessary by WAC standards. Johnsons also allowed themselves to receive a bit of good natured ribbing, with frequent references to Racine by the McGees.

Probably the single-biggest way in which Johnson's sponsorship differed from other programs was the way in which Harlow Wilcox was integrated into the story at more or less than middle. Wilcox could turn the most innocent remark into a paean for a Johnson's product. Everyone knew a commercial was being delivered but somehow it didn't seem like one. The McGees poked fun at Harlow's obsession, but never at the products themselves (true to Quinn's remarks). In one program, McGee stated that Wilcox "thinks the Seven Wonders of the World are pyramids, Hanging Gardens of Babylon, and five cans of GloCoat®."

Don Quinn apparently, and by his own account, wrote, or helped write those, mid-story commercials. As Horton points out, this was the best place for keeping the audience attentive to the sales message, by integrating the commercial into the entertainment itself (GH, p.105).

Jack Benny also used the technique, but in a different way. Benny, first of all, played himself, not a fictional character like "Fibber." Everyone knew that Don Wilson was going to try to sell them something, from Jell-O® to Lucky Strike® cigarettes. Somehow, Fibber's audience was expected to accept Wilcox as just another character in Wistful Vista, understanding, but ignoring the fact that it was simply a device to make the commercial entertaining. This was even more extraordinary when one remembers that Wilcox delivered the "straight" commercials at the beginning and end of the program.

It is assured that agency writers did the "straight" commercials. Horton points out that "any product could enhance America's fighting power and help the war effort. Johnson's Wax® was frequently touted for its life — prolonging qualities in a time of shortage." Examples will be provided in the next chapter (GH, p.99.)

Johnson's avoided the blatant use of what Horton (GH, p.99) call "brag" commercials in which the sponsor boasted of the significant contribution of a single product to victory by America. There *were* references to the use of waxes in various ways by the military. More often the listeners were reminded of ways in which *their* use of this product was consistent with the war effort.

The Johnson Company won numerous awards for production efficiency during the war. In 1944, according to Kelly M. Semrau, vice-president of Global Public Affairs and Communication at S.C. Johnson and Son, Inc., the employees of the company were awarded an Army Ordnance Award "for meritorious production of war materials for the Armed Forces. This award entitled us to fly the Army Ordinance Flag over the plant for the duration of the war." They were also given credit for sponsoring one of radio's most actively patriotic programs. The company had a personal relationship with the Jordans, who visited Racine fairly often.

According to my source, the decision to discontinue sponsorship was largely that of Jack Louis at the agency, who became disenchanted with the level of comedy provided. Another version is that The Johnson Company wanted to put their money into television, a medium which did not prove to be right for the show.

In any case, this fifteen-year (1935-1950) marriage ended amicably. The Johnson family went on to other programs and products and Fibber McGee and Molly found a new sponsor in Pet Milk.

CONCLUSION

In the next chapter, I will treat the reader to examples of the words that won the war as written by Quinn and Leslie, acted by the Jordans et al, and sponsored by a remarkable company, Johnson's Wax®.

Fibber McGee and Molly was not the only "war effort" program sponsored by Johnsons. In June 1943, the Johnson Wax® Company consented to sponsor a program with a message, but at that time no sponsor, *Words at War*, as a summer replacement for Fibber. The program dramatized contemporary war books. It was failing dismally until Jack Louis heard one of the programs and convinced Johnsons to sponsor it. Within four weeks it "had established itself as the summer's most powerful program and one of the best contributions to serious commercial radio in many a year." (*Newsweek*, July 1943)

By 1942, the Johnson Company had lost many of its employees to the service. They consolidated the output on products for the War effort.

STARS IN THE WINDOW FOR JOHNSON'S WAX®

The 1970s were the beginning of a wave of nostalgia, especially in radio. That continues today, usually under the label, "Old-Time Radio" (OTR), on "Classic Radio" or "Radio's Golden Age." The Johnson Company has shown its acknowledgement of its role in that era. In 1978 the Johnson Wax® Company sponsored a full year of repeat broadcasts of the old *Fibber McGee and Molly* program over station WRJN in Racine. As a public service, the Johnson Company used the available commercial air time within the broadcasts to promote community activities in the Racine area.

In the S.C. Johnson and Sons website, one of the company's representatives stated Core Values is "an unparalleled commitment to doing what's right for communities . . . In sponsoring these broadcasts in the way they did, the company lived up to its commitment to "Community U.S.A." In recent years, the company was still giving 5% of pre-tax profits to charity, following the example of its founder who gave 10% of his income annually to civic improvements.

In 1994 Columbia University awarded the Lawrence A. Wien Prize to S.C. Johnson Company for "global and local philanthropic activities and care of the environment."

Fibber McGee and Molly would have been proud.

PHOTOGRAPHS

Fibber, Molly and Johnson Products.

Cast and Staff of The Johnsons Wax Program.

FOLD BACK

UNITED STATES
OF AMERICA
War Ration Book One

WARNING

1 Punishments ranging as high as *Ten Years' Imprisonment or $10,000 Fine, or Both*, may be imposed under United States Statutes for violations thereof arising out of infractions of Rationing Orders and Regulations.

2 This book must not be transferred. It must be held and used only by or on behalf of the person to whom it has been issued, and anyone presenting it thereby represents to the Office of Price Administration, an agency of the United States Government, that it is being so held and so used. For any misuse of this book it may be taken from the holder by the Office of Price Administration.

3 In the event either of the departure from the United States of the person to whom this book is issued, or his or her death, the book must be surrendered in accordance with the Regulations.

4 Any person finding a lost book must deliver it promptly to the nearest Ration Board.

OFFICE OF PRICE ADMINISTRATION

No. 169703 -97

World War II ration book.

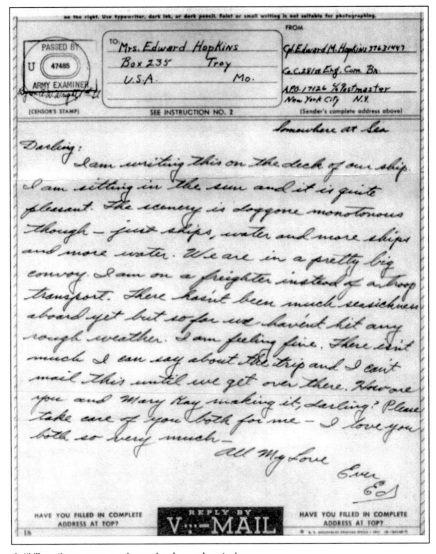

A "V" mail message to the author's mother in law.

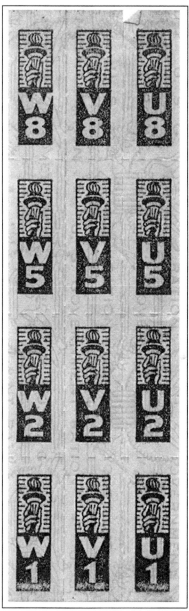

Ration stamps.

Head writer, Don Quinn.

L-R: Jim Jordan, Bill Thomson, Marian Jordan.

L-R: Harlow Wilcox, "Molly," Don Quinn, Phil Leslie, "Fibber."

The Jordans with Phil Leslie, writer.

Harlow Wilcox with "Fibber" in costume.

The "real" Kremer's Drug Store.

Kremer, selling a carton of scarce cigarettes.

The Jordans in Racine, meeting President S.C. Johnson for the first time with Bill
Thomson in costume.

Cast of the show leavng for Canada for a Bond rally.

Canadian crowd for the Jordan's Bond rally, 1945.

Jim Jodan and memories of a job well done.

PART II
WORDS THAT WON THE WAR

In the November 1946 issue of the *American Legion Magazine*, a fellow named Fibber McGee published an article entitled, "The Big War and Me." It tells the story of how, on December 8, 1941, he was (with great difficulty) getting into his World War I Army uniform. Fibber was headed for the Army recruiting office to "tell 'em McGee was ready." The recruiting sergeant mustered all his sarcasm: "You're the kind of man we need for our shock troops. When those Heinies see you, the shock'll kill 'em. No use wastin' a man like you in the early battles, Pop. We'll save you for the reserves. When the Japs lay siege to Kansas City, we'll call you."

After being escorted out by a pair of MP's, McGee decided the best way to serve his country was as air raid warden. With McGee in charge, "enemy planes never even came within a thousand miles of Wistful Vista." He went on to say that "It makes a fellow feel pretty good to know the enemy still remembers him from the Big War. Yes sir, they still remember the Big Three from the Big War — a General, a Sergeant, and a Private! Pershing, York, and McGee!"

In fact, no episode of the radio show had McGee as an air raid warden. He was, however, a part of a small, elite army of goodwill and patriotism. It consisted of himself, Molly, a great supporting cast, some gifted writers, and Harlow Wilcox speaking on behalf of Johnson's Wax®. In the period between Pearl Harbor and the official V-J Day of September 2, 1945 (the original V-J Day had been August 14, the day when the Japanese accepted the surrender terms), *Fibber McGee and Molly* aired 139 times (the show was not on the air on the latter date, having been replaced for the summer by Victor Borge). Of these 139 shows, at least 28 had a theme directly related to the war or contained special material (not just a random remark or commercial) on the subject. Clair Schulz in his exhaustive guide to the show, *Fibber McGee and Molly on the Air*, remarked that the May 26, 1942 program was "one of the few episodes during this period in which . . . there is no mention of the war or any concern related to it." (CS2, p. 92)

The war effort on *Fibber McGee and Molly* took several forms:

- Theme shows as above, which were dedicated to a single war-related issue (e.g. gas rationing)

- Remarks by Fibber and/or Molly, usually the latter, worked into the context of the story

- Remarks by the Jordans (*as* the Jordans), directly asking listeners to do something specific (e.g. buy War Bonds)

- Remarks by other members of the cast

- Musical selections

- Messages from the sponsor, Johnson's Wax®

WARTIME THEME SHOWS

While doing research for this book, I was frustrated at my inability to assign full credit for the decision to devote so much air time and creativity to the war effort. At the end of the June 22, 1943 broadcast, Fibber announced: "This last season, as you know, the makers of Johnson's Wax® dedicated every fourth program to the presentation of some government message. Some phase of the War effort which we thought we might make a little clearer to you in our own peculiar way. We want to thank Mr. Elmer Davis and his Office of War Information (OWI see Chapter 3) for the highly efficient cooperation we have had in getting our facts straight and elimination conflict with other programs."

Given the history of the Johnson's Company, it seems certain that the idea originated in Racine (thanks to Clair Schulz for this observation). Certainly the company had to be committed to the plan and clearly the stars. The writers and the agency embraced the concept with brilliant results.

HISTORICAL NOTES

Scattered among the pages that follow, I have provided historical notes concerning the war. These are intended to provide context to remarks and allusions that may not be familiar to some readers.

It seems unnecessary to begin these notes with any description of the events surrounding Pearl Harbor. It is well to remember, however, that *Fibber McGee and Molly* was broadcast live, with most writing being done just days before the broadcast. The December 9, 1941 program aired just two days after the Pearl Harbor attack was just one of many which would be heard days and sometimes hours after the listeners and those on the program learned of important war developments.

The United States declared war on Japan on December 8, 1941. On December 11, Germany and Italy declared war on the United States, and America responded in kind.

HISTORICAL NOTE:
WARTIME GOVERNMENT CONTROLS

RATIONING

On the broadcast of November 10, 1942, Molly described Fibber this way: "He's as proud and happy as a man can be who doesn't own a car, can't eat sugar, and hates coffee." This was only one of hundreds of references to rationing during the war.

Rationing is a method of making sure that everyone receives his fair share of scarce goods, foods, or other items. Governments usually impose rationing only during emergencies, such as wars. During World War II, when supplies of almost every commodity grew scarce, the governments of most warring countries used rationing. Controls were severe in Great Britain, Russia, and other countries — and less strict in Canada and the U.S.

There are two primary reasons for rationing. First, the government must take steps to conserve materials vital to its war effort, such as gasoline. Second, it must control the distribution of materials regarded as essential for a strong civilian economy or for good civilian morale, such as coffee. In both cases, rationed items are already in short supply or soon will be.

Rationing is directly related to price controls. Workers receive high wages during a war, and can afford items they might otherwise consider luxuries. If they can buy all the luxuries they want, they soon compete for scarce goods, driving prices rapidly upwards. The government sets legal limits on prices, and also sets legal limits on how much of a given item any consumer may buy, by rationing it.

There are two basic systems for rationing. In one, a civilian consumer proves to his local ration board that he really needs a particular item for work connected with the war effort. The board issues him a *certificate* to buy the item he needs. The board has only a limited number of these items available, and gives certificates on the basis of real need. If the consumer needs another item, he must apply to the board a second time, proving his need all over again. During World War II, ration boards used certificates for automobiles, tires, typewriters, and stoves.

The *coupon* system is used for items that consumers must buy again and again, such as foods, gasoline, and shoes. The ration board issues coupons to all consumers (or to all qualified consumers, such as automobile owners). The consumer then takes his coupons with him when he shops, and surrenders a certain number for each rationed item he buys. If he uses up his coupons before the ration period ends, he cannot buy any more rationed items until the next period.

In World War II, rationed items in the United States included automobiles, bicycles, fuel oil, gasoline, kerosene, shoes, stoves, tires, typewriters, and many foods. Sugar was rationed longest, from May 1942 to June 1947.

PRICE CONTROLS

Governments sometimes introduce controls to keep prices from skyrocketing, especially in time of war or emergency. In price control, prices are not allowed to rise above certain levels, in an attempt to fight inflation and establish a stable economy.

During World War II, the price control program of the United States was carried on by the Office of Price Administration (OPA). It could place *ceilings* (top prices) on rents and many commodities. By fall of 1946, most federal price controls (except rent) had been lifted.

DECEMBER 9, 1941: TWO DAYS AFTER PEARL HARBOR

One can only try to imagine the atmosphere in the studio only two days after the surprise attack on Pearl Harbor. The show had already been written! Indeed, the finishing touches would have been put on the script on the very day Pearl Harbor was bombed. Uncertainty and apprehension must have been rampant, but the show when on.

The broadcast began with the announcement: "NBC will be on the air with the latest war news at the beginning of every program day and night. The British radio, heard by NBC, has reported that the Sultan of one of the little Malay states has handed control of his country right over to the British to make it easier to repel the Japanese . . . The United Press in New York, the United States has banned Germans, Austrians, and Italians from American citizenship until further notice . . . The Bolivian cabinet has decided to adhere to any joint action by American nations . . . From United Press in Vichy, British planes have blasted the German-held port of Calais in the most savage raid on the that city in months . . . Associated Press in Manila, a number of new fire stations have been opened up today in thickly settled parts of Manila. All firemen are equipped with steel helmets and gas masks. All civilians are being evacuated to areas near American military bases. We thank the sponsor of this program for relinquishing its time in order to bring you the latest news from the NBC Newsroom."

It was up to Harlow Wilcox to open on a seemingly ordinary note. But not for long: "We have just received this message for our listeners in a telegram from the President of S.C. Johnson and Son, Incorporated, our sponsor. In these serious days, there can be no division of opinion. The United States is at war. We are all ready and eager to do our part. The makers of Johnson's Wax® and GloCoat® believe it is in the public interest to continue programs as entertaining as *Fibber McGee and Molly*. They have a place in national morale. So you can continue to hear *Fibber McGee and Molly* and still be in touch with latest developments. We have asked the National Broadcasting Company to feel free at any time to cut into our programs with important news flashes and announcements,' Signed, H.F. Johnson, Jr.'"

The program continued more or less as usual. There was no reference to the war in the program proper. There just hadn't been time to work in war messages, especially in a way, later perfected, that did not interfere inordinately with the flow of humor.

The program centered on Fibber's supposed ability to buy things wholesale. Bandleader Billy Mills was heard speaking, which was a rarity. Mrs. Uppington had so much money she wasn't interested in any bargains. The neighbor, Mort Toops, was interested in buying a short gun.

When Harlow Wilcox knocked on the McGees' front door (the signature doorbell was not yet being used). He was carrying a box of cigars, bought as a gift for the man who coined the phrase, "Your linoleum will be your pride if Johnson's GloCoat® is applied." Fibber, in an aside, says: "That's it folks. It's the stuff that keeps Wilcox working, you waiting, and us eating." This was yet one more example of the good-natured kidding that personified the relationship between the stars and their sponsor.

Mayor LaTrivia comes by and McGee agrees to get him a globe wholesale. Wallace Wimple wants dumbbells for his wife, also wholesale. Everyone, it seems, is Christmas shopping.

The McGees go to the wholesaler, who agrees to deliver all the purchases. Later, all of the people for whom he made 40-percent-off purchases parade in to complain about the shoddy merchandise they received.

This was, admittedly, not a great show, but everyone had other things on their minds. Harlow Wilcox seemed to confirm this by saying, "Ladies and gentlemen, we know everyone is anxiously awaiting the words of President Roosevelt." In the meantime the makers of Johnson's Wax® have this message for you. America has answered the treacherous attack of the Japanese by declaring war until the victorious end. To assure our victory, we must turn our dollars into guns and our dimes into bullets. Buy United States Defense Bonds and Stamps at your post office, bank, and savings and loan office. Get them from your newspaper carrier boy or your retail dealer . . . Don't delay. Do it now."

The show closed with a moving rendition of "My Country, 'Tis of Thee" (also known as "America"), sung by the live studio audience.

FEBRUARY 24, 1942
THE MCGEES BUY A HORSE

The show opens with this message from Harlow Wilcox: "Many of you have already heard about, or seen, or even signed the Consumer's Pledge being sponsored by the Government's Consumer Division. For those of you who haven't seen one, here is the three-point pledge that women have been asked to sign voluntarily: I will buy carefully. I will waste nothing. I will take good care of the things I have. That makes sense, doesn't it?" (Of course Johnson's Wax® provides one the means of keeping that pledge.)

The premise of the show is that Fibber McGee has bought a horse because his tires are getting thin and he anticipates difficulty in replacing them because of wartime rationing. (Never mind that the only place for the horse is in the garage.) But Fibber doesn't know how to break the news to Molly. He starts by describing his tires as "looking like burlap bags with sidewalls." He floats a trial balloon about getting a horse and meets with a heavy dose of Molly's practicality. Of course, he can't give up. The deed is done!

When the Old-Timer arrives, asking "Where do you want the hay?" Molly begins to wonder. Fibber tries once again. He thought maybe he could stuff the tires with hay. Fibber tries the horse idea, but Molly says he knows nothing about taking care of one.

"Remember," she says introducing a vintage Quinn remark, "You were only a groom for one day."

Next, McGee takes a few pails of water out to the garage. He's "washing the car," he explains, but wishes he was washing a horse. What would Molly say, he wonders, if he bought a horse? She responds that her answer might necessitate having her mouth washed out with soap.

Sooner or later we know the truth will come out. Mrs. Uppington, the next arrival, likes the idea of a horse; she was once an avid horse woman, after all. After a bit of banter about Fibber's experience as a horse rider, she leaves. At that moment, Harlow Wilcox arrives. Wilcox thinks buying a horse to save tires is a good idea. "This is a time for conserving," he says sagely. We know what's coming, of course. And it does, with GloCoat® contributing not only to conservation but to morale in the home (because of the bright, shining surfaces).

On Wilcox' departure, Teeny turns up. She knows he has a horse because she saw it in the garage (after her baseball went through the window).

There is a brief musical interlude, after which we hear Molly screaming: she has discovered the horse. Her protests are interrupted by the arrival of Wallace Wimple. His wife, "Sweetie Face," is at home teaching jiu jitsu to soldiers. Nearly half of the soldiers take the full course. The other half "will be all right . . . in time."

After Wimple leaves, Molly says it's unpatriotic to keep a horse now: "Think of all the glue that's needed for the back of Defense Stamps."

Mayor LaTrivia is next. Amazing enough, he wants to *buy* the horse! The city has decided to supplement motor vehicles with the horse-drawn variety "because of the rubber shortage." Fibber insists on bargaining with the mayor over a price, even though they have already agreed on $100.

Harlow Wilcox winds things up with a note about the adjustment necessary for the new Daylight Savings Time. Anything to save electricity will help the War effort. And by the way, kitchens will be brighter when one uses GloCoat®.

HISTORICAL NOTE: WAR BONDS

Bonds, sold by the government to help finance the war and slow post-war inflation were called War Bonds. Prior to Pearl Harbor, they were called Defense Bonds. The bonds yielded only 2.9 per cent in interest. A $25 bond was purchased was for $18.75 for ten years before maturity. War Stamps were available for 10 cents, an encouragement to young people, and could be collected until enough of them were bought to allow purchase of a bond.

Some 85 million people (essentially half the population) bought bonds and/or stamps for a total of $185.7 billion. Jim and Marian Jordan, as well as others in the cast, were actively involved in promoting bond sales. Their efforts were not limited to the program, but included appearances at bond rallies and other activities. They received a number of awards for these activities.

MARCH 24, 1942
"FIBBER WRITES A SONG"

This program focuses on Fibber's Musical composition, "The Defense Stamp Stomp."

It opens with Harlow Wilcox noting that many more people will, with the war, be planting gardens: "It helps the family save and the country conserve." Of course, he is able to tie in this message with the sponsor's product, GloCoat®. Because use of the product saves time, that time "can be used in your vegetable patch." In addition, the dirty shoes from the garden won't be a worry if the floor is protested with GloCoat®.

The set-up finds Fibber McGee writing a song. He feels "like Stephen Foster." His title for the song, as told to Molly, is "The Defense Stamp Stomp." Molly approves, but is a bit "leery of your lyrics." (Billy Mills had already agreed to write the music.) Fibber is not even slightly discouraged when Molly informs him that the first line of his song —"There's a long, long trail a'winding" — has already been used in a song.

Then Molly doesn't like the title because she read that they're changing the name of Defense Stamps to War Bonds: "We're going to stop defending and start fighting." Very well, then — Fibber is willing to change the name to "War Stamp Stomp." He's flexible, in fact he's been "maulin' over" in his mind another song: "Ballad for America," which he thinks would be great for a singer like Paul Robeson (a popular yet controversial black opera singer). Molly tells him there already is such a song, sung by Paul Robeson. By now Fibber is sure someone is stealing his ideas. A bit of banter follows during which Molly notes that Sullivan, of Gilbert and Sullivan, wrote *The Mikado*. Fibber calls Sullivan a "dirty traitor" for corresponding with the Japanese.

The discussion is interrupted by the arrival of Mayor LaTrivia. What follows is what will be the first of many occasions in which the McGees drive the mayor into a babbling rage by intentionally misunderstanding him. This time his Phi Beta Kappa key is at issue. At one point the Mayor says the key has "no utilitarian purpose whatever." McGee can't understand, then, why the mayor wears it. When the mayor asks, "What good is that American Legion button?" Fibber is wearing, he gets a strong patriotic response.

After the mayor's departure the McGees decide to give the assignment of writing the lyrics to their friend Wallace Wimple, who fancies himself an amateur poet. On their way to his house they meet the wealthy Mrs. Uppington who decided to walk to the Bonton Department Store (at 14th and Oak) to save time and rubber. Naturally, her chauffeur later meets her with a car and drives her home!

The next encounter is with Billy Mills. During that conversation Fibber reveals that they have been trying to get Uncle Dennis to lay off the booze. Molly told him to "lay off the little Brown Jug until we lick the little yellow mugs." (The audience greets this racist remark with enthusiastic applause.) Uncle Dennis would make a "great air raid warden: he's out all night anyway."

Rather than go to Wimple's house, the McGees agree to meet him at the radio station, McGee with Billy Mills' music and Wimple with the lyrics. They do so, and Wimple relates that he'd like to send "Sweetie Face" over to General McArthur. "She's built like a tank," he explains. He does have the promised lyrics:

Dig down deep into your rompers
Lay it on the line you stompers
For the right, for right is might
Jump into it. Don't be tight
And stomp, stomp — stomp, stomp, stomp . . .
Oh, there's none behind the man behind the gun . . .

Fibber is too impatient to let him finish.

When Fibber gets to meet the manager of radio station MEOW, he learns that *another* song with his chosen title, "Just Come to Me," has been played over the air for the past two weeks!

At the close of the show, Molly commiserates: "I'll bet if you ever published your song and everyone started singing it, it would be an awful pain to Berlin."

"Berlin, Germany?" he asks.

"No — Berlin, Irving," she answers.

HISTORICAL NOTE: BATAAN

In April 1942 Bataan (in the Philippines) surrendered to the Japanese. General Edward P. King, Jr. signed the surrender document at 12:30 p.m. About 35,000 American and Filipino troops fell into Japanese hands. Almost immediately, the prisoners began the forced "Bataan Death March" from Balanga to San Fernando.

As news of the brutality of the Death March was revealed, America's enmity toward Japan increased, if that was possible, and the recapture of Bataan became a high priority. In February 1945 American forces returned to Bataan, and — except for a small Japanese pocket around Mount Natib — was retaken by U.S. forces, who suffered a total of 50 casualties in regaining an area which was contested four years before at a cost of thousands of lives.

MOVIES: *Bataan* and *Back to Bataan* capture the horror and American resolve of this chapter in the war. *Back to Bataan* is described in one movie review book as a "good, sturdy World War II movie. John Wayne does his usual heroic job in avenging the Bataan Death March."

APRIL 7, 1942
"THE SCRAP DRIVE"

According to Claire Schulz, (CS,p.90) this was the first show to be devoted entirely to a war theme, although strong allusions to war-related issues had been made in prior broadcasts. A case in point was the McGee's purchase of a horse on the rather far-fetched premise that they would make rubber and gasoline.

This episode opens with a visit from the rich and ever-affected Mrs. Uppington. She is chairperson of the Wistful Vista Reclamation Committee (Read Committee to Collect Scrap). McGee doesn't think they have much of that stuff. The program is obviously intended to educate him and, of course, the listeners on the subject. This leads to the incorporation of the show's most famous running gag — the hall closet — into the story. Strangely, opening the door does not *immediately* result in the sound-effects-generated avalanche of odds and ends. A few seconds later the expected eruption occurs, however what follows is a give and take on what to give to the government — an aluminum coffee pot. They decide to make three piles: metal, rubber, and paper. After some discussion, they decide to keep Fibber's old ukulele.

Harlow Wilcox arrives just in time to wax eloquent over an empty can of Johnson's GloCoat® found among other items in the debris. His pitch is actually quite short.

Next to arrive is the precocious Teeny, who provides the perfect reason for McGee to deliver a paean to "Uncle Sam." Teeny wants to know if Uncle Sam is a real man. Fibber assures her that he is and that "Nobody ever had a better uncle. When we get in a jam he's always there to back us up and when he gets in a mess we rally around him." He admits that "Like all relatives he annoys us now and then but it really doesn't mean anything." And — "He's the only rich uncle in the world that the whole family hopes will live forever."

An unusual exchange with Mayor LaTrivia results in the McGees arguing between themselves while the mayor escapes unscathed. Enter Wallace Wimple, who informs them that he had tried to join the Marines that morning. (No more unlikely recruit could be imagined!) Sweetie Face went down to "*give her consent.*" Wimple was rejected for a variety of reasons although the Marines accepted Sweetie Face, as an instructor in armed combat!

At the finish, McGee notes that the masseuse at the Elks Club was in the Army, Molly expressed surprise because of his age.

Fibber's response was vintage Don Quinn: "I guess the Army wants all the old rubber it can get." (*Masseuse! Get it?*)

HISTORICAL NOTE: AIR RAID ON TOKYO

James A. "Jimmy" Doolittle, a noted American flier, led the first bombing raid on Tokyo in World War II. He led sixteen B-25 twin-engine bombers, normally land-based planes, from the deck of the aircraft carrier U.S.S. *Hornet* in the surprise attack on Tokyo on April 18, 1942. Congress awarded him the Medal of Honor for this daring raid.

A lieutenant colonel when he led his raid, Doolittle rose to lieutenant general during World War II. He commanded the 12th Air Force in the North African invasion in 1942, and later the 15th Air Force in the Mediterranean area. In 1944 and 1945, he was commander of the 8th Air Force, which bombed Western Europe. He also commanded the 8th Air force on Okinawa after Germany surrendered.

This was a real morale booster, by genuine heroes, coming as it did only four months after Pearl Harbor. It couldn't have helped the morale of the Japanese, either. Some of the planes reached Tokyo using a practice air alert, and most Japanese were first confused, then startled when actual bombs started falling. Yokohama, Kobe, and Nagoya were also struck. One plane was hit by antiaircraft fire, suffering only minor damage. Eight of the aircraft bombed their primary targets. Five others had to select secondary objectives. Only one failed to drop its bombs on Japan. Favored by an uncommon tail wind, the planes continued westward, most of them to China and safety. One landed near Vladivostok, and the crew was interned by the Russians. Two crews came down in Japanese-occupied China (three of the men were executed by the Japanese; five were made prisoners, and four were freed at the end of the war). Little damage was inflicted on the Japanese cities, but the Doolittle raid gave

Japanese military leaders pause and was a factor in their decision to consolidate their vast holdings rather than expand even further. For the allies, the attack was an antidote for the painful doses of defeat.

The Doolittle raid was not mentioned on the *Fibber McGee and Molly* show. I surmise that this omission in part by the uncertainty over the fate of some of the flyers.

Movie: *Thirty Seconds Over Tokyo* is highly recommended as a cinematic account of what is always referred to as a "daring raid." Spencer Tracy plays General Doolittle; he is supported by a fine cast and an excellent script by Dalton Trumbo. The film won an Academy Award for its special effects.

APRIL 28, 1942
"McGee's Old Straw Hat"

"Save what you have, conserve, make it last a little longer. That's the watchword nowadays." With these words, Harlow Wilcox introduced another program.

Molly thinks restoring McGee's shabby straw hat is carrying conservation a bit too far, but McGee is adamant. "The government wants us to conserve and by the million merry men of the mighty McArthur," he says, "[and] I'm gonna conserve!" He wants to try art gum on the hat, although Molly says that would be like bombing Tokyo with confetti.

Teeny comes along with some rather bizarre ideas about what one can plant in a Victory Garden. Her ideas about the *reasons* for Victory Gardens are serious, however: "How can we win this war if everybody says I've been thinking about a garden, but they never do it? My teacher says that every single vegetable we grow means more food for our soldiers and sailors. She says we have an ocean between us and Australia and an ocean between us and Europe, and if we have a nation that we can sit around and do nothing we're gonna get smacked." Her teacher said that whether it's buying bonds or planting vegetables, there's only one thing to do and that's *"Dig, dig, dig!"*

The Old-Timer is next selling Christmas cards (in April?). No war talk. With Harlow Wilcox, there is only mention of how important it is to conserve in wartime, as well as a quick pitch for Johnson's products.

The mayor arrives to ask McGee to serve on a committee: "To organize others to write more letters to their friends and relatives, sons and brothers and fathers in the Army and Navy. Give them more news from home." Fibber is happy to help in a good cause. LaTrivia says he was a captain in the Army in the last war (Gale Gordon would join the Coast Guard in *this* war), and he knew how welcome were letters from home. The McGees drive the Mayor to distraction, as usual, by pretending to confuse Annapolis with the Army Academy.

Wallace Wimple comes by. Sweetie Face is going to take him up in an Army blimp (as ballast). Wimple is not even surprised to learn that "ballast" is usually thrown out. After McGee dyes the hat blue, Molly covers it with fruit to make a hat for herself. Fibber leaves to buy a *felt* hat. "That was the last straw," he cleverly remarks.

Harlow Wilcox finishes with: "At no time does a woman's role in life become more clear than when a country is at war and homes are threatened, because those homes are only as strong as the women who guard and keep them. Most men would admit either openly or secretly that no job is more important than home management. Especially when budgets must be watched closely, when things must be conserved and made to last. Really, they have several jobs rolled into one: feeding their families the right food, making mending clothes for the youngsters and, certainly not the least, keeping the house clean." He's given homemakers everywhere a well-deserved pat on the back. He adds that they save kitchen fat and salvage scrap materials for war production. They study first-aid and enlist as air raid wardens. "Yes," he says, "*you* are the guardians of our homes. The makers of Johnson's GloCoat® and Wax® salute you, the housekeepers and homemakers of America."

Fibber's serious message is to announce that an address by the president follows (as it often did on Tuesday nights). He promises that "everyone will do his share to support the Commander-In-Chief. Molly adds that "We'll all be listening, Mr. President."

May 5, 1942
"Sugar Substitute"

Once again, an episode is based on the subject of rationing. This time it's sugar. When the show opens Harlow Wilcox tells us: "The government says there will be enough sugar to go around if we don't go around too fast. So solid citizen McGee, whose cocoa has taken more than one lump in the past, is determined to find a chemical substitute for sugar."

McGee has a collection of chemicals ready, but no idea what to do with them. Of course he is not deterred. He is motivated by the fact that two-thirds of America's sugar is imported, and one-seventh from the Philippines (now held by the Japanese). Shipping had to be diverted that ordinarily brings the sugar in order to take food and equipment to Australia.

Molly, for once, is cautiously encouraging — McGee wants to make sugar from alcohol. He knows they make alcohol from sugar. He abandons that plan when Molly points out the folly of making alcohol from sugar so he can make sugar from alcohol.

The Old-Timer arrives with a load of skepticism, based on McGee's previous experiments, and suggests he take an aspirin and give up the idea. Mayor LaTrivia, who arrives next, is equally skeptical. He has come by to see if Molly has registered for the Ration Board. The mayor observes that rationing is the only way to handle what sugar there is: "This way the government makes sure that everyone, regardless of how much or how little money he makes, or whatever he does, or wherever he is, will get his fair share of sugar. And when 132 million people register it'll be the greatest registration job ever tackled." He is confident that *every* American citizen will cooperate.

When Harlow Wilcox arrives, he thinks, based on the odor in the house, that Fibber is still cleaning his straw hat from the previous week's show. When he learns that a sugar substitute is in the works, he is reassuring: "Oh, there'll be enough sugar, Fibber, only *everybody* has to cooperate."

McGee plans to continue: "Do you realize that Hitler has substitutes for almost everything?

Molly *does* realize this, adding, "Do you realize that one of those days they'll need a substitute *for Hitler?*" (The audience loves this.) Wilcox uses the subject to introduce his favorite subject, Johnson's Wax®.

After a visit by Teeny, and a musical interlude, Fibber is looking for a guinea pig on whom to try out his invention. Enter Mrs. Uppington. Unfortunately, she has given up sugar in her tea. Nevertheless, McGee finds a way — *his* way — to sweeten it. When she leaves, Molly is impressed by his cleverness.

Wallace Wimple is the next experimental arrival. He loves tea — and, yes, he *does* take it with sugar. He finds the tea quite sweet and delicious. When he leaves, Fibber reveals to Molly that he did *not* put sugar in Wimple's tea. All he did, for Wimple and "Uppy," was rough up the bottom of the cup. When they stirred, they felt the "sugar" on the bottom. (This may have been the first recorded use of the placebo effect in foods.)

Wilcox's final commercial is built around the need to conserve. He is followed by another serious message.

FIBBER: Ladies and gentlemen, if you haven't already registered for sugar rationing, may we urge you to do so within the next two days. Cooperation with the authorities in this matter is as vital to our war effort as almost anything you can do. Your local newspaper will tell you the exact place of registration in your neighborhood.

MOLLY: Remember now, that every pound of sugar we don't use means so much more ammunition for our soldiers. It takes a fifth of an acre of sugar cane to fire a big gun just once.

FIBBER: So, let's raise cane where it counts.

May 12, 1942
"McGee Is Trailed by a Spy"

Everywhere he goes, Fibber spies a photographer taking pictures. Has he spied a spy? *He* thinks so! Molly shows her usual skepticism, especially when she hears that he took pictures of the Elks Club. How could that be a military objective? She answers her own question. The Elks Club might be classified as an ammunition dump: "There's so much lead sitting around there."

The key to Fibber's suspicion is that every time he looks at the picture-taker he looks away. Molly observes that if everyone who chooses not to look at her husband 24 hours a day is a spy: "The whole country could end up in a concentration camp."

When the mayor turns up, McGee tells him of his suspicions and demands action. The man carries a camera under his coat and McGee hears a *click, click, click* every time he's around. The mayor offers to have him picked up for questioning but McGee, fearful of being sued for false arrest, decides to capture the "spy" himself.

McGee is convinced that *he* is the target of surveillance because he is working on a project for the Signal Corps, *a* "triple cross" bird. This hybrid combines the qualities of a homing pigeon, a woodpecker, and a parrot. It will fly to the right place, knock on the door, and speak the message. Not to be outdone, Molly suggests adding an ostrich to the mix. If pursued by the Nazis, this remarkable fowl can stick its head in the sand and they can't hear what it says.

Throughout all of this, the "spy" stays across the street with an eye on the house.

After the King's Men sing "America is Calling," the McGees attempt to lure the picture snapper into following them. It works, and Molly begins to fear they will be kidnapped and "taken to Germany on a submarine."

They meet the ubiquitous Mrs. Uppington on the street and explain their suspicions of the picture-taking spy. She has a little trouble believing this, but she does worry a little, as she would be unhappy in a concentration camp. It is difficult for her to concentrate.

McGee calls the FBI who arrives almost at once and surrounds the man. Soon, the FBI reveals that the "spy" is, in fact, a photographer for a national magazine doing a story on how a small town busybody (Fibber) spends his day.

Harlow Wilcox rounds out the show by a question for listening housewives. "Have you joined the Scrap Brigade? Any old rags or rubber or metal today, ladies?" He refers them to an ad in the current issue of *Life* magazine on how to salvage valuable materials for war production. The ad, sponsored by Johnson's, tells how patriotic housewives can help their country while doing their own spring housecleaning. There are, of course, also some suggestions about how to use the sponsor's product.

HISTORICAL NOTE: GUADALCANAL

On August 7, 1942, the U.S. Marines landed on Guadalcanal. It was their first major offensive in the Pacific, the first time American and Japanese soldiers had come face-to-face on land. The fighting was bitter, and control of the island seesawed for several months. In February 1943, Army troops under Major General Alexander M. Patch finally cleared Guadalcanal.

American Forces learned very hard lessons about Island Fighting and the Army and Navy about coordination during this effort.

MOVIE: *Guadalcanal Diary*, based on the best-selling book of the same name, is one of the very best World War II epics. An all-star cast captures the drama and horror of the battle.

OCTOBER 13, 1942
"McGEE CONVERTS THE FURNACE"

This episode is devoted almost exclusively to war-related themes. Fibber has been talking to himself about distribution problems affecting heating fuels. He's decided to convert his oil furnace to coal — by himself. Molly supports the idea of the conversion, but not his do-it-yourself proposal. This is the theme which the other messages surround.

It begins with McGee asking for the paper to see what the weather will be *today*. Molly reminds him that in wartime the newspaper only prints what the weather was *yesterday* (to avoid giving valuable information to the enemy).

The Old-Timer turns up for the by-now-familiar exchange of marginally funny puns, including "There's no fuel like an old fuel." When "OT" departs, Fibber starts on a crossword puzzle. "What's a four-letter word for an article attached to a heel?" he wonders aloud. The only word *he* can think of is "swastika." (The studio audience responds with sustained applause.)

Molly suggests that while he is in a working mood, he should weather-strip the windows. He says they don't need it. *She* says they *do*: "The dining room has a draft that would shake a married man with seven children." (The *military* draft granted deferment based on the potential draftees family obligations.)

Enter Abigail Uppington. She is collecting for the USO and hopes the McGees will contribute by attending a dog show. Mirth ensues over remarks about her dog, Fifi. She leaves in a huff — or a limousine.

Molly suggests that Fibber put on old clothes for his furnace job, but he reminds her that all his old clothes went to the Red Cross. Coveralls would do, but they went to the Red Cross, too!

Harlow Wilcox arrives on cue to slip his wax commercial into the storyline. The writer (Don Quinn) contrives cleverly to have Fibber actually deliver the pitch. Wilcox reminds Fibber that he should have checked to see which fuel was best for Wistful Vista. Fibber had done it. McGee knows the rules of wartime fuel conservation.

When Wilcox leaves, Molly goes upstairs so Teeny can appear at the door. McGee tells her he has a job to do — "It's almost for the government."

"Why?" Teeny asks, using the word for the ninth time since she arrived.

"Because the government wants us to conserve fuel," McGee says.

"Why?" one more time.

McGee delivers a short lecture: "In wartime, the Army and Navy needs all the oil and coal they can get. So the ordinary citizen has to use a little less. And we've got a transportation problem. Training boats needed for hauling soldiers and supplies. So we gotta cooperate and use whatever fuel is handy. And the supply of oil being a little shorter than coal, the government wants us to change over our oil burners to coal burners wherever possible."

This technique of explaining war needs in terms even a "child" can understand is used effectively many times during the war years.

McGee goes downtown to get much-needed supplies and coveralls, followed by Wallace Wimple. "Sweetie Face" has been pinching his cheeks — with a pair of tongs. No war conversation ensued, but when Mayor LaTrivia arrives there is *plenty* of conversation. Unfortunately, the conversation ends with LaTrivia in his usual state of exasperation rage, but again without any war reference. Meanwhile, Molly calls a legitimate firm to do the furnace conversion.

Harlow Wilcox begins the wrap-up: "In these days when all of us need to put forth an extra effort, we certainly don't want to add unnecessary work in the home." The listener knows what's coming but as is so frequently the case, the commercial message is preceded by a wartime reminder. "It's imperative to take extra good care of the things we have." Johnson's call it "Protective Housekeeping."

This show demonstrates the advantage of live broadcasts and weekly script writing. The 1942 World Series (won by this author's beloved St. Louis Cardinals) was mentioned twice, making the broadcast very real. Jack Benny and Bob Hope used this technique as well, usually with college football references.

OCTOBER 27, 1942
"THE OLD-TIMER HIDES OUT"

This is the most prominent role The Old-Timer (played by the versatile Bill Thompson) ever had on the show — he even interrupts Harlow Wilcox' introductory remarks. The Old-timer is in a panic; he needs to hide out! The cops and the FBI are after him, or so he thinks. He hides behind the "davenport" when Mrs. Uppington arrives. The McGees go through various machinations to keep her from knowing that the Old-Timer is there, especially when she says she's going down to the FBI.

"Why?" Fibber wants to know. "Find a German spy in your sauerkraut?"

In fact, she's going to register her fingerprints in the voluntary civilian file. On her exit, the Old Timer tries another hiding place. You guessed it—the hall closet!

The McGees have a hard time getting to the facts of the Old-Timer's concern. Finally, he says: "I've been un-American. I'm a traitor to my country. I'm just a dirty old Benefit Arnold." His confession is interrupted by the band leader, Billy Mills, who stays just long enough to plug the McGees' new movie.

Before "OT" can get to the facts, Harlow Wilcox comes in for his commercial. He says he's with the FBI — "Floors Brightened Instantly." He also mentions his oft-repeated admonition to conserve during wartime.

Another doorbell delays the Old-Timer's confession. This time it's Mayor LaTrivia. A discussion of a local eatery gives the mayor an opportunity for a wartime message: "Remember what happened in 1920 when people starved in the midst of plenty? We ought to be much smarter now. If we want milk, let's feed the cow. Let's all be ready when this is over. And start today to plant the clover. Let's all buy Bonds and pay our debts, for the man what has is the man what gets." This poetic thought, it turns out, was penned by Wallace Wimple.

Still no answer from the Old-Timer — and the program's nearly over. Molly takes him into the kitchen for a sandwich, giving Teeny a chance for a visit. She poses a riddle: Why are toy banks in the shape of pigs? The answer came in verse form:

> Because sailors wear little white caps
> And the sea has little white caps, too
> And it makes the waves pretty
> And my momma's pretty too
> And she just joined the WAVES
> And the waves wash the beach
> And the beach is full of sand
> And so is spinach
> And farmers grow spinach
> And they have to get up at 5 o'clock in the morning

And that's "Twearly"
And so's a pig's tail
And you can bank on that, I betcha.

Finally, the Old-Timer admits that he's a hoarder. He knows very well, Molly is sure, that hoarding causes shortages, which cause prices to go up: "It's greedy and selfish and un-American," she says emphatically.

"Pour it on," says the Old-Timer.

There is a misunderstanding as the McGees listen to his tale. They think he's hoarding tires, and the country is desperate for tires. It turns out he's hoarding United State War Bonds!

A long way to go for this message, but the point can't be missed when Harlow Wilcox weighs in at the end: "You hear it said by our enemies that we are soft, wasteful people. Well, let them have what solace they can from that thought, because by now they have learned that we are anything but soft. Before we're through with them, they'll know that we're only wasteful because we have had so much of everything. Such a high standard of living. But every day in talking with friends and neighbors you realize that we can certainly make whatever sacrifices we are called upon to make. Also that it's probably very good for us to be more saving and learn to take better care of our things." A very short two-sentence commercial follows.

The show closes with a brief discussion by the McGees of a speech by former presidential candidate, Wendell Wilkie, the night before. He said that after the war we would all be neighbors: "First arms, then hands across the sea."

HISTORICAL NOTE: NORTH AFRICAN CAMPAIGN

The British fought a seesaw campaign against the Germans and Italians in North Africa, taking and losing ground over and over again. In May 1942, Rommel's Afrika Korps, aided by Italian troops, began a powerful offensive. Capturing Tobruk in Libya, they moved toward Egypt. By July, strong British resistance and Rommel's supply shortage had halted the Axis attacks at El Alamein, Egypt. In October, the British Eighth Army under Gen. Sir Bernard

L. Montgomery took the offensive, and rolled on to Tripoli and Southern Tunisia. This victory was a major turning point of the war.

Along with the British offensive in Tunisia, the allies planned an invasion of French North Africa with the code name of "Operation Torch." They hoped to force the Axis armies out of Africa, and also to relieve pressure on the hard-pressed Russian forces, which were reeling under a new German offensive. Lt. Gen. Dwight D. Eisenhower commanded an Allied force that landed on the coast of Algeria and Morocco on November 8, 1942. About 500 troop and supply ships, escorted by more than 350 warships, transported Allied troops from the United States and the British Isles. The invasion caught the German high command completely by surprise.

Early in 1943 President Roosevelt and Prime Minister Churchill conferred at Casablanca, Morocco. They announced that the Allies would accept nothing less than unconditional surrender from the Axis nations. While U.S. troops pushed eastward across Algeria, the British Eighth Army advanced into southern Tunisia. On May 12, 1943 the last organized Axis army force in Africa surrendered. The allies had killed, wounded, or captured about 350,000 Axis soldiers, and had suffered about 70,000 casualties in the North African campaign.

MOVIES: *Immortal Sergeant, Tobruk, Sundown.* A real "sleeper" is the seldom-seen Humphrey Bogart movie, *Sahara.*

NOVEMBER 17, 1942
"FINDING MONEY IN THE SOFA"

After Billy Mills and the orchestra open the show with Irving Berlin's "This Is the Army, Mr. Jones," Harlow Wilcox reminds the listeners that "most men are working harder today than ever before in their lives." He adds that women are working harder than ever, too, especially with war work. Of course, this leads to a short commercial on "protective housework."

Molly is intent on cleaning the attic, a task that Fibber resists until she tells him his old Army uniform is up there. "Did it have my sharp shooter's medal on it?" McGee wants to know. Seems he used to hold his rifle over his left shoulder, a looking glass in his left hand, and knock a cigarette out of a soldier's mouth at 200 yards. The unfortunate volunteer soldier was "One-Ear Coggins."

Teeny drops by and learns that McGee was in the last war. "Were you a General?" she wants to know. McGee admits he was not, but implies that the reason for this oversight was "petty politics." When Teeny hears he had a sharpshooter's medal, she wants to know why. He had claimed, after all, that he "hit the bull's eye 99 times out of a hundred."

"Didn't it hurt him?" she asks.

"There was no bull," he tries to explain.

"No bull?" asks the departing Teeny: "*Ninety-nine* times out of a hundred . . .?" (*We* know what she means.)

Finding the uniform, Fibber waxes nostalgic. (Forgive me, dear reader; after listening to scores of these shows, the word "wax" just creeps in, unbidden, to one's vocabulary.) He remembers how he got a bayonet tear in the shoulder by falling on his rifle. Molly thinks he might have been in the Air Force because there are wings on the shoulder of his uniform. But it's a moth.

They find a twenty-year old newspaper. The 1922 headline reads: "German printing presses pour out 100 billion marks every day." (This has an unpleasantly familiar ring).

"Why were they printing all that money?" Molly wonders.

"Inflation," McGee explains. "Terrible mess. In Germany after the last war, it took a bushel basket of money to buy a pair of shoe strings, if anybody had the shoes to put 'em in."

Molly wants to know if every war does that. "Not necessarily," Fibber responds. "That's why the government wants us to buy War Bonds, and pay off our debts and buy only what we need. If they keep things under control then after the war our money will really be worth something."

The McGees then discover a note from Fibber's grand uncle saying $20,000 is hidden in a horse-hair sofa. But *which* horse-hair sofa?

Harlow Wilcox stops by to find Fibber verbally spending the money he doesn't have. McGee, affecting an upper-class accent, pretends not to know for whom Wilcox works. Wilcox straightens him out.

In the end, the McGees find the $20,000—in Confederate money.

DECEMBER 1, 1942
"GAS RATIONING"

Nearly a year has passed since Pearl Harbor and mileage rationing has just come to Wistful Vista and "in spite of its being a meatless day," announces Harlow Wilcox, "get a load of the 'beef' being put up by an average citizen as we meet — Fibber McGee and Molly."

Fibber is in a rant: "I tell you it ain't fair, Molly. They can't do this to me. Four gallons a week! That's ridiculous."

The ever-pragmatic Molly tries to reason with him: "You don't *need* four gallons."

This is not what McGee wants to hear! He thinks mileage rationing is a "dirty deal . . . Everyone will stay home, and giving every car owner a measly little medicine dropper full of gasoline is an infringement on private life."

Molly points out to her husband, and to the listeners, that the main reason for gasoline rationing is to save tires: "Don't you know that if we continue like we have been, the majority of automobiles will be off the road next year?"

"Good," McGee says, "there's too much traffic anyway! Get the cars off the road." Except for his car, of course. He'd write to his congressmen or his senator, but he can't recall either one's name.

Molly continues a reasoned approach with her unreasonable spouse: "Our government has asked us to take less gasoline so we'll drive less and save the country's rubber. And if you haven't got enough interest in the government to know who your representatives are, you haven't got any right to stand around and stomach ache." (The writers avoided the word "belly," as it struck them as a bit coarse.)

McGee wants to know what happened to that sympathetic (synthetic) rubber. Harlow Wilcox arrives early (for him) in the program and begins what will be a series of putdowns for Fibber's attitude. But first he announces that Mayor LaTrivia (Gale Gordon) has joined the Coast Guard and Harlow does a quick tribute to the

Coast Guard: "Do you realize the first boats ashore in the Solomons and North Africa were Coast Guard boats?"

Molly tells Harlow that McGee has been raving about gas rationing all day. Harlow wants to know what business requires Fibber to use more gasoline. Molly supplies a little sarcasm. Fibber is the "sole support of three pinochle players at the Elks Club." Wilcox is not persuaded or amused. Fibber "talks like a chump," he says. "Mileage rationing is the only fair way to cut down non-essential driving when the rubber this country has is gone. It's gone."

Fibber thinks "They should have foreseen that and 'took' care of the situation." When Harlow asks if *Fibber* is that farsighted, she responds in the affirmative: "He's the one who said we'd lick the Japanese in ten days, remember? . . . He's the one who said Germany would fold up from starvation last April . . . He's the one who said we'd never ship a soldier out of this country."

The sarcasm is, of course, lost on McGee, and Wilcox says he's a little bit ashamed of him: "If you had the brains of a seahorse, you'd realize what a spot this country is in regarding rubber. England does almost no civilian driving. Canada has had mileage rationing for months, and you stand there and squawk putting your pretty little private life against the importance of winning this war. Only a monkey could consider doing business as usual — and we haven't got time for monkey business."

Wilcox leaves and, as happens in other programs, the people at Johnson's have given up their commercial time for a war message. It is well-received by the audience and even Fibber begins to see the light, but only dimly. He still thinks *he* deserves special treatment.

Of course, Fibber decides to go right to the Ration Board, by phone, which means a chat with Myrt, the operator. (No war messages here.)

Molly is just about to give Fibber another lecture when Abigail Uppington arrives. Fibber tells her to "tear off a few (ration) coupons and we'll gas a while." It seems she wants Fibber's advice about how to get the utmost mileage out of a gallon of gas. Like most conscientious citizens, she wants to drive under 35 miles per hour and wants to know if it would help to drive with the emergency brake on. Fibber wants "Uppy" to know how he's been mistreated by the Ration Board. She isn't buying it: "As usual, Mr. McGee, you are being stupidly self-centered. Every intelligent person knows that every extra unnecessary mile of wear on times is equivalent to sabotage."

Fibber is nearly speechless by his visitor's strong language, but is still unconvinced as she takes her leave.

Molly suggests Fibber write a letter to Mr. Roosevelt. When he says it's a matter of principle she suggests he put his idea in another bank as he's not getting any interest. He does like the idea of the letter, however.

"Dear Mr. President . . ." No, that's too formal.

"Dear Chief ..." — *that's* it. "I know you must be pretty busy these days . . ."

The doorbell rings.

"Excuse me, Frank," McGee says to the absent president, "there's somebody at the door."

It's Teeny (Molly is in the kitchen). McGee launches into his rant again: "Who do they think I am?"

"Who do *you* think you are?" Teeny responds. *Her* father is getting by quite nicely on his gas ration, thank you very much. "How do you think we can keep doing it over there if we don't do more over here?" She leaves on that precocious note.

Mayor LaTrivia is the next to turn up. He is leaving for the Coast Guard the next day. When McGee learns that the mayor is going in as an ordinary apprentice seaman, McGee is sorry that he didn't have a chance to use his "influence" to get him a commission. (McGee's "influence" will be a highlight of later shows.) La Trivia doesn't want a commission until he earns it! When McGee asks LaTrivia to use *his* influence on the gas problem, the mayor observes that McGee is one of the "moaners and groaners . . . one of those astigmatic individuals who thinks the war is being fought only by soldiers and sailors and marines. Everything you do in your daily life has some effect on the War effort." LaTrivia offers an eloquent explanation of why McGee is wrong and how desperately the country needs rubber. He leaves on this note: "McGee, when you do drive, if you get up to 35 miles per hour, think of somebody who didn't get a rubber lifeboat."

This comment really hits home. McGee does 180 degree attitude change. It's time for him to set an example "for these guys that are crabbin' about not getting' enough gas."

When Wallace Wimple drops by for a brief visit, McGee watches out the window when he leaves to be sure he's walking not driving.

The next arrival is a young woman with a baby looking for Mayor LaTrivia. She's the mayor's sister. When the baby fusses, the mother gives her a teething ring. Fibber snatches it away. It's made of rubber! When McGee changes his mind, he *really* changes it.

Wilcox finishes with a commercial softly listing the ways Johnson's Wax® helps in transportation, "so critical in wartime." Executives in the transportation industry are encouraged to write to Racine for more information. At the end of the show, there is another service message.

Jim Jordan tells the audience that Gale Gordon is one of many members of the broadcast team who are serving in the military. He wishes them all well and promises a warm welcome on their return.

Marian adds: "And if all of you give that big show everything you gave our little one, your new sponsor, Uncle Sam, will be very happy."

DECEMBER 8, 1942
"WOMEN IN THE WORK FORCE"

There's a war on, but Fibber is only interested in the battle of the sexes.

The show opens with the McGees, Fibber especially, worrying over a vacuum cleaner that refuses to work. In the process Fibber succeeds in insulting the entire female gender — they don't know much of anything. Molly isn't buying it, of course, and informs him that she had to call the telephone company because the phone is out of order. Someone is on the way over to fix it.

When the repair man arrives, "he" is a repair *woman*! Fibber's reaction is predictable: "*This is gonna be good!*" She can't possibly fix a phone. She's an 'Alexander Graham Belladonna.'" She fixes it in minutes, to McGee's chagrin, but that gives him a chance to talk to Myrt, the telephone operator, with the usual confusing result.

The McGees prepare to go to the hardware store for a part. They will walk because Fibber is still grousing about his gas ration from last week's show. Molly goes to go "fix her face." In her absence, the paper boy comes to collect. The paper "boy" is a paper *girl*! All the way to the hardware store, Fibber mumbles about women in men's jobs. Molly stops him for a moment where she tells him they have a female delivering the milk, too. McGee doesn't "know what this country is coming to."

They encounter Mrs. Uppington who, she says, is now a "working girl," in spite of her wealth. McGee can't believe that either. The next encounter is with Harlow Wilcox, who is confronted by McGee's question: "Are you still working for Johnson's Wax®?" (This is meant as a commentary on women seemingly taking over men's dominance in the work force). In fact, they had just been "bawled out by a lady cop" for crossing against the light. Wilcox, of course, has a ready answer. Johnson's Wax® wouldn't be in business if it weren't for women. They were the ones who realized all the advantages of using the Johnson products.

McGee stops to buy a cigar, and guess what? *The clerk is a female.* It turns out she knows a great deal more about cigars and tobacco than he will ever know.

As they pass the courthouse, Molly wonders what "Uppy" is working at. (She never told them, after all.) Fibber thinks she might be enforcing the "blackout" because he can't think of any other job a "dim-bulb" like her could handle. (Citizens were expected to show no lights at night due to potential air raids.)

Arriving, finally, at the hardware store, McGee asks to see the manager. Another female! She immediately launches into a technical explanation about vacuum cleaners that leaves Fibber speechless. She selects the correct part, which Molly buys for fifty cents.

Now McGee is scared, a point he makes known audibly. Wallace Wimple, overhearing this, wants to know exactly what scared his neighbor. McGee responds that he is afraid that the fighting men will have a tough time getting their jobs back after the war. Wimple isn't worried. After all, he's married to "Sweetie Face."

It's the Christmas season and on the way home, the McGee's encounter a "Santa Claus." It's Mrs. Uppington. Mystery solved!

At the end of the show, Molly "fixes" the vacuum cleaner. It wasn't too difficult — she merely had to plug it in!

This program did not directly address the importance of women fitting in for the men in the military; it did so by implication, while making the strong point that women are totally capable of doing as well as men — and maybe better.

HISTORICAL NOTE: WOMEN AND THE WAR

As men went into the armed forces, women took their places in war plants. By 1943 more than two million women were working in American War industries, in shipyards and aircraft plants. "Rosie the Riveter" became a common sight. In twenty-one key industries, officials discovered that women could perform the duties of eight of every ten jobs normally done by men.

As in World War I, women other than nurses joined the U.S. armed forces. They enlisted in the Women's Army Auxiliary Corps (WAAC), which later became the Women's Army Corps (WAC); the Women Appointed for Voluntary Emergency Service in the Navy (WAVES); the Women's Auxiliary Ferrying Command (WAF); the Women's Reserve of the Coast Guard Reserves (SPARS); and the Marine Corps Women's Reserves. Women had a more important role than in World War I, when most of them were clerks.

MOVIE: *Keep Your Powder Dry* is somewhat condescending, but women in the military (nurses in particular) are sympathetically portrayed.

JANUARY 19, 1943
"MRS. UPPINGTON JOINING THE WACS"

Harlow Wilcox opens the show with some good news: The National Safety Council has presented the Johnson's Wax Company with a special wartime award for distinguished service for safety: "The Council is conducting an accident prevention campaign at the request of President Roosevelt to save manpower for war power. Although working under pressure and devoting a good part of their plant to making finishing products that serve the war equipment, manufacturers, S.C. Johnson and Son, reduced their accident frequency rates this past year by eighty-three and one-third percent.

The Council reports that in the first year of the war the number of American workers killed by accidents was six times as great as the number of Americans killed on all battle fronts. The time lost by industrial accidents during this period could build 100 aircraft carriers or twenty-tree thousand bombing planes."

Sure, it's a plug for the company, but not a commercial for the products. Further, Wilcox adds that it is important for workers to try to be well and accident free to back up the boys in North Africa and Guadalcanal.

Fibber continues the show by recounting a dream in which he is able to buy steaks. Tonight he's going to dream he buys a pound of butter!

The first guest, whom Fibber guesses might be "a fireman from Berlin looking for a cool place to sit down," is in fact, the indomitable Mrs. Uppington. She's come by to announce that she is about to join the WAACS (The Women's Army Auxiliary Corps). Inasmuch as McGee's regular comments lead one to believe that "Uppy" is about the size of a Clydesdale, this meets with some surprise. She hasn't applied yet, but she believes she has the basic qualifications and proceeds to enumerate them for the McGees — and any listeners:

- U.S. citizenship

- Proof of birth

- Generally good health, height, and weight

- Pass a written test

- Two good character references.

Molly agrees to go to the recruitment center as well and announces that she has considered joining herself. Fibber erupts. It would be too hard on him! He thinks "Uppy" just wants to strut around in uniform. Molly straightens him out. "I know a little bit about the WAAC's myself. They're wonderful! Every one of them is releasing a man for front line duty. And they don't strut. They work. They rig parachutes. They drive Jeeps, and repair motors and operate radios. It's the only authorized women's organization, except for nurses that serve with the Army."

She reminds Fibber that the Marines said Fibber was too old, the Army said he was out of condition, and the Navy said they didn't want him — and the Air Corps just laughed. (This established that McGee *did* try to enlist.)

Horatio K. Boomer enters in time to stop Fibber from trying to convince Molly to give up the WAAC idea. This old reprobate says he has a job in a defense plant, having concluded that crime doesn't pay . . . enough." Asked to see his badge, Boomer makes his usual pocket search and finds only "a check for a short beer." The only time alcohol is ever mentioned on the show is in reference to Boomer or the unseen Uncle Dennis.

Fibber is still worried about Molly joining the WAAC's. He can imagine her over in Egypt and himself at home with a star in the window. Harlow Wilcox comes in (without knocking — was the sound effects man out on a coffee break? No, there *was* the sound of a door opening). Harlow is pleased to learn of Uppy's military plans. He can't wait to turn WAAC's into wax — at least Fibber thinks so. Of course, he does have a commercial to offer, this time with music on a phonograph records. They're funny, and a painless sales job.

Molly joins Mrs. Uppington, leaving Fibber for a visit by Teeny. She thinks the idea of Molly joining the Army is "peachy." She notes that Fibber used to be in the Army. He tells her he was in France in the last war. After a little whimsy about "*Parlez-vous,*" she leaves.

The musical interlude which follows is "I'd Rather Be a Private with a Chicken on My Knee than a Colonel with an Eagle on His Shoulder." After that, we find Uppy and Molly at the recruitment office where Uppy becomes nervous. The lieutenant explains the Women's Army Auxiliary Corps to the ladies, and to any listener who might consider enlisting: "It is a corps of women in military uniform, under military discipline, receiving military pay. We serve officially with the Army and when we have recruited our necessary 150,000 members, it means that 150,000 men are released for combat duty."

When the lieutenant asks if Uppy speaks any foreign languages, Molly says she speaks "pig Latin." That's of no value, says the officer, as they have very little contact with the German General Staff" (Big laugh). On a more serious note, she "feels that this is a great opportunity for American woman. Many of them will develop special skills which will be very useful after the war."

McGee is at home trying his hand at cooking, using "graduated" sugar, when Wimple shows up, followed closely by Molly. She didn't join the Army, of course, but wanted McGee to worry about it a little while.

When Wimple leaves, Harlow Wilcox takes over with a message about conservation — a theme that is mentioned on many programs.

Molly has a message just for the ladies at the end: "The Women's Army Auxiliary Corps (WAAC's) really does need 150,000 members. This is the answer to the question lots of you have been asking, 'What can I do to serve?' "

Fibber agrees: "Yes, and after seeing some of those snappy-lookin' women, I think they ought to change the old slogan to, 'Join the Army and let the world see you.' "

HISTORICAL NOTE: THE RUSSIAN FRONT

In April 1941 Japan and Russia had signed a non-aggression pact; a similar agreement existed between Russia and Germany. Nevertheless, in June 1941 the Axis invaded Russia. This initiative proved to be a strategic mistake, but not before millions of Russians had been killed. Sieges of Leningrad and Stalingrad took a terrible Russian toll. Russia's stiffened resistance and this, combined with the cruel Russian winter and Germany's over-extended supply lines, finally resulted in victory. In February 1943, Germans at Stalingrad surrendered and in January 1944, the Russians broke the siege at Leningrad. The Russians, of course, not only survived the German attacks but aggressively began to acquire neighboring countries.

FEBRUARY 16, 1943
"FINDING WAR WORKERS"

This time the McGees work together on the need for skilled workers on the home front. The mailman turns out to be a mail *woman*, because the regular mailman is in the Army. It's the first time Fibber calls the post-person a "bagette." The mail includes a letter addressed to "Householder." After a discussion of whether to open it (they don't know anyone by that name), they do so and it's from Uncle Sam. It reads: "The Government needs workers with special skills. If you are a tack welder, plate hanger, mixer operator of explosives, or are skilled in any similar work, please report to your nearest United States Employment Service office now."

This appeal was specifically requested by the government of the McGee team, and they took up the challenge. It was, after all, not the usual material of which comedy is easily made. The writers make it work, but they were obviously challenged.

The McGees have no idea of what any of the people in the named occupations *do*. But they immediately set about to help.

After a note that Fibber is trying to decide whether to spend his ration coupons on sugar or shoes, and a phone call from Mrs. Uppington (An interesting switch: Molly on the phone and *not* with Myrt), they discuss the issue with Harlow Wilcox. No surprises here. Mayor LaTrivia arrives next in his Coast Guard uniform. He's on leave with some other military men who "just completed a course in Japanese anatomy at Guadalcanal." He mentioned the real name of the commander of the naval base at San Clemente, but knows what a tack welder is. He also noted that the Coast Guard "joins the Navy in wartime and fights wherever the Navy and Marines fight." Unfortunately, he mentions his executive officer was "Chief" Petty Officer, which leads to the kind of purposeful confusion into which the McGees have for years led the mayor.

Wallace Wimple is "just peachy" when he shows up. He is experienced in "plate hangin'," but not the kind the government wants — only the kind "Sweetie Face" uses.

Jim Jordan concludes the episode by saying, "No foolin', the government does need skilled workers," and tells the listeners how to apply.

Molly adds: "Don't forget. It's your sons at toil that will help put those Nazis under soil."

MARCH 23, 1943
"FIBBER VOLUNTEERS FOR THE RED CROSS"

In this episode, Fibber McGee is appointed to collect funds for the American Red Cross. He "couldn't turn 'em down." Humility requires him to admit that he is not national chairman, not state chairman, not for Wistful Vista, not for the neighborhood — not even for both sides of the street. He's proud of his assignment, "to raise fifty bucks," however. "Do you realize," he asks Molly, "the Red Cross has already turned out with 550 million surgical dressings; they operate 150 service clubs for the guys overseas?" Not surprisingly, he doesn't have to convince Molly of the merits of the Red Cross.

The Red Cross needs $125 million and McGee intends to pick the pocket (figuratively speaking) of everyone who visits their house on this day. When Molly notes that he may have trouble getting people to reach into their pockets just after paying income tax, Fibber's response is a winner: "This ain't a matter of reaching into their pockets. It's a matter of reaching into their hearts. One gives to the Red Cross on the basis — of one's belief in humanity is his view. He becomes so emotionally involved that he vows to double his quota to $100 and cover it with his personal check if he doesn't raise it himself.

The parade of visitors begins with Abigail Uppington. She, to Fibber's chagrin, had sent the Red Cross a large check on the previous day. McGee offers to shoot dice with her, winnings to go to the Red Cross. She feigns ignorance of the game until the sport begins, at which point (with a $20 bet) she suddenly blurts out, "Come on, baby, talk to Momma." Fibber is being hustled! As the dice jargon flows from Uppy's mouth, Fibber realizes he's out $20.

McGee's next target is the mailperson, in this case a female whom he again describes as a "bagette." She has already signed a pledge for her neighborhood but at McGee's urging agrees to "cut the cards" for the amount of $3.30 (all the money she has with her) — with the winnings go to the Red Cross, of course. McGee pays . . . again.

Harlow Wilcox is the next target. He wants to put him off for a few days, but Fibber can't wait. After a discussion of mutual debts, Fibber agrees to repay Harlow if he will give the money to the Red Cross. The deal is done and Fibber is out another $25.

Wallace Wimple arrives with the news that he has sold one of his poems. The poem, which is not worth repeating here, allowed the writers to address — subtly — the censorship of mail from the military by cutting out portions that might have military significance. In the poem, Wimple has written a soldier friend in the Aleutian Islands. The soldier's response, after "surgery" by the censor consisted of this message: "Dear Mr. Wimple . . . Yours very truly, Joe." The set up to deliver this message by poetry was a brilliant bit of writing. Fibber has eyes for the $17 check Wimple got for the poem and bets him that amount that their famous "hall closet" is, surprisingly, cleaned out. *Not* surprising, the closet erupts as usual, and Fibber is out the $17.

After the King's Men entertain with "Sky Anchors Aweigh," Teeny shows up (Molly is upstairs making the bed). Fibber even tries to get her fifty cents for the Red Cross by a coin flip. He loses, of course, only to learn that she called "heads" when she flipped her own coin, which had two heads.

By this time, McGee knows that he will be overdrawn at the bank and the couple goes to the bank president to ask him to cover the overdraft. After a hilarious exchange where the president learns McGee lost the money "gambling," Molly straightens things out by telling him the money is going to the Red Cross. His tune changes rapidly. He has a son in the Army, a nephew in the Air Corps, and a niece in the WAAC's. He is emphatic that the Red Cross needs all the support they can get, "not only for their work with the military, but in feeding starving children all over the world, making life bearable for prisoners of war, saving lives with blood plasma, training nurses for all branches of the service." Needless to say, he covers the overdraft. (The part of the bank president was played by Arthur Q. Bryan, who would later be "Doc" Gamble when Gale Gordon [Mayor LaTrivia] joined the Coast Guard.)

Historical Note: Black Market

"Black Market" is the sale or distribution of goods or currency in violation of ceiling prices, quotas, rationing, and priorities established by a government. Anyone who buys or sells rationed goods or controlled currency through illegal channels or above the established ceiling prices becomes a dealer in the Black Market.

The Black Market was a special problem during the rationing of World War II. It was, of course, illegal.

April 27, 1943
"Fibber Buys Black Market Meat"

This is one of the best-known war-themed shows. The subject was actually quite serious: Black Market meat.

Harlow opens the show with the observation that this is normally the time of year for spring cleaning but this year housewives may have less time for the annual task: "War work, civilian defense, Red Cross, Victory gardens . . . are our number-one obligations." Of course, those housewives have a "silent partner" in Johnson's Wax®.

Harlow continues with the show's introduction. "When a man is out of meat (ration) coupons and hungry for a big thick steak, his mouth is liable to water so much it drowns his conscience." Sure enough in the alley behind the pool hall a "little business transaction" is being conducted between Fibber and "a man (who shall be nameless) though there is a (prison) number waiting for him. Fibber can't wait to "fling a fang" into the porterhouse steak he's buying (illegally). "Eddie" assures him the steak is good and names his price: "Five bucks, please." When Fibber mentions ceiling prices, Eddie reminds him that he's an "alley butcher . . . and alleys . . . don't have no price ceilings." Fibber doesn't even *see* the steak; it's already wrapped, and in spite of Eddie's unintentional hints that the steak is in danger of spoiling, Fibber leaves happy.

On the way home, Fibber voices the thoughts of what must be thousands of listeners: "Don't catch me standing in line like a dummy! When I want something bad, I get it." When he gets the Black Market meat home, he puts it in the refrigerator and tells Molly not to open the wrapper.

Mrs. Uppington is the first to appear. She is upset — she is hosting a dinner party for a group of naval officers and she can't buy any meat. Her butcher is out of meat and says the Black Market dealers are taking so much that the legitimate dealers have a hard time getting their quota. Does this bother McGee? No! "It's all in knowing the right people, Uppy. I can arrange for you to get some meat." He begins to direct her to the alley behind the pool hall to meet "Eddie." Uppy is incensed. "This sounds suspiciously like the Black Market to me," she says. Molly wants to know how Fibber knows about this. He dissembles and both Molly and Uppy jump on him, the latter wondering if Fibber thinks she could face the naval officers after dealing in the Black Market. "To offer them something that was damaging the legitimate businesses of the country they're fighting for," she says indignantly. Indeed, she adds, "If you believe that, you know as much about me as a hyena knows about international law. And if you've read the reports from Japan, you know how much that is!" She leaves, slamming the door behind her.

Molly is very suspicious. Fibber tries a comparison with Prohibition when everybody bought illegal spirits. Molly is ready for that one: "That was a law that everybody knew would be repealed. You can't repeal a war."

Enter the Old-Timer. He doesn't worry about meat because he doesn't eat meat. He eats chicken and eggs of all kinds. He ignores Fibber's attempt to send him to Eddie.

Harlow Wilcox is next to arrive. He's out of meat at home, too. Molly quickly interrupts Fibber before he can suggest a visit to the "alley butcher," but he won't be stopped. He insists on giving Harlow his meat tip. Harlow is quick to ask: "What is this? Black Market meat?" Harlow isn't so hungry for meat that he's willing to buy it from "a rat in an alley." He is truly incensed that McGee, a "pretty decent guy," would support "the dirtiest racket to come out of the war." The Black Marketers, he continues, are not only selling meat without inspection or sanitation and "throwing the whole system of supply and demand out of killing how can the Army and Navy get the meat they need when so much of it is chiseled away into the Black Market?"

Harlow "waxes" eloquent on the subject and finally finds a way to tie in his product, which has "years of conscientious quality behind it." By the time he takes his leave, he is convinced that McGee was only joking.

Light is beginning to dawn, albeit slowly, on Fibber. "You know, Molly," he says, "this Black Market might be a serious thing at that." Of course it is, Molly agrees, as Teeny enters. (A rare occasion, Molly stays in the same room, however briefly, with her alter ego.) The Black Market issue doesn't come up.

Wallace Wimple is the next visitor to the house at number 79. He mentions that he has to go buy some meat for Sweetie Face. McGee can't leave it alone. He starts again about Eddie as Molly objects. Wimple, it seems, "has enough coupons."

By this time, Molly has had enough and demands to know the truth about the meat. Before she gets the truth, Doc Gamble — Fibber's verbal sparring partner — arrives. He can't linger because of an epidemic of ptomaine in town. He blames it on the Black Market meat some people are buying. Fibber timidly inquires: "You mean the meat ain't good, Doc?" The Doctor replies, "Why should it be good? Does it go through the hands of government inspectors? Is it properly refrigerated? Do Black Market operators care if it's sanitary or not?" The answer to all of these rhetorical questions is, of course, in the negative. "As long as they get their filthy money," he says cynically, "they don't care if their customers live or die." He goes on, noting that many parts of beef needed for medical uses (insulin, e.g.) are discarded by these criminals. Noting that McGee is "looking bilious," he prescribes a milk diet and leaves.

"I've been a fool," McGee announces. He rushes to the kitchen, gets the meat, and throws it out the window. A neighbor's dog sniffs it and walks away.

At the end of the program, Jim Jordan finishes with another serious message noting that "There's nothing humorous in children becoming ill from eating doubtful meat. It isn't particularly amusing to find crooks and saboteurs disrupting a legitimate system of distribution of food. So in this interest of your own health and Americanism, buy only from a reputable dealer."

"Meat from the Black Market is probably a 'bum steer,'" concludes Marian Jordan.

MAY 25, 1943
"TRAIN TICKETS ARE HARD TO GET"

Another example of McGee believing that, "the rules don't apply to me." This time it's travel restrictions that bother him.

Harlow Wilcox's commercial is straightforward, but even when noting that use of Johnson's Wax® saves time, he adds "and that's important now for all of us" — a short and subtle reminder that the war is still on.

The scene changes to a discussion by Fibber and Molly about a trip they are about to take. McGee is close-mouthed about the purpose of the trip and Molly is suspicious that it is silly and unnecessary. McGee demurs. The trip will "affect the whole post-war travel industry in America." It's the McGee system of world travel, and it's simple: "Just buy up a couple of old aircraft carriers. Get a few planes and some good pilots. I can land tourists anywhere in the world without docking the boat."

Molly still feels a little guilty. "We shouldn't travel unnecessarily now," she says. "And if I stay home that's one more seat for a soldier or sailor." McGee wants to know what they've got to do that is as important as *his* mission.

"Just win the war. That's all. Nothing urgent," Molly retorts.

McGee argues that a "couple of seats on a train ain't gonna lose the war."

Wallace Wimple comes by for a chat. Sweetie Face is away, but she has written that the trains are very crowded.

"Yeah," says McGee, "between the Army and the Navy and the civilians, the railroads have almost bitten off more than they can choo-choo."

Sweetie Face has been a teacher at a two-week Army commando training course.

At the train station, McGee notes the many service men on benches looking very thoughtful — "must be the Army of preoccupation." Molly is especially on target with her familiar comment: "T'aint funny, McGee!" The Old-Timer turns up and advises them to get on the streetcar and go home. "Look at all them boys in uniform. Bad enough for 'em to be fightin' Japs and Germans without having to fight Americans for a seat on a train. Think it over." He leaves.

McGee is not dissuaded, even by the lady at the ticket counter who reminds him of wartime restrictions on civilian travel. McGee is incensed. *His* business is *important.*

Molly tries sarcasm: "What if some soldier or sailor does have to spend his ten-day furlough in a train station because some civilians grabbed all the accommodations?"

Harlow Wilcox offers no condolences to Fibber: "You heard about the war, pal? You see, it all started when the Japs smacked us at Pearl Harbor . . ."

Fibber interrupts, but Harlow continues: "You ought to know better than to try to travel on trains these days. They've got all they can handle with soldiers and sailors and government employees, and military suppliers." How is Wilcox to work a commercial into this conversation? No worry! "These days railroads are like kitchen linoleum," he says. "When they have to handle too much traffic, something has to be done about it." His simile does a terrific job of selling wax *and* a wartime message.

After a real putdown by a railway officer, McGee still has to deal with Mrs. Uppington. She wonders aloud if Fibber is carrying important documents. When she hears his loud but weak explanation, she says that his not being able to get a ticket is "splendid." She has a nephew in the Marines who had five days of liberty but had to return to camp because there was no room on the train. Civilians had taken all the extra space. She suggests that if McGee insists on being bull-headed, he should take a cattle car.

McGee is getting absolutely no support for his position. Molly observes that "Anybody would think this war is a plot against you personally."

Doc Gamble then arrives with a load of acerbic comments. If it's not a matter of life or death, he says, "Why don't you stay home? There are a lot of home-hating hoboes with more money than sense gumming up the nation's transportation system with their little penny-ante projects and their fishing trips. When I see self-inflated little big shots keeping servicemen from getting seats on trains, keeping them from seeing their families before they go some place to save the country for people like you, I know Darwin was right. We certainly are descended from monkeys." Saying which, he takes his leave.

Is Fibber abashed? Hardly! When a train arrives a passenger alights. He is the man Fibber was going to see and is on his way to Washington with a travel innovation — exactly like Fibber's!

Wilcox winds up the show with a straight commercial for Johnson's Car Nu.®

Jim Jordan follows with a serious note: "Ladies and gentlemen, when you have sons and brothers — yes, *and sisters* in the service — it's nice to have them come home, when and if they can. And it's heartening to know that the railroads of this country are doing a tremendous job of transporting essential military and civilian supplies. So let's not get in their way. Let's not do any traveling that isn't absolutely necessary."

"That's right," Marian adds. "The fish will still be biting and the scenery will still be there after the war. So let's all pack our suitcases — back in the closet."

This ranks with the Black Market meat episode as one of the toughest McGee had to endure. It is a little short on laughs, perhaps, but heavy on message.

One item provides, I believe, a little insight into Don Quinn's creativity. During one of Fibber's tirades, he threatens to write to the government person in charge of trains. Informed that the man's name was Eastman, Molly says they have used one of his cameras (Eastman-Kodak). The local railroad representative encourages McGee to write Mr. Eastman: "I'm sure he'll be happy to send you a negative," she says cleverly.

Exactly how many listeners grasped the double meaning, I don't know, but I suspect Quinn was very happy with it.

HISTORICAL NOTE: THE ITALIAN CAMPAIGN

On September 3, 1943 Italy signed a secret armistice with the allies (the American forces had landed in Italy that day).

Italy became a "co-belligerent" and declared war on Germany on October 13, 1943. The allies hoped that Italian soldiers would attack German garrisons in all parts of the country. But most Italians allowed themselves to be disarmed by the Germans. The Germans continued to fight allied advances into the country.

The allied drive up the Italian boot proved to be a slow struggle against a 400,000-man German army led by Field Marshal Albert Kesselring. The allies also faced floods, mud, mountains, and winter cold.

Early in November 1943 the allies reached a line about 75 miles south of Rome, but they could not pierce the German defenses. Naples had fallen to the allies after landings near Salerno. Late in January 1944 the allies tried to outflank the German lines by landing troops near Anzio, 33 miles south of Rome. But the Germans held the high ground overlooking the coast, and hemmed in the invaders on a small beachhead. The town of Cassino stood about halfway between Naples and Rome. The allies bombed the famous monastery on top of Monte Cassino, thinking that Germans were using it. The Germans later claimed they had not used the monastery until after the bombing. The allies finally captured Cassino and pushed northward. The Italians made Rome an *open city* by announcing that they would not defend it. On June 4, it became the first Axis capital to fall.

Two months later, the allies captured Florence. The Mediterranean Allied Air Forces supported the ground forces by attacking German troops and supply centers. The allies finally reached the Gothic Line, a German defense system four miles deep across northern Italy.

MOVIE: *A Walk in the Sun* is recommended.

OCTOBER 5, 1943
"THE MCGEES GET A NEW BOARDER"

This program highlights two wartime topics: the housing shortage and the role of women in the workforce.

Before the comedy begins, Harlow Wilcox has a serious message: "The air is full of rumors these days, but common sense tells us not to accept them as truth or help spread them, especially when they concern the war. But there are other kinds of rumors about individual companies that often need to be corrected. You may have been told, for instance, that you can't get Johnson's Wax® and Johnson's Glo Coat® because the company isn't making these products anymore. Well, it is a fact that the makers of Johnson's Wax® have been turning out millions of packages of protective finishes for war uses. And they're proud to be doing so. But without interfering with that important job, they're also able to make good quantities of the products you know so well . . . Every dealer gets his share though not always all that he asks for, of course. He tries to keep you and his other customers supplied with Johnson's Wax® products of all kinds."

The McGees are about to take in a war worker as the episode begins. Molly is cleaning up the spare bedroom and talking on the phone with a neighbor, Mrs. Toops (Mort's wife). Doc Gamble has vouched for the new roomer, but the McGees haven't met him. McGee interrupts the phone call, wild with excitement: "Look at the paper! Germany surrenders!" Turns out the newspaper he was reading was dated 1918; he had found it in the closet. While cleaning up the spare room, Fibber also found his doorknob collection. This prompts him to relate a tale about his old friend, Fred Nitney, from Starved Rock, Illinois. Nitney collected hairpins and compacts and every time his wife found one in his car he'd say, "Don't throw that away; it's part of my collection." (I include this because it's virtually the only time a show ever hinted at anything off-color.)

The new roomer's name is Al Darling. Fibber bets he "carries his lunch in a knitting bag." He is already prejudiced against the name, but he is ready to welcome the new roomer. After a virtuoso performance by the sound effects men consisting only of the stumbling footsteps of Uncle Dennis arriving home from Joe's Tavern, Uncle Dennis actually speaks (he is usually only heard *of.*) McGee has moved his moose head into Uncle Dennis's room and, while Uncle Dennis is accustomed to seeing pink elephants, a moose head startles him.

The work on the spare room continues as Harlow Wilcox arrives. Molly confirms the rumor that they are taking in a roomer because the town is so crowded with war workers. They'll use the extra money to buy War Bonds. The new roomer works in an airplane plant and Fibber notes: "He'll be handy in case we want to build a wing on the house." Wilcox wants to see the spare room and uses the occasion for a tribute to the beautiful linoleum floor, courtesy of Johnson's GloCoat,® of course. (McGee says Wilcox has been turned town three times at the blood bank. "All they could get out of him is GloCoat.®")

Molly goes upstairs and, of course, Teeny drops by. When McGee tells her they're taking in a roomer, Teeny says her dad says it's silly to listen to them. Fibber explains the difference, but she already knows. Their "roomer" has been promising to pay his rent for three weeks, and her daddy says it's silly to listen to rumors!

It's getting near the end of the program and it's about time the roomer shows up. The next doorbell, however, is Mayor LaTrivia (Gale Gordon on leave from the Coast Guard). Molly explains that she felt sorry for war workers who didn't have a proper place to live. The McGees do their usual number on LaTrivia pretending to believe he went to barber college. As usual, he leaves in a rage, but not before Molly observes that if LaTrivia gets his hair cut in the Coast Guard, it must have been done by a "Coast Guard Cutter."

The doorbell sounds again, this time signaling Doc Gamble's arrival. He has brought "Al" with him. When McGee complains about all the furniture he had to move, Doc Gamble fires back: "Your muscles have less tone than a dime store harmonica." When "Al" walks in, the McGees (and we) learn that "Al" is short for Alice. Their surprise is reflected in their voices.

Alice Darling was one of Don Quinn's finest creations, played brilliantly by Shirley Mitchell. She was perfect for the war; a loving stereotype of the quintessential "Girl Back Home." Although not a "Rosie the Riveter" type, she *did* work in an aircraft factory. Somehow she continued to keep a number of "boys" on the string and simultaneously at arm's length (the number of phone messages she received daily was often mentioned by McGee). Alice was by no means stupid, but her sentence structure could be unconventional. "The boy that his father owns the airplane plant," is but one example of her mixed-up syntax.

In spite of that mild idiosyncrasy, Alice Darling exemplified all that was best in America's young womanhood in a time of war.

OCTOBER 12, 1943
"FIBBER USES HIS INFLUENCE"

Fibber McGee has a great deal of influence from Washington, D.C. to the Wistful Vista City Hall. Unfortunately, he's the only one who knows it!

Harlow Wilcox's commercial includes the fact that Johnson's Wax® finishes have been called upon to render "protective service to countless products used in the war. Wax coatings for steel shell casings, airplane finishes, black wax for bayonets . . . It even includes paints impregnated with wax, and special wax finishes to render soldiers' uniforms and tents water repellant. The makers of Johnson's Wax® have turned out many millions of packages of these special products for war use. And they're proud to be able to do so . . . Remember that Johnson's Wax® has gone to war."

Fibber is going through the mail, most of it from soldiers for Alice Darling, the new roomer. The phone rings — and that's for Alice, too. But there is *one* letter for McGee. It's from the frequently mentioned Fred Nitney of Starved Rock, Illinois. He and Fibber were in vaudeville together. Fibber reads the letter aloud, pausing at a blank space where Fred went out to sharpen his pencil. Nitney's child, Anita, is coming to town and wants to use McGee as a reference in order to join the WACs. Predictably, Fibber is sure he can "wangle her a commission," a thought which Molly immediately tries to quash. McGee is undeterred. He's done plenty of political maneuvering. He has "more angles than a folding ruler," as he puts it.

Alice Darling, just arisen, interrupts. She had worked the night shift at the airplane factory. She regales them with her romantic liaisons, especially with Bruce: "He's tall dark and time and a half," she says dreamily.

The McGees head downtown to the recruiting office for the WACs, Fibber is intent on getting a colonel's commission for Anita Nitney. He implies that he pulled the strings to get General Pershing *his* commission from President Wilson in World War I. Harlow Wilcox arrives just as McGee is figuratively pinning oak leaves on Anita's shoulder. When Molly says colonels have *eagles* on the shoulder, Fibber vows to scare 'em away.

Wilcox, when he learns of McGee's boastful plan, is quick to warn him: "Before you make a complete chump of yourself, don't start monkeying around with the Army . . . The WACs are slightly allergic to hot-shot civilians messing up the details." Wilcox has a cousin who is a WAC lieutenant and he knows that one cannot pull wires to get a commission: "Promotions are strictly a matter of merit." He tells Fibber to go ahead if he insists, but adds "I know my WACs!" And the *audience* knows that a WAX commercial is next. But Harlow fools them, for a bit anyway. When the McGees urge him to go ahead, he finally does.

The McGees meet Doc Gamble on the sidewalk and he, too, is derisive of McGee's plans. But McGee doesn't want Anita Nitney to go in as a "doe private" (a female "buck private"). Doc Gamble answers, "The Army doesn't take advice from civilian fatheads."

Fibber takes offense and accuses the doctor of barely graduating from an "aspirin academy." The doctor, who is medical examiner for the local WACs, goes along with them to the recruiting office where Fibber gets a proper lecture from the WAC Sergeant. (She also does a fine job of plugging the WACs).

"After five weeks of basic training," she explains, "you may apply for officer candidate school, where you learn the right things to be an officer. In the WACs you come under the influence of the best instructors the Army can supply. In a short time a WAC is in [better] health than she's ever experienced in civilian life. Her posture is better and she has new poise and assurance that will last her the rest of her life." When McGee calls the sergeant naïve, (which he mispronounces as "nave") because she says influence will not get anyone a commission, she makes it clear that *he* is the naïve one.

She goes on: "For every woman who joins the WACs, a man is free to move up to the front lines. We need hundreds of thousands of women to join us, so our Army will be that much stronger. There are now a hundred and fifty-five jobs a woman can do just as well as or better than men. And the sooner those jobs are filled, the sooner we'll have the strength to win the war. WACs receive regular Army pay and receive all the extra benefits that men do. A private receives fifty dollars a month free and clear of all expenses, which is more than most of them ever had left at the end of the month in civilian life."

McGee has been trying to interrupt throughout those remarks. When he does get a chance to suggest some kind of deal, the sergeant says his offer is "tantamount to bribery." McGee says "tantamount has nothing to do with it, I did tell a few guys from RKO" (he obviously thinks tantamount is the movie studio.) She doesn't think that's funny — she is *serious*. "I must inform you, that an attempt to use undue influence on an officer of the United States Army is a Federal offense and in wartime approaches a crime of treason!" Doc Gamble is really pleased with that response.

The surprise ending comes when the sergeant learns McGee's name. Seems she often heard her father mention him. Seems also she's Anita Nitney, Fred's daughter! She had been carrying her father's letter around for six months, had just found it, and mailed it.

"Well I'll be a monkey's uncle," says McGee.

"Your genealogy has nothing to do with it," responds Sergeant Nitney.

Fibber is unabashed by his treatment. Indeed, this is the first time he had ever argued with a sergeant and didn't end up peeling potatoes.

Fibber ends the program by urging qualified young women to apply to the WACS and Molly adds: "Remember, a WAC with the knack can really back the attack."

Good night, all.

(A minor footnote: Wilcox said, "Johnson's Wax® has gone to war." He provided plenty of evidence of that. The makers of Lucky Strike® cigarettes were already using the slogan, "Lucky Strike Green has gone to war." This was based on the claim that their green package used copper needed for war materials. According to Wikipedia®, however, the switch to a white package was mainly a marketing ploy to attract more female smokers and improve the look on the shelf. The patriotic claim seems specious.)

MARCH 7, 1944
"SPEECH FOR THE RED CROSS"

The opening commercial has Harlow Wilcox wondering if the listeners "realize that manufacturers of war materials took a tip from your housekeeping methods and are using wax to protect the surfaces of many war projects." He gives the housewives credit for setting an example but, "Of course the makers of Johnson's Wax® helped them to discover these war uses for these wax polishes but it was your use . . . that really showed them the way . . . I guess you ladies should take a bow" (a clever tie-in between the sponsor and the listener in the war effort).

The show opens with Fibber at the typewriter composing a speech for the Red Cross:

". . . And so I say to you listening in tonight — if all of us do our part, part of us won't have to do it all."

As he prepares to read his speech over station WVIS, Jim Jordan as Fibber McGee — a legendary figure in broadcasting — pretends to be nervous at the prospect of appearing on radio.

Fibber starts by identifying himself to the listening audience because the announcers at WVIS have been so busy reporting Russian War news they might have trouble with a simple name like McGee.

McGee continues composing:

> Ladies and gentlemen, the Red Cross needs your money. This campaign is to raise $200 million. The Red Cross is the greatest symbol of practicing humanity in the world today, and when you give generously to it you are helping people all over the world. Remember that it's as easy to give a dollar as it is to pass the buck.

Alice Darling, who arrives at this point, is invited to join the McGees at the radio station. Before she can offer her excuse, McGee jumps to his usual wrong conclusion: She "can't let her bobby sox cool off for a minute." Doesn't Alice realize "that between January and November of 1943, the Red Cross packed over five million, three hundred thousand food parcels?" McGee is "typing his fingers to the bone and what is Alice doing?" Dancing — or so he thinks. In fact, Alice rolls bandages for the Red Cross every Tuesday night for four hours. Fibber was (almost) suitably abashed. She also spent another night a week dancing with service men at the canteen.

During a musical interlude, Fibber has finished typing. His speech ends thusly:

> And so, ladies and gentlemen, in conclusion may I say that the Red Cross is the link between the serviceman and his family back home. So give generously to the Red Cross in this campaign for funds so we can give every possible service man every possible service.

Mr. Wellington turns up next asking if Fibber has his speech ready; he wants a copy for the newspaper: "For a cause of this scope and magnitude the widest possible publicity is desirable." Wellington leaves, carrying his short cane (he's just out for a short walk).

Molly wants to know if McGee included in his speech that the Red Cross operates 350 service clubs and recreation centers overseas. He did, but the most important thing to him was "the fact that the Red Cross gets information about war prisoners wherever possible. My gosh, that alone is enough to make you sit down and write 'em a big check."

Harlow Wilcox is next; he'll be at the radio station, too. He does some "spot announcements" about how Johnson's Wax® gets rid of spots. His commercial is a show case for the sound effects man.

Fibber's departure to change clothes gives Molly a chance to read the speech aloud — for the radio listeners:

> During the past two years, the disaster preparations of the Red Cross have been widened to include storage of strategic points of blood plasma, blankets, cots, and clothing for emergency use. We hope enemy action may never strike our own cities, but if it does, the Red Cross stands ready.

Beulah is next. (The audience seems especially surprised to see a white man reading her lines.) She has just arranged to work one day a week for the McGees. It's *her* idea. She *wants* to be their housekeeper (and will be full time until Marlin Hurt leaves to start his own show).

A short patriotic song, "The Kid with the Rip in His Pants," follows, giving the McGees plenty of time to reach the radio station, where they are joined by Doc Gamble.

Fibber has lost his copy of his speech, or so he thinks. After a moment of panic, McGee finds it (in fact, he was holding it the whole time.) The doctor wants to know if McGee is "going to mention the [Red Cross] home service for soldier's families, or the 50,000 Red Cross nurses serving all over the world, and 180 Red Cross service buildings already up or under construction." As a doctor, Gamble is well aware of what the Red Cross does, "a terrific job for every boy and girl in the service and for their families at home."

When they arrive at the station, they find Wellington on the air delivering McGee's speech! It is his own petard on which Fibber is hoisted, however. A week before he had salted down Wellington's coffee at a luncheon and Wellington was unable to give his luncheon speech. Fibber was quick to fill in!

The finish of the program is to be expected:

FIBBER: Ladies and gentlemen, the goal of the 1944 Red Cross War Fund is $200 million. It's important that they get it — important not only to us and our families and our country, but for the comfort and well-being of all our men and women in service. Remember, the Red Cross is not a government agency. It is dependent on you and me for support. So let's see that they get it.

MOLLY: Send your check to the Red Cross in your community tomorrow morning. Wear the Red Cross on your lapel. It will show where your heart is.

Surely, this program demonstrates forcefully where the hearts of the stars, writers, and sponsor were.

APRIL 18, 1944
"FIBBER'S NEIGHBOR IS A NAZI SPY"

In spite of the serious subject matter, this episode is played mostly for laughs. It opens with Harlow Wilcox noting that the series is starting its tenth year. After a little music, he notes that Victory Gardens are again in the limelight. Johnson's Wax®, of course, is the answer to keeping the gardening tools clean and easier to use.

We join McGee, who is spying on his neighbor across the street. He is convinced that the man is a spy. "Look at him," he says disdainfully. "The dirty Nazi — I'll bet he blows up the post office before the week is out." Molly is not convinced. The neighbor's name sounds German to McGee, and that's enough to make him a dirty "Sabatini." Molly corrects him. He means saboteur. "*Sabatini,*" she explains, "was a writer."

"Sure he was a writer," replies McGee, "and in code, too."

It seems the catalyst to McGee's suspicion was the neighbor's refusal to loan McGee his
lawnmower. McGee responds to Molly's skepticism: "When they hang this guy in the electric chair . . . ." He is interrupted by their roomer, Alice Darling. Alice *likes* the neighbor. He seems nice, she says, and she has seen him often near the airplane plant where she works. McGee's suspicions get an adrenalin rush, especially when he learns that the neighbor is taking pictures.

When a milk truck backfires, McGee hits the floor. "Can't be too careful," he says. The guy, after all, has a German name, accent, and haircut — and McGee has seen him with sheet music under his arm written *by Berlin*! He decides to call the FBI, which means an encounter with Myrt. What Molly hears is that Myrt's cousin in the Army is "chief pretty officer." Molly says it's not *pretty,* it's *Petty* (a reference to the popular pin-up artist).

McGee says, "Petty ought to see *this* officer. She's a WAVE."

A call to the chief of police only brings disdain.

Mr. Wellington arrives. "Are you playing G-man, Junior, or junior G-Man?" he asks sarcastically. Wellington continues to be derisive throughout his visit. When he leaves, he is succeeded by Harlow Wilcox, who gives him even less respect for his suspicions. Indeed, he thinks the neighbor is a "typical American. He left his engine running outside the gas ration board and then went in and yelled for forty minutes about how they were making things so tough for him."

Fibber, though, is steadfastly suspicious. As a precaution, he will even have dinner on a card table by the window. Informed of Fibber's suspicions, Beulah threatens: "You get a Nazi spy around me and I'm gonna Gestapo him with a fryin' pan." McGee says to make it a *roasting* pan since his goose will be cooked very soon.

The arrival of Doc Gamble assures even more ridicule for McGee's concerns. And the listener is not disappointed. Gamble says McGee "wouldn't recognize a spy if he saw him coming ashore in a rubber boat." He leaves saying, "hypo my dermis" — not for the first time on the show.

Teeny, who comes in next, is the only one to give any credence to McGee's concerns. She's ready to help by breaking the neighbor's windows and letting the air out of his tires because she doesn't want him using "unsanitary" (incendiary) bombs. McGee tries to curb her retaliatory enthusiasm, but fails. She leaves intent on action.

Can you believe it? The next segment sees the arrival of police, complete with gunfire to arrest the neighbor who really *is* a German Spy.

This was one of the extremely rare times when McGee is actually proven right!

Harlow Wilcox has a word or two to say about conservation and the role of GloCoat® in this effort. Jim Jordan ends the show with an appreciation of Johnson's Wax®, Don Quinn, the National Broadcasting Company, and the listeners. Oh, and McGee hopes the spy left his garage unlocked. That's where he kept his lawn mower.

HISTORICAL NOTE: D-DAY

Preparations for the invasion of the Normandy coast began early in 1943, when the Allies set up a planning staff. The invasion plan received the code name of "Operation Overlord." Roosevelt and Churchill selected General Dwight D. Eisenhower as supreme commander of the Allied Expeditionary Force. Hitler had appointed Field Marshal Karl Gerd von Rundstedt as commander in chief of the western front to defend *Festung Europa* (Fortress Europe). The

Germans built the *Atlantic Wall*, with fortifications stretching from Norway to Spain.

The British, Canadians, and Americans assembled almost three million men, and stored 16 million tons of arms, munitions, and supplies in Britain for the great invasion. The allies had 5,000 large ships, 4,000 smaller landing craft, and more than 11,000 aircraft. Months before the invasion, allied bombers pounded the Normandy coast to prevent the Germans from building up their military strength. The invasion had been set for June 5, but storms forced Eisenhower to postpone it one day. Paratroopers went ahead to cut railroad lines, blow up bridges, and seize landing fields. Gliders brought in men, jeeps, light artillery, and small tanks. Allied warships fired 200 tons of shells per minute at the German coastal batteries.

Eisenhower told his forces, "You are about to embark upon a great crusade." The first wave of infantry and armored troops, commanded by Montgomery, crossed the choppy English Channel under a cloudy, overcast sky. They waded ashore on a 50-mile front at 6:30 a.m. on D-Day, June 6, 1944. There was no air opposition because the allied air forces had completely subdued the German air force. To the west, U.S. First Army troops landed on both sides of the Vire River. To the east, British and Canadian infantrymen of the British Second Army pushed ashore near Caen. Allied engineers devised prefabricated harbors in which to unload troops and supplies.

The invasion opened Europe to Allied ground attack for the first time.

MOVIE: For all its detractors, *The Longest Day* remains the most ambitious account of D-Day.

NOVEMBER 14, 1944
"FIBBER AND MOLLY FIGHT INFLATION"

As the war continued, inflation became a very real concern. Getting the message of the dangers of inflation across in an understandable yet entertaining way presented the writers with a sizeable challenge. But Don Quinn and Phil Leslie (the latter for the first time getting on-air credit on a regular basis for his writing) were up to the task.

The premise of this particular episode has Fibber going to night school. During the set-up, Fibber gives his reason. While he and a "bunch of the guys were standing around the cigar store and he, by his own admission made a fool of himself, or as he put it: "I made a triple-plated, five-star, rhinestone-studded jackass out of myself."

"How" Molly asked, "— *this* time?"

When asked by the "guys" what he thought of inflation, he had to bluff because he "didn't know from nothing." He responded that he thought it "would be a fine thing for the country." The other guys *and* the cigar store owner ridiculed him, and worse. By his own admission, he didn't know there was nothing to be said in favor of inflation. Although ignorance might be bliss, Fibber could not tolerate having *his* ignorance exposed (hence, his motivation to attend night school).

During the course of the various discussions, Alice relates that she tried to find a correspondence course in Latin for a boyfriend over in Italy. A hog-caller in civilian life, he wanted to learn "pig-Latin." Beulah offers her own views on inflation: "Of course, there is certain aspects of the problem that eludes me, but I got me a fairly comprehensive grasp of the basic principles."

When Fibber asks her to "break it down," she does so: "The whole concept of preventing inflation lies in the control of prices. Therefore, if both the dealer and the consumer play fair with ceiling prices [a wartime phenomenon] retail goods will remain at a predetermined and reasonable level, thus obviating the necessity of raising wages and expanding production costs, which, in turn, raises prices again. Reducing the problem to an understandable perspective: If the article is ceiling priced at 32 cents and you pay 33 cents for it, you're on your way to inflation." (Beulah admits she learned it all in night school.)

When Doc Gamble makes his weekly appearance he, too, has something to say about inflation (after Fibber calls him "pulse pincher"): "It's just a matter of teaming up to keep prices down. That's all. If prices stay down, the cost of things stay down. Prices go up, costs go up. Then prices go up again; and climb in kids, we're off to the poorhouse." After a quick gratuitous insult ("Fever Lover"), McGee asks for a ride to the school. Doc refuses, as it would cause him trouble with the gas ration board. "Getting rid of

McGee for three hours would definitely be considered pleasure driving," he explains.

Fibber is later found at the Elks Club, playing "hooky" from night school, because all his life he's wanted "to play hooky without getting in trouble at home."

After a short Johnson's commercial at the end, Jim Jordan comes on with another serious message: "Ladies and gentlemen, we had fun with inflation tonight, but there won't be much comedy in inflation if it comes."

"And it needn't come at all," Marian injects.

Jim Jordan continues: "Because although it's a very real danger, prevention is comparatively simple. Whenever you buy things in a store, check the prices with the ceiling price posters. The responsibility rests with *both* the retailers and the customers. And we know everybody will back up our fighting services by fighting against the increase of prices at home."

"Remember," Marian concludes, "there's a certain paperhanger* who hopes we'll neglect our ceiling . . . Good night, all."

HISTORICAL NOTE: THE BATTLE OF THE BULGE

After the exhilaration accompanying the successful D-Day invasion, hopes for a quick end to the war in Europe were quickly dashed. In December, after six months of hard fighting across Western Europe, the Germans mounted an offensive which became known as the Battle of the Bulge (so named because of the appearance of the battle lines on the map).

Before the allies could cross the Rhine, they had to face a last-stand German onslaught in the Ardennes Forest. Hitler personally planned a swift breakthrough to capture Antwerp and Aplit the Allied armies in two. Field Marshal Walter Model, army ground commander under Von Rundstedt, directed the assault, which had the code name, "Watch on the Rhine." Under cover of fog, 38 German divisions struck along a 50-mile front on December 16. Mechanized units overran several First Army positions.

---

* The paperhanger referred to, of course, was the failed house painter, Adolf Hitler.

Model's armies drove the allies almost to the Meuse River, and surrounded Bastogne in the southern Ardennes. Asked to surrender, Brigadier General Anthony C. McAuliffe of the 101st airborne Division at Bastogne replied, "Nuts!" Third Army armored units pierced the German lines from the south and relieved Bastogne. By early January 1945 the allies had recovered all ground lost in the battle. The Germans had 110,000 men taken prisoner, and about 100,000 casualties.

MOVIES: *Battleground* is excellent, as are segments of *Patton*.

NOVEMBER 28, 1944
"WALLACE WIMPLE HOME ON LEAVE"

On *leave?* Surely Wimple couldn't qualify for military service! The truth is even more unbelievable.

The show opens with McGee running home in a state of excitement. He just got a hot tip: "They're going to open a carton of cigarettes at Kremer's Drug Store (please refer to the broadcast of December 12, 1944). Reminded that neither he nor Molly smokes, he is disappointed at his own excitement even though "Men who know tobacco best [part of a contemporary cigarette commercial] can't get it."

The *real* news is a post card from Wallace Wimple, the poster child for meekness. Wimple is arriving from the Great Lakes Naval Base where he is a physical instructor. Neither McGee can believe it; Alice Darling is skeptical as well. Molly says he "used to come in here black and blue [compliments of "Sweetie Face," his "Big Old Wife"] and it'll be nice to see him come in here just in Navy blue." Alice offers that the Navy *does* change men. She uses as an example a beau who, before entering the Navy, was afraid to sit on the porch swing with her. When he came home on leave he could "whistle with his eyes."

The Old-Timer's arrival is announced by the ringing doorbell. As it turns out, he is in the Sea Bees! (So, too, was Bill Thompson, the man who voiced the part of the Old-Timer.) He's "a seagoing carpenter boy — a salt with a saw." Apparently, the Sea Bees aren't concerned about his age. After a lame joke about a skeleton crew and an encounter with the famous hall closet, he leaves.

Fibber decides to call the Wimple house, giving him an excuse to talk with Myrt. His end of the conversation goes like this: "What? Your *brother*? A lieutenant junior grade? Good for you, Myrt; that was a real promotion."

Molly wants to know *what* promotion? "He was home on leave for Thanksgiving and when he left he was a *full* lieutenant." (Admittedly, this was not the writers' finest hour.)

Doc Gamble is next. He can't believe Wimple is a physical instructor, either: "That anemic little sparrow? You can't make an old salt out of a little mug with no pepper." McGee is reminded of his experience in the army in 1918 — "The Big War" — when he was in *great* physical condition. The two men trade a series of insults before the doctor leaves.

Harlow Wilcox arrives. He thought Wimple was in the Coast Guard, but he is reminded that it is Mayor LaTrivia in the Coast Guard. When Wilcox mentions the word "protection," the McGees immediately think "floor wax." But the announcer surprises them: "The protection I have in mind is the protection of your own future and the protection of every man in the armed forces. Have you bought any bonds in the new bond drive?"

They have.

"Did it cramp your budget a little?" he asks.

"No," says Fibber.

"Well, then, you didn't buy enough. This is the time when every cent you don't need for absolute living expenses ought to go into War Bonds. Who do you think is going to pay for arms, ammunition, and medicines for American soldiers and sailors, if not Americans? Over in Europe, they're fighting from house-to-house; over here, too. And put 'service stars' in the windows of your bank book." (Stars in a home's window indicated one or more persons in the military.)

Harlow asks Fibber to go down to the bank with him to buy more War Bonds. Fibber wants to wait until tomorrow morning.

"Okay," says Wilcox, "and I'll send a cablegram to General Eisenhower to tell him to quit fighting until tomorrow morning."

Molly suggests (and Harlow agrees) that his remark is a "little farfetched." But he observes that the "supplies to the South Pacific have to be pretty 'farfetched,' too. And we've got to keep 'em going. It's a wonderful feeling when you buy that extra $100 bond. To think that you're buying some guy a few extra rounds of ammunition he needs in a tight spot. Or that you've given a sea-going flyer a rubber boat, or some wounded sailor much-needed morphine. To me, that extra War Bond is a certificate to show that I've accepted a little more responsibility in this war . . . If we let up over *here*, we're letting them down over *there*. Tie a string around your hearts to remind you."

This was another dramatic example of the Johnson Company giving up commercial time to support the war effort.

McGee notes on Wilcox's departure that "We give the Japs and Germans the bird while we feather our own nests." Beulah is called and informed that the McGees will be cutting down on the groceries to buy more War Bonds. Beulah is wearing a hat. She, too, is going out to buy a War Bond. She happened to be "eavesdropping" when Wilcox mentioned the sailor — and Beulah's brother is in the Navy.

After a little music, the long-awaited Wimple arrives, with his patented but irreproducible on paper, "Hello, folks" (You just had to hear it). Exactly what does he do in the Navy, he is asked. He answers that he builds men's bodies and wishes he could build one for himself. His description of his activities in teaching fitness is hilarious. He's a "specialist third class." Basically, he's afraid to go home and face "Sweetie Face." She's angry with him for running away and joining the Navy. When an angry man who has tripped over McGee's rake threatens a poke in the nose, Wimple (the man called him a knee-high Nimitz) steps in! He not only intervenes, he throws the man through a window! But he's still afraid to go home alone!

Wilcox finishes with a plug for the housewife as a household manager. He's "glad his company lends her a hand."

Again, at the end of a program, Jim Jordan reflects on his and Marian's visit to a Navy base as part of the sixth War Loan Drive. The Jordans, courtesy of Navy transport, have been all over the country selling War Bonds. Marian welcomes Bill Thompson, Specialist First Class, who portrays the Old-Timer and Wallace Wimple. Several admirals are mentioned by name and thanked for their help in the War Bond Drive.

DECEMBER 12, 1944
"CIGARETTE SHORTAGE"

The underlying theme for this show is the shortage of cigarettes during the war. Depending on your point of view, this wasn't such a big deal; certainly not as important as gasoline rationing, meat shortages, or restrictions on travel. But given the times, the difficulty in finding cigarettes was a very real hardship to some. Fibber smoked only cigars, but his verbal sparring partner, Doc Gamble, smoked cigarettes and Fibber, in spite of their frequent bouts of insults, set out to find some for him. (The reader is reminded that this episode was the one referred to in Chapter 2 when the *real* Kremer's Drug Store was described.)

When Doc Gamble shows up at 79 Wistful Vista, the usual banter follows. Fibber tells Gamble he has "the profile of a basketball smuggler." Gamble responds that with his "pot," Fibber "ought to be standing under a rainbow." With that banter concluded, Gamble asks for a cigarette. Fibber offers a cigar, but the doctor "just wants a smoke, not to fumigate." It seems he can't find a "gasper" anywhere in town.

After Doc Gamble leaves, the McGees discuss the doctor's nicotine needs and after agreeing that he is a "sweet old character," decides to find him some cigarettes. But it's not so easy! Fibber tries every drug store (including Kremer's) and tobacco shop in town and . . . no cigarettes.

At this point, Molly says she'd like to have a package of cigarettes herself. Reminded that she doesn't smoke, she responds: "I know, but that's how these shortages affect people. If somebody started a rumor that there was a shortage of War Bonds, the country would buy over its quota."

A quick exchange with the telephone exchange follows. Fibber tells Molly that Myrt's sister "went into the waves last week." Molly, as per the usual running gag, misunderstands. Believing that "waves" refers to men in the Navy, she says: "Oh good for her! How old is she?"

"Eleven," Fibber replies; "she went fishing on the lake with her old man and fell out of the boat."

Fibber's last resort is a radio quiz program, *Smokes for Folks.*

(When Beulah is told of his plans she responds: "Well, strike me pink — if possible.") After a visit from "Teeny," who tricks him into giving answers to her homework questions under the guise of "warming up" for the quiz, it's off to the radio station.

McGee's performance on the quiz show is predictable, albeit amusing. In spike of hints from the master of ceremonies, he barely survives to the final challenge: "Name ten American Indian Tribes." When he gets through nine, he can't think of a tenth, even though the M.C. says, "I hope you won't sue [Sioux] me." The clue is lost of McGee.

Fortunately, Molly sneezes phonetically and he comes up with "Apache."

It turns out that first prize is only a cigarette *holder*. The guy who came in *second* won the cigarettes.

January 30, 1945
"The McGees Take in a Sailor"

Although there is reason for optimism, the McGees don't want their listeners to become complacent. The war isn't over yet, after all.

The show begins in the Biltmore Hotel where Fibber has stopped to buy a cigar. There is a line as people try to book one of the scarce hotel rooms. Molly notes a sailor (Tommy) sitting on a suitcase and looking discouraged. They decide to give the "nice-looking dad" a kind word. He couldn't find a room at any hotel in town. The conversation reveals that he is in the Merchant Marines and his "hitch is up."

"We'll stand in front of it if you want to hitch it down a little," McGee volunteers.

When the young man says he may now try to get a shore job, Molly asks if there is any more important job than making "shore" and win the War.

Reluctantly, the young man agrees to accept the McGee's invitation to spend the night. Fibber immediately launches into a tale of his seafaring days on the Illinois River, filling the air with meaningless, inaccurate (but hilarious) nautical gibberish. The prime reason for his acquiescence is learning that the McGee's boarder, Alice Darling, "has a smile that would make Himmler follow her into a Russian restaurant."

Fibber tells Tommy that he had read that after the war, the Merchant Marines would be one of the "great American industries." His experience would count for a great deal, and his wife (when he got one) would be proud of the job he'd done during the war.

When Harlow Wilcox turns up, he learns that he and the seaman have a mutual acquaintance: the captain on a cruise ship. When Wilcox asks if the captain's parrot still swears, Tommy replies that following an attack of "Jap Zeroes," all the parrot says is, "Oh, my goodness." Not surprisingly, Wilcox finds a way to tell how Johnson's Wax® helped to keep the ward room ship shape. The captain insisted on it.

Wilcox weighs in on the effort to convince Tommy to re-enlist: "Trained seamen are pretty scarce."

"You know what General Eisenhower said about you fellows? He said every man is his Allied Command is quick to express his appreciation for the loyalty, courage, and fortitude of the officers and men of the Merchant Marines. They've never failed us yet, and we know they never will." (This is yet another example of the Johnson's people giving over part of their middle commercial time to a war message.)

As they prepare for dinner (Fibber had invited Doc Gamble, whom he refers to as "that bedside bandit"), Beulah is summoned. During the ensuing conversation, she uses the phrase, "Dark as Japan's future."

Doc Gamble (to McGee's chagrin) also had Marine experience as a ship's surgeon. This is almost more than McGee can handle, as everyone at the table (except Molly) corrects his use of nautical terms.

By the time dinner is finished, Tommy has decided to re-enlist. Doc Gamble applauds the decision: "You'll have a secure job in a tremendous industry." Alice adds her own words of encouragement.

McGee leaves for the kitchen to escape the sea-wise criticism, only to learn that Beulah was a stewardess on an ocean liner for seven years!

At the end of the program, Jim Jordan finishes with a serious message: "Ladies and gentlemen, there really is an urgent, almost desperate need for men in the Merchant Marines. Experienced able-bodied seamen, mates, cooks — men of all classes are needed immediately."

Marian adds: "Three new merchant ships are launched every day, and we must have men to man them. This is a vital war job with a great post-war future . . . Get out on the water, men, for the land's sake. Good night, all."

HISTORICAL NOTE — MERCHANT MARINES

Ray Doerhoff lives in St. Elizabeth, Missouri. During World War II, he was a Merchant Mariner. As part of a history of Merchant Marine radio operators, he wrote the following account (which has been only slightly edited).

The unique thing about Merchant Mariners is that each of us found our way into the service through a wide variety of routes and methods. I was a neophyte rural school teacher in the Missouri Ozarks and looking for a job during the summer of 1941. The state employment office informed me that the only thing available was a U.S. maritime Service Radio Training School in Boston that paid you while you trained.

I filled out an application because I felt getting paid $60 a month for going to school might be better than getting $60 a month for teaching.

Then came December 7, 1941, a day that none of us will ever forget.

In May of 1942, I received my induction notice from the county draft board, but on the same day I received a letter from the U.S. Maritime Service saying my application had been approved and they were in urgent need of radio operators to man merchant ships. I took both notices to the draft board and asked them what I should do. They told me I could take my choice since I would be serving my country both ways. Since radio school was an unknown quantity, and the draft notice was more of an unknown quantity, I chose the troop to Gallups Island. I have never regretted that decision.

I was assigned to a new Liberty, the *S.S. Clarence King*, and along with a skeleton crew helped bring her from the shipyards. We zigzagged our way to Brisbane, Australia, with a load of bombs and vehicles. From there we shuttled back and forth between Australia and the fighting front in New Guinea to such places at Port Moresby, Milne Bay, and Lae, loaded with either bombs or high-octane gasoline. Port Moresby had the only dock facilities in New Guinea so most of our unloading was done into army "ducks" who kept shuttling from ship to beach 24 hours a day.

After nine months of shuttling to New Guinea, we returned to San Francisco. The union office said there was a shortage of operators on the East Coast so I boarded a train to New York, signed on another Liberty, the *S.S. Cardinal Gibbons*, formed a convoy, and headed for India via the Mediterranean. We hugged the North African coast, but a group of German torpedo bombers found the convoy and hit it with deadly accuracy. Once again, our ship was fortunate to escape a hit. After this, I concluded that there was no comparison between the accuracy of the German pilots and that of the Japanese pilots around New Guinea, and if I had a choice, I was headed back to the Pacific.

I returned to Baltimore. Since my hometown girl-friend and I had previously decided on marriage after this trip if at all possible, I headed for Missouri. We were married on August 10, 1944. We spent our honeymoon in an upper berth on a three-day train trip to San Francisco.

I signed on another Liberty, the *S.S. Edward N. Westcott*, while my wife found a job with the Federal Reserve Bank in San Francisco. The *Westcott* went to New Guinea and formed a convoy heading for the first invasion of the Philippines at Leyte Gulf. The gulf was literally crowded with merchant ships waiting to unload while Major "Bing Bang" Bong, and his squadron of P-38s kept the sky clear of Jap planes. While the P-38s were in the air, all ships were ordered not to fire. This gave us a ringside seat for the dogfights overhead. We finally had our cargo unloaded and picked up another load in Australia. We formed a convoy and headed for the Lingayen Gulf invasion in the Philippines.

I always rigged a long extension of my earphones, so as usual I was standing watch on the catwalk behind my cabin and the Captain's cabin and had a ringside seat. The tenth plane turned away but our rear gunners burst a five-inch shell directly under him and he started trailing smoke. He immediately turned back toward our corner of the convoy and I suddenly realized that those flashes coming from both wings of the plane were from his gun muzzles. I headed back to the shack, which was protected by reinforced concrete. He strafed the decks all the way in, but our gun crews stayed on him, causing him to explode just before hitting the ship. After the hit, I looked out on deck and on the same catwalk — not five feet from where I had been standing — was the engine from the Jap Zero. The pilot lay crumpled on the deck below with pieces of plane and deck cargo scattered everywhere. We had injuries (mainly due to the strafing), but no deaths.

After unloading in Lingayen Gulf, we returned to San Francisco with three Jap flags painted on the ship's funeral, of which our gun crew was rightfully proud. We had a crew that "stuck to their guns" when we needed them.

I signed on a "C" ship, the *Cape San Blas*, and headed for the Philippines to await further orders. Two weeks out to sea, I was copying press when the news about the A-bomb attack on Hiroshima came in. I had to keep my "ears on the wire" constantly until the second bomb hit Nagasaki. Two days after that we received a message to pull into the nearest harbor and await further orders. We anchored in some isolated lagoon for four days, and then received orders to return to San Francisco, still loaded with our cargo.

Shortly thereafter, my wife, Rosetta, and I returned to our hometown of St. Elizabeth, Missouri, where she taught biology and I was superintendent of schools for 41 years, along with teaching physics. We have five sons who found five wonderful wives, resulting in fourteen wonderful grandchildren. They all help to make our retirement very enjoyable.

Doerhoff lost a good friend, George Hord, as a result of a collision at sea. He provided statistics, showing that Merchant Mariners lost to death the highest percentage of their serving number

(3.16%). This was higher than that of any branch of the military. One in 32 was killed. Only the Marines came close — one in 34.

February 27, 1945
"Red Cross Drive"

Molly is collecting money for the Red Cross. Fibber is trying to drum up business for his latest invention. As it happens, *Fibber* had volunteered, again, to help raise money in his neighborhood for the Red Cross. But the Red Cross had decided on someone else to do the job. Fibber is irate and loudly expresses his irritation when the letter of appointment arrives. No one could possibly do the job as well as he. Well, maybe. *Molly* has been appointed.

Alice Darling drops downstairs to tell the McGees about her boyfriend whose ship is laid up because they broke their rudder. Fibber wants to know "their 'udder' what?" and the puns continue through udder (as in cow) and steerage (where they put the steers on a cattle boat). There are more that don't warrant repeating. Alice wants a three-cent stamp to mail her Red Cross War Donation. Alice had already donated at the war plant where she worked but she had just learned that the Red Cross had located her cousin who had been missing in action, in a concentration camp (but uninjured). She felt compelled to increase her donation to the Red Cross.

Doc Gamble ("Tonsil-tester" to McGee) was next, on his way to start on *his* Red Cross drive. He's a captain in his district as is Molly is here. Fibber bets him five dollars that he and Molly will raise more money.

When the doctor leaves, Fibber reveals his plan to accompany Molly and try to sell his "Magnifico Low-Freeze Ice Box." Molly is not pleased, but McGee is undeterred.

Their first encounter is with a lady who has doubled her normal donation because the Red Cross has taken good care of her son. Surprisingly, she expresses some interest in the ice box.

The next stop is at the home of Mr. Sarpus, who lives up to McGee's attempt at "synonimity"(?). He really *does* seem to be a sourpuss. Molly tries persuasion.

"Mr. Sarpus," she says, "there are several million men fighting for us. The Red Cross is like a mother to all of them." Mr. Sarpus wants to know how he will know where his "dough" goes. Molly tells him the Red Cross financial records are public.

Sarpus didn't know that. "Here's twenty-five bucks, and I do begrudge it," he says. "No — make it *fifty* — might as well begrudge a lot."

Mrs. Smith, the next stop, has a check ready for them. She wishes there was more, but her daughter has been in the hospital. With the shortage of nurses, a Red Cross nurse's aide was looking after her. Molly suggests that Mrs. Smith consider being an aide herself. Molly is joining a class, and the lady immediately plans to join her. (She slams the door when McGee starts *his* pitch.)

Mr. Kiner, the next stop, answers the door with, "Here's my hundred bucks for the Red Cross. Good day!"

Slam.

Mrs. Dixon, next door, asks them to wait a moment.

"Take your time," Fibber says, "Rome wasn't built in a day, and Berlin won't be, either."

It just so happens that Harlow Wilcox is in the house delivering a wax commercial. He has already donated at the office. For her part, Mrs. Dixon is happy to give even more than she had planned, as her nephew is a prisoner of war in Manila. He had written about what the Red Cross does for the boys in prison camps: "Food, medicine and communication. I felt I had to give more." When Fibber mentions the ice box's built in butter slicer, she loses interest. She doesn't have any butter! (Butter was hard to get during the war, of course.)

When the McGees return home, they are greeted by Beulah; she is interested in their collection success. (They had collected $595!) Beulah gives five dollars of her *own* money. "It ain't much," she says apologetically, "but it represents several months of self refusal in the candy department." She leaves to fix sandwiches because McGee's stomach is "as empty as a campaign promise."

Enter Doc Gamble. It's time to settle the bet. The doctor wins, only because the *McGees'* Red Cross contribution goes on the doctor's list!

Following a Harlow Wilcox commercial, Jim Jordan delivers one of his serious messages: "Ladies and gentlemen, the collectors for the Red Cross War Fund will come to *your* house one of these days. So give generously to them."

Marian adds: "If we give till it hurts over here, it will help a lot of the boys who are hurt over there."

Good night, all.

MARCH 27, 1945
"CLOTHING DRIVE"

Harlow Wilcox's opening commercial is a bit of a stretch. His latest recommendation for using Johnson's Wax® is to use it to bring a shine to the visors of military officer hats!

As the show opens, the McGees are sorting clothes for the United National Clothing Collection for Overseas Relief. As usual, Fibber thinks they may be giving too much away. Molly, of course, is the voice of reason and humanity. He protests when she proposes to give away his old basketball sweatshirt. Same with his old pair of corduroy pants which are "only too small around the waist . . . and around the seat." He plans to take off twenty-five pounds "one of these days." Molly is not convinced. "There are people in France and Greece and Poland and Holland that have taken off *seventy-five* pounds the hard way."

Doc Gamble ("Arrowsmith" to McGee) is the first to arrive. His comment about the sweater for McGee by Aunt Sarah must have been done before Fibber "got so broad-shouldered in the hips." The usual exchange of insults follows.

Molly, again, brings the conversation back to the real world: "To me, it's no joke that there are people in the world suffering for lack of clothing."

The McGees offer the weary doctor a shower, which he accepts. Meanwhile, the McGees continue sorting clothes. The hard decisions come a little easier as Molly observes that "It's hard to realize that 125 million people are desperate for shoes and clothing while we are . . ." She interrupts herself when she realizes McGee has tossed the doctor's clothes onto the pile. She talks him out of *that* ruse.

Alice Darling arrives and, after receiving thanks for *her* clothing contribution, says her former golf pro is flying a bomber now. "He says his game was still good," she relates. "He flew over some Japanese airplane plants and made a hole in one." Alice also remembers another of her many suitors —"That nice looking boy that went in to the Chemical Warfare Division."

Molly remembers him: "He always had such a nice smell of mustard around him," she says, reflecting the politically incorrect times.

Alice leaves with the note. "I'm glad I can help dress some destitute women in Europe or the Philippines," Alice says. "That's me: Cover Girl Darling."

Molly says Alice is good hearted, as are most people, "but it's pretty hard to convince people that there are millions and millions that need clothes. They think, what good will my little donation do, among that many?"

Even McGee can figure out that "if millions give, millions will benefit."

A standard encounter with Myrt the telephone operator follows in which the word "paratroopers" is, in fact, in reference to a "pair of" (police) troopers.

Enter Harlow Wilcox for his middle commercial. Wilcox is on the local committee for the clothing drive and mentions that Henry J. Kaiser (C.E.O. of an ill-fated automobile manufacturer) is national chairman. This is the largest clothing drive in U.S. history. In Holland there is only one blanket for every five people. In Norway, they even sew Nazi propaganda leaflets together and wear them. In Belgium, there's only one usable shirt to a family of seven. "This isn't just a drive to keep war victims warm," Harlow notes. "It's a matter of restoring their self-respect, too. It's pretty hard to keep your chin up when you have to keep looking down to see if your feet are frozen."

Harlow leaves without a word about the sponsor's product. As Molly observes (and I agree), Harlow and the Johnson's people have a nice sense of proportion. No commercial!

Beulah is also donating to the drive. "The way I figures, they's two kinds of folks in this world — the 'gots' and the 'ain't gots.' And nobody got more sympathy for the 'ain't gots' than them that ain't got much." (This is another beautiful bit of writing by Quinn and Leslie.)

When the doorbell rings, it is for Mrs. Carstairs (a new character), played by the inimitable Bea Benaderet. The show needs a new character and the versatile Bill Thompson (Old-Timer and Wimple, among others, and Mayor LaTrivia (Gale Gordon) are in the military. Carstairs is quite similar to Mrs. Uppington. She, too, is rich, but she has arrived in her station wagon to pick up the clothes. Immediately, McGee calls her "Carsty," and will continue to do so in future episodes.

Whoops! McGee forgot that Dog Gamble's clothes were taken away by Mrs. Carstairs.

After Wilcox delivers a straight-forward commercial there is another serious message from Jim Jordan: "Ladies and gentlemen, the United National Clothing Collection starts April first. Use the time until then to go through your closets and attics and trunks and storerooms to see what you can spare for the millions of suffering people in war areas. The goal is 150 million pounds of clothing."

"This is *not* a charity drive," Marian insists. "It's an opportunity for you to do what you can to spare the health and self-respect of war-ruined families."

Jim Jordan continues: "Greatly needed are infant's garments, particularly knitted goods and all kinds of warm, sensible clothing, shoes and bedding for boys and men, women, and girls. There will be receiving stations set up everywhere — in churches, schools, factories, and clubs. So get ready, won't you?"

Marian has the last word: "You wouldn't like to be in their shoes, but they'd like to be in yours — if you'll send them."

Good night, all.

APRIL 24, 1945
"A RIDE TO THE ELKS CLUB"

Molly wants Fibber out of the house so she can do spring cleaning. He's willing to go to the Elks Club, but he needs a ride. This simple premise is the framework around which to fashion a wartime message.

Alice is going to the airplane plant — maybe Fibber can get a ride with her. She's leaving early to instruct some new employees on (Are you ready for this?): "How to adjust the centrifugal equalizer on the universal compensator in the hydraulic mid-section booster gears." (This from a girl who has trouble putting a sentence together properly!) After a brief note on cosmetics — Alice's boss said they could assemble four bombers which she was correcting Nature's mistakes — Alice tells him there's not room for him in her car pool (six in a coupe).

It's a little stretch but Alice is able to work in another message: "The whole idea is to conserve tires. There's a terrible shortage of tires and cars and gasoline, and it'll get worse. Did you know that already over four million cars have had to be scrapped?"

When she leaves, Fibber complains that he didn't have any trouble getting a ride during the *last* war. "In the last war . . ." he begins.

"We didn't have any B-29's using more gas in an hour then an average driver uses in a year," Molly says, adding perspective to her husband's lament.

Mrs. Carstairs is McGee's next target for a ride. She hasn't her own car, however: *she's* driving a station wagon. That's okay with McGee, who thinks she means a *police* car. In fact, the station wagon belongs to the Red Cross, and she is not permitted to use it for anything but official business. "Carsty" takes an opportunity to tell how important it is to save cars: "Automobiles are wearing out at a simply appalling rate. People absolutely *must* use their cars only for necessary driving. Save them in every way possible."

Harlow Wilcox drops by, but he has the company car — which looks great because of CarNu®. Of course, Wilcox can't use the company car for Fibber and he, too, has a few words about the transportation situation: "Much as I'd like to do you a favor, I'd rather do [Generals] Eisenhower and MacArthur a favor just now. Do you realize that the stockpile of new cars is down to what would have been a two-day supply before the war? Have you heard that there are over twenty-three million cars on the road today and if the number falls to twenty-one million, our transportation problems will be something horrible."

The use of wartime vernacular is highlighted when Beulah says her boyfriend, Ira, "established a beachhead on her cake."

McGee is pleasantly surprised when his verbal adversary, Doc Gamble, says Fibber can go downtown with *him*. The surprise turns to chagrin when McGee realizes the doctor is *walking* downtown. (The resulting action requires a *lot* of footsteps from the sound effects man.)

Just in case anyone missed the message, Jim and Marian Jordan tie a ribbon on it at the end . . .

JIM: Ladies and gentlemen, today there are more than two million American-made military vehicles running on American-made rubber tires. Mostly, they don't run on modern concrete highways. Mostly, they run in ruts, over rocks, through forests, and across the ruins of towns and cities. Three out of five of those tires don't wear out. They're cut to pieces.

MOLLY: That's one of the many reasons we have to conserve tires.

JIM: And the need of our Armed Forces for gasoline is tremendous — twenty-five million gallons a day.

MARIAN: Which is why we have to use as little gasoline as possible here at home!

JIM: So pool your cars wherever possible. The kind of car pooling that really means something is where members rotate the use of their cars and ride together. So see if you can't adjust your necessary traveling to car pooling.

MARIAN: You know our fighting forces are getting places by smart planning, and so can we.

Good night, all.

HISTORICAL NOTE: PRESIDENT ROOSEVELT DIES

Franklin D. Roosevelt, the 32nd president of the United States, and the only president to serve more than two terms, died on March 29, 1945. He had been in very poor health, but his death still came as a shock to most Americans.

Roosevelt was succeeded by Harry S. Truman, a man with neither the charisma nor the confidence of the people enjoyed by his predecessor. He had not even been told of the development of the Atomic Bomb, which he would decide to use less than six months later.

Nevertheless, most historians share the opinion that Truman went on to become one of America's great presidents.

HISTORICAL NOTE: ADOLF HITLER DIES

Although Adolf Hitler's death has been the subject of much speculation (his body was never found.) The most popular belief was that Hitler and his bride, Eva Braun, committed suicide on April 30, 1945. The Russians, apparently, saw their remains. The Third Reich's minister of Popular Enlightenment and Propaganda, Goebbels, and his wife killed themselves and their six children at the same time.

HISTORICAL NOTE: V-E DAY

On May 8, 1945, the war in Europe was declared ended. Prime Minister Winston Churchill and President Harry Truman declared V-E (Victory in Europe) Day. Not all German forces had surrendered, but they did so (in various locations) in the days ahead.

MAY 22, 1945
"THE SEVENTH WAR BOND DRIVE"

There is a big War Bond rally on Wistful Vista, and McGee has managed to be appointed director of ceremonies.

The first order of business is to organize an event to decorate an auditorium; Fibber, however, only manages to *dis*organize it. The first visitor is Mrs. Carstairs, whom McGee had edged out as director. Fibber knows all the theatrical jargon (but not necessarily its correct usage) from his vaudeville days.

"Carsty" is worried — and with good reason. "This is Wistful Vista's golden opportunity to show the world its interest in and support of the Seventh War Loan," she says, and she feels that McGee is running the operation like a flea circus.

McGee defends himself by saying "it's better to put on too many fleas than too much dog."

Already, the stage hands are losing confidence in their boss. He has commandeered the job of keynote speaker and can get "Carsty" on the stage if she buys a big enough bond. In fact, she and her husband have each purchased five thousand dollars' worth of extra bonds, and she eschews a chance to sit on the stage.

Billy Mills and his orchestra are tuning up and Fibber wants to help. Billy calls him a "Tosca-little-Ninny." Fibber interprets that to mean he has an ear for music.

The musical interlude which follows is "This Little Bond Went to War," and details some of the ways in which the bond money is used at home and abroad. The song is a Billy Mills original.

Meanwhile, Molly has been writing Fibber's speech. So far it reads: "The war in Europe against Germany and Italy is over, but the war against hunger, privation, and distress will go on for many, many months. It is our money, yours and mine. The money you put in War Bonds which will fight this war to an end. Seven billion dollars is the quota for individual purchases in this seventh War Loan. With this money, we will bring order in Europe and continue the war against the Japanese in the Pacific."

Fibber thinks she has made a good start while he has been working on the musical arrangement.

Alice Darling arrives, and expresses surprise that Fibber writes music. Alice is "raffling off" a date with her for the bond dance. The boy who buys the biggest bond wins the honor of being her date. The two leading contenders are, respectively, "the boy who his father owns the airplane plant" and "the boy that he works at the bench next to me which he naturally hasn't got as much money as Freddie, who's the boy that his father owns the plan."

Harlow Wilcox is next. He says a good start to Fibber's speech will be to note that: May 27 is National Maritime Day, "a day on which we pay tribute to the courage and tenacity of our merchant fleet and its men who have contributed so much to the winning of the war in Europe and the maintenance of vital supplies in the Pacific. Many of these men have performed feats of heroism equal to those in the Armed Forces. Their casualty rate has been high and will continue to be high until the final victory in the Pacific. These men in 1944 carried eight thousand tons of supplies every hour, every day! Arms, ammunition, and medical cargo bought and paid for by your purchase of War Bonds. It's up to us to keep those supplies going to fighters who need them. Let's send them over the bounding waves on a sea of waving bonds." (Don Quinn — or possibly Phil Leslie — does it again!)

This was not the first time that the McGee's show had highlighted the often-overlooked Merchant Marine. Neither was it the first time that the Johnson's Wax® people gave up commercial time for a war message.

Enter Doc Gamble for another verbal skirmish. He wants to know who put Fibber in charge of the rally — the Japanese embassy, perhaps?

McGee calls him "Artery Pincher," and reminds him that one has to buy a War Bond to get into the rally. The Doctor, of course, already had his bond — a "thousand-dollar certificate which he bought instead of new X-ray equipment. I've worked on hundreds of men back from the Pacific. Believe me, a trip through a veteran's hospital is a sure cure for complacency. And if any bonds I buy will help shorten this war by one split second, [then] they can have the gold out of my teeth. If anybody thinks he can sit back and let the world come to a state of milk and honey, he better start buying a cow and get the bees out of his own bonnet."

The curtain finally raises, and a radio announcer notes that every member of the audience was required to buy an extra bond. He then introduces Billy Mills to lead the Wistful Vista Philharmonic. The music doesn't start immediately because McGee has forcibly taken over the orchestra. When he waves the baton, the "music" is indescribably discordant. (Indeed it is difficult to imagine how, even on purpose, someone could have written it. The audience, by their applause, evidently agreed with me.)

In a way, all ends well. The audience agrees to buy another bond to get out of the auditorium!

After a commercial, Jim Jordan addresses the listening audience:

"Ladies and gentlemen, there are *some* shows you can't buy your way out of, except at the price of blood, sweat, and tears. There's a show like that going on in the Pacific right now. And it's up to us to buy an end to it."

Marian chimes in: "We can do it with our purchases of War Bonds in this mighty seventh War Loan. We can buy the guns and ships and planes and tanks that are needed to overwhelm a tough and determined enemy."

Jim adds: "We can buy more than that. Your War Bond purchases are merely loans to your government. That means you are purchasing postwar security and a controlled economy for our fighting men to come home to."

Marian concludes: "So buy your extra War bonds today — all you can afford, and a little more. Let's prove that when it comes to buying bonds, America's clothing has no "pockets of resistance."

Good night, all.

HISTORICAL NOTE: V-J DAY

On August 18, 1945, the Japanese government asked the allies if unconditional surrender meant that Emperor Hirohito would have to give up his throne. The allies replied that the Japanese people would decide his fate. On August 14 (in the United States), the allies received a message from Japan accepting the Potsdam terms. The allies appointed MacArthur supreme commander for the Allied Powers.

On September 2 (Tokyo time), aboard the battleship *Missouri* in Tokyo Bay, the Allies and Japan signed the surrender agreement. MacArthur signed for the Allied Powers, Nimitz for the United States, and Foreign Minister Mamoru Shigemitsu for Japan. President Truman proclaimed September 2 as V-J (Victory over Japan) Day. Three years, eight months and twenty-two days after Japan bombed Pearl Harbor, World War II ended.

Fibber McGee and Molly were enjoying their annual summer hiatus on V-J Day, but we can be sure they enjoyed the day immensely.

MORE WISDOM, WARNINGS, WIT, AND WHIMSY

I have presented some details and comments on the thirty broadcasts which were devoted entirely to war themes. By no means, however, was this limit of the programs commitment to the war effort. Indeed, only a few programs were broadcast without any mention of an allusion to the turmoil in Europe.

In this section, I have included representative excerpts and comments from some of the non-war-themed shows. There was never any letup in reminding the listeners that there was a war on.

JANUARY 20, 1942
"MRS. UPPINGTON'S BROKEN WINDOW"

"Uppy" has a broken window. Is McGee the culprit? He's not sure. Maybe he dreamed it! That's the story in this episode, continued from the previous week.

There is no specific war message, but the program does finish with an appeal by the Jordans for funds to fight infantile paralysis, a disease which had afflicted President Roosevelt.

JANUARY 27, 1942
"THE BLIZZARD"

There is a record-breaking blizzard in Wistful Vista. The weather is so devastating that Fibber deems that it's "Not a fit night out for a man or Hitler." McGee then claims he wouldn't put his face outside "for all the retreads in Detroit."

When a stranger braves the storm to knock on the door with a message from the governor, McGee is gratified: "I've volunteered for everything from air raid warden to mixin' macaroons for Marines." The stranger is joined by the Old-Timer. Noting the knitting in Molly's lap, he wants to know if she's "knittin' for Britain or crochetin' for the Malayans." He then leaves to try to find his girlfriend under some snow drift.

Yet another fugitive from the frigid air — Mrs. Uppington — arrives. Fibber can't understand what brings her out. "This weather is only good for one thing;" he insists, "to keep the Germans from rushin' back from the Russian front." "Uppy" is followed by Harlow Wilcox. (The blizzard seems to have brought everyone out.) Wilcox finds a way to work in a commercial. After that, another foul-weather friend appears at the door: Mayor LaTrivia, who reminds Fibber that his driveway needs shoveling. A search for the snow shovel allows for the door to the venerable hall closet to be opened.

After a musical interlude the McGees try, not too subtly, to suggest that their "guests" go home. They don't take the hint. This time it's a visit from Wallace Wimple.

By now McGee's patience is wearing thin. He still doesn't know what is in the stranger's message from the governor. The "governor," in fact, is an automotive device to prevent a driver from driving too fast.

At the end of the show Jim Jordan steps out of character again with a serious message: "Ladies and gentlemen, this country has a big job ahead of it and won't stop until it's done. We've got to get in there with our money, and our work, and our loyal 100% support.

Marian concurs: "Yes, Uncle Sam has rolled up his sleeves and now what he needs is more sleeves."

"So let's give him our shirts," Jim concludes, giving voice to one of Don Quinn's lesser lines.

This may have been one of Don Quinn's lesser lines, but it's the *thought* that counts.

MARCH 10, 1942
"FIBBER MAKES A FOOTSTOOL"

Harlow Wilcox opens this broadcast by noting that the word "home" expresses "everything we are fighting for . . . liberty, freedom, family. And it's a word that tells the part you women play in the war." He means, among other things, *preserving* the home — with the help of Johnson's Wax®, of course.

Mrs. Uppington provides an unusual view of the wartime blackout policy. McGee is an air raid warden and has had complaints about her; it seems she needs to get some heavier curtains. She agrees to do so, but thinks the whole thing is silly. "If the Japanese *or* the Germans should come to Wistful Vista they'll be far too busy to go about peeping into people's windows."

After the final commercial, the Jordans stay in character for this final bit:

MOLLY: McGee why don't you settle down?

FIBBER: I can't help it, Molly. I want to do something about this war. I want to get in and help.

MOLLY: Well, my goodness, you've been buying Defense Bonds for all you're worth!

FIBBER: Yeah, but that's no sacrifice. That's just a darn good investment. I wanna really get in there and pitch. I wanna fight!

MOLLY: You're a little over-aged for that. I'm afraid you're gonna have to be one of the men behind the men, behind the guns.

FIBBER: I'm not so old. I'd make a wonderful captain of artillery.

MOLLY: You just stay on the radio, dearie, and be a colonel of *corn*!

April 14, 1942
"Fibber is Grand Marshal in a Parade"

Mayor LaTrivia has a wartime message. He has been making his "belt buckle" speech at various places. It's about the war effort and the mayor has been traveling to offices and plants with the following: "I tell them that if we expect our boys to 'belt' those Japs over there, we have to buckle down and work over here. My whole purpose is to get people to realize that this war won't be won by giving up two golf balls, a new inner tube, and a teaspoonful of sugar. This thing involves everything we have and everything we are. It's twenty-four hours a day, seven days a week. And, by George, if a nation of freedom-loving mechanical geniuses can't smash the kimonos off a bunch of little thieves who couldn't invent a dollar watch on their own, we're not the people I think we are. And I think we are!

June 9, 1942
"Pot Roast"

Considering the meat shortage, it may be surprising to find a program featuring pot roast. It's Fibber McGee's favorite meal, and he can hardly wait to eat. Unfortunately, people keep dropping by (as they do every week).

The first visitor is the mayor, who wants an opinion on the new big bulletin board on the city hall steps. "It's a huge poster affair," he explains, "on which we post, air raid information, rationing information, direction about enlistments and that sort of thing." In his haste to taste, Fibber tries to urge the mayor's departure. The mayor *nearly* departs after a typically hilarious exchange with the McGees. The mayor, however, has obviously decided to outlast the McGees: *He wants some pot roast.*

The Old-Timer drops in and doesn't recognize LaTrivia. The mayor attempts to establish his credentials: "Princeton, '32 . . ."

The Old-Timer immediately tops him: "Lockheed, '42, Welding School."

In a little twist on war shortages, the Old-Timer says he's not worried about getting gas. His radishes are already up in his garden.

The mayor continues to be "The Man Who Came to Dinner"— at least he longs to be. He stays through a wax commercial and continues to stay, and stay.

Next to arrive is Mrs. Uppington. She invites the McGees and the mayor to dinner. Fibber declines, for obvious reasons, and the mayor "doesn't want to desert McGee when he isn't feeling well." (He's hungry!) Uppy leaves, disappointed that the McGees can't join her for a dinner of *bourguignon*. LaTrivia knows the word — it means pot roast.

Finally, the mayor leaves. But the pot roast has cooked dry.

The serious message at the end of the broadcast deals with the need for Navy pilots.

JIM: Ladies and gentlemen, the Navy wants and needs 30,000 pilots a year to be trained on a twelve-month program of flight training. The requirements are simple: They want young men between eighteen and twenty-seven, high school graduates who have been American citizens for at least ten years. All those successfully completing the course will be commissioned as an ensign with pay and allowances of over $200 a month!

MARIAN: Yes, it's a wonderful and thrilling opportunity for young men to find a new glory under Old Glory.

FIBBER: Join the Navy and see the world — made into a decent place for free people to live in.

Harlow closes by telling the listeners that the broadcast will be sent overseas by short wave.

JUNE 16, 1942
"MOUSE IN THE HOUSE"

There is a mouse in the house at 79 Wistful Vista, and Molly doesn't like it one bit. Fibber is assigned with the task of getting rid of it. He says he needs to find out where the rodent is coming from; he's going to "tail him." For once, Molly says, "That's very funny, McGee", not "T'aint funny." The audience loved it.

Molly refuses to allow Fibber to use any violence, so McGee, typically, launches into a strategic plan that even Eisenhower might envy.

The Old-Timer drops by and drops this piece of wisdom: "One feller says t'other feller, 'Is it true the Japs are attacking Alaska just to save face?' 'Can't be,' says t'other feller, 'I've seen their face and I don't know why you'd want to save it.'"

Harlow Wilcox, after working in a short commercial wants to know where the McGees are going on their summer vacation.

"We haven't decided," says Molly, "what with saving tires and gas and cutting down on pleasure driving, we probably won't be doing anything very fancy."

The mayor's arrival provides an opportunity for another war message. He has dropped by to inquire about the McGee's scrap rubber. Molly promises that the next day Fibber is going through the house to collect scrap rubber and take it to the filling station. She describes one of her ingenious ways to conserve rubber. She has taken Fibber's hip-high fishing boots (over his objections) and cut rubber rings out of them to use in canning fruit in jars. "Any kind of rubber will do;" says the mayor, "old hot water bottles, garden hose, tennis shoes. If it's made of rubber and you can possibly spare it, give it." One of the filling station men had coined a slogan: "Bring your scrap over here so we can finish that scrap over there." (A one-cent a pound fee was allowed for scrap rubber.) Molly offered her own slogan: "Turn in your rubber, a pound or an ounce; it will all help our soldiers give Hitler the bounce."

The mayor doesn't escape without a verbal dose of intentional misunderstanding from the McGees. On his way out, McGee asks him how *he* would get rid of a mouse. The mayor would "import a few Russians. They seem to be pretty good at exterminating rats."

A brief encounter with Mrs. Uppipngton on the subject of women wearing slacks finds Fibber with a somewhat Victorian attitude: "Why do they call them slacks?" he asks. "The only slack in them is around the ankles." One bit of Quinn's writing is too good to omit. McGee says "Uppy" has a skin as thick as a cantaloupe and that's probably why she can't." (You figure it out; it took a while for the audience).

Harlow Wilcox finishes by noting: "One good thing seems to be coming out of this war — greater neighborliness among all of us. Haven't you noticed this in your own community — block captains, air raid wardens, first-aid courses? They're bringing us closer together to meet our common problems. Right now those problems are pretty serious. But there are other less serious problems on which neighborly advice is helpful." It's about wax, of course, but why not?

JUNE 23, 1942
"PACKING FOR VACATION"

In the middle commercial Harlow Wilcox calls attention to the current edition of *Life* Magazine: "It's got Fibber and Molly's picture in it," he says, "and a double-page spread about what Johnson Products are doing in the line of war duty. The ad tells all about how Johnson protective coatings are used on airplanes, army textiles, housing projects, special wax finishes for leather belts, holsters, and boots. Believe me — that advertisement gives you a new slant on Johnson Wax® products. *We've* got a sponsor that knows there's a war going on."

The incongruity of the picture of these plain folks from Wistful Vista in *Life* and a casual reference to their sponsor was something the listeners were quite willing to accept.

December 15, 1942
"Fortune Teller"

The war messages included in this episode start with the comment that Magee keeps something more valuable than money in their sugar bowl, namely "sugar." (He has lost fifteen dollars that he had been saving to buy Molly a Christmas present.) He may hire the Internal Revenue Service to help find it. "They could find money in a caraway seed." The only government agency not immune to criticism on the McGee shows was the I.R.S.

There is one other allusion to the military when it is suggested that McGee see a fortune teller for help in locating the money, he scoffs: "Those bargain-basement gypsies couldn't tell the future of a blue-eyed blonde with the fleet in."

He does, in fact, see a fortune teller with no positive results. He tells Wilcox, "The way she clipped us, she should have been a barber in a boot camp."

Next, the McGees are confronted by a man at the door. He has noticed that McGee's car has an "A" (gas ration) sticker on the windshield." He has a number of questions. Does McGee do any pleasure driving? Can he see McGee's draft registration card? How much coffee do they have? And, for that matter, how much sugar?"

When McGee protests the quizzing, the man retorts, "McGee, this is war."

"Yeah," Molly chides, "we read about it in the papers."

More questions follow: "Have you been buying War Bonds?"

"Yes," McGee says, "we've been buying War Bonds until we're red, white, and blue in the face. And I've licked the back of so many War Savings Stamps, everything I eat tastes like glue."

The questioner is unstoppable: "Did you buy that suit after restrictions were put on clothing? The government doesn't want you to buy anything you don't need. They're trying to keep prices at a reasonable level, encourage buying Bonds and paying off debts. We want this country to be on a sound financial footing after this war is over. *Now remember that.*"

This totally incongruous interruption is explained away by the fact that the impertinent interrogator has just moved in next door and wants to get to know all about his new neighbors.

In the denouement, Fibber finds the money in a copy of Charles Dickens' *A Christmas Carol*, where he hid it for a logical reason: "nobody opens that book until Christmas."

JANUARY 12, 1943
"BILLY MILLS IN THE HOSPITAL"

Orchestra leader Billy Mills is in the hospital. McGee has volunteered to be a hospital visitor to patients there and is surprised to learn who his patient is. Before he can leave, the Old-Timer drops in. "OT" has been to Chicago where he "got to talk to a sergeant just back from the front. Told me all about the war."

McGee hopes he "didn't spill any military secrets."

The soldier, apparently, was too smart for that: Every time he came to a secret he'd just say some vegetable instead. Here's how the encounter went, according to the Old-Timer: "He tells me his troop ship, the *S.S. Rutabaga*, left the harbor in Sweet Potato on the Lima Bean of Green Pea. Says they were escorted by three Golden Potatoes and a small fleet of Turnips with four motored Onions flying overhead." He goes on: "They arrived at north Succotash about the fourteenth of Celery and went into action immediately. Says they killed a thousand Cabbages and captured six hundred Radishes." Then comes the vital news: Inside information is that the war will be over "by the Squash of April 19 hundred and Garlic."

Molly says: "We won't breathe a word of it."

(Well, not everything Quinn wrote could be a knee-slapper.)

Mrs. Uppington is at the hospital when the McGees arrive. She notes that she "must go buy my War Bond, thanks to Mr. McGee." It seems that every time she sees him she thinks of inflation! "And when I think of inflation, I think how important it is that this country maintains financial controls during and after this war. Which means everyone must buy all the War Bonds he possibly can. So [this to McGee directly] please stay out of my sight for the rest of the week. I'm over my budget already."

The show ends with Fibber regaling Mills with some really bad jokes. Having eaten the fruit cake, candy, a malted milk, and six doughnuts he brought for Billy, Fibber ends up in the hospital himself!

February 23, 1943
"Poker Game"

Fibber wants to play poker with the boys, but doesn't want Molly to know. She is, of course, suspicious of his sudden need to "go to a meeting." The meeting in question (at least according to Fibber) is about war efforts, labor problems — some of the businessmen want to see if they can get some "good hands." Everyone is going to "lay his cards on the table; we're going to try to see that everyone gets a square deal." After hearing this, Molly claims to be proud of her patriotic husband, but we suspect that she is doing this tongue in cheek. Concerning efforts to meet some of the labor needs she "wouldn't gamble on it." The double entendres continue.

Teeny comes by in one of the few episodes where she and Molly are in a room at the same time. It's obvious from her seemingly naïve comments that her father is headed for the same poker game. McGee becomes increasingly uneasy as the conversation continues.

The Old-Timer drops in asking for help in planning a wedding. McGee thinks it's a bad time for a wedding. "Who's gonna spend three ration coupons just so they can throw rice at a couple of chumps?" he asks indignantly. "Who's tyin' old shoes on the back of an automobile with no gas in it?"

The program continues to be filled with words having a double meaning. A few examples: Fibber has to fix Harlow Wilcox's "poker" that he broke and Harlow has to meet an old auntie (ante) tonight. (His auntie's name is Philpot.) This byplay continues even into the commercial — "give your linoleum a new deal . . . next time you have a full house for a party . . .

enjoy that royal flush of pride." (Well, you get the idea.) The writers must have had a great time with this. They didn't have much time left over for war talk. Fibber did slip in a note to Mrs. Uppington to take off her shoes, as "you only get three pairs a year (because of rationing), and you're pretty hard on them."

At program's end, we learn that Molly knew of Fibber's plans but wanted him to leave so she could go play bingo.

MARCH 30, 1943
"BROKEN WASHING MACHINE"

Harlow Wilcox opens the show by thanking the listeners who have written in hoping that Johnson will continue to sponsor the program. Harlow says: "The makers of Johnson's Wax® feel a strong obligation to continue the shows — in spite of such problems as packaging, labor and material shortages that every manufacturer has to contend with these days. In spite of the large volume of Johnson's Wax® finishes that are going directly or indirectly to war work, the management of the S.C. Johnson Company have made it clear to all of us that the program should be made as helpful as possible to the war effort, not only as entertainment but also as a means of giving you valuable service information. We shall certainly carry on with that thought in our minds."

In the opening, Fibber falls victim to a rumor mill and panics because there is going to be a shortage of some gadget he has never even seen. Molly, as usual, tries to apply a little common sense suggesting that they go buy some "flandeckers." This mythical object "goes over the mouth of a rumor monger to keep him from blowing his top." Having made her point about the dangers of spreading rumors during wartime, she finally gets McGee to look at a washing machine that has gone berserk. Molly has already tried to fix it herself but now, "I haven't seen so many crooked parts since my nearsighted uncle sold his barbershop."

Fibber picks up a newspaper and finds an ad featuring a used washing machine for sale. (There are no new ones during the war.) He quickly tries to make a call, but is briefly sidetracked by Myrt, the telephone operator. The standard one-sided conversation has McGee repeating that Myrt's sister is studying to be a gunner because the sailor she's going with wants to be a gunner's mate.

The program continues at the butcher shop where they get a quick lesson on how foolhardy it is to waste war ration stamps on food you don't eat. They also learn that the butcher's delivery boy is in Guadalcanal.

After a hilarious bit of confusion involving Harlow Wilcox and his twin brother, Paul, the McGees search frantically for the address of the washing machine owner. At the Old-Timer's house, they learn that his girl friend Bessie is missing. She could be in Africa, Alaska, Solomon Islands, Iceland, or Texas. It seems she was working in an airplane factory and must have welded herself into a wing. Nobody knows *where* she is.

The search continues without bearing fruit for most of the program until the McGees do find the washing machine owner, who shows them the date on the newspaper. It's two years out of date!

APRIL 6, 1943
"FIBBER HAS NO PEP"

"There's one thing they teach a boy in the Army — to be neat and tidy. There's nothing like a little stretch of Kitchen Police (KP) for giving a man respect for little things like keeping shoes shined, buttons sewed on, guns spotless and gleaming."

So ran Harlow Wilcox's opening to this episode. Not surprisingly, he was reminded (by himself) "That S.C. Johnson and Son are making for the Armed Forces millions of cans of a product for keeping those rifles clean called Rifle Bore Cleaner . . . It's just one of a number of war products made by Johnson's Wax®.

Well, it's time for spring cleaning and Fibber McGee "got no pep, got no energy." He will use that phrase so many times during the show that the audience starts to join in.

This was one of very few wartime shows with no other wartime message.

APRIL 13, 1943
"UNCLE SYCAMORE ON THE RADIO"

This episode does not have a *single* wartime theme, but the war is a factor in the broadcast. The McGees are waiting to hear Fibber's Uncle Sycamore on the radio. This is a chance to *talk* about radio. In a rather feeble attempt at humor, Fibber says that his uncle (who is about ninety) tried to join the Marines because he read that they were the oldest branch of the service.

Fibber has been "fixing" the radio and as a consequence the dial no longer conforms to the station. Molly notes that it's illegal to change radio wave lengths without the government's permission. Hilarity ensues while McGee frantically tries to tune the radio in time for the broadcast. All he can get is a western drama.

There is a bit of support for international cooperation when Rosita comes by with an almost unintelligible Spanish accent to observe that if North Americans and South Americans knew each other better, they would all be just Americans. (The reason for this message at this time is obscure, at least to me.)

During the middle segment, Harlow Wilcox read letters from servicemen expressing gratitude for being able to hear the show on short wave. Also, actress Claudette Colbert appears as a guest to urge support for the Second War Bond Drive.

MAY 4, 1943
"MCGEE CHANGES HIS NAME"

McGee has tried to join the Army but was rejected. He's not taking it well. The first guest is Teeny, which is something of a surprise since Molly is still in the room. Teeny wants to see his uniform having heard that he joined the Army. Fibber explains that the Army decided to save him for a real emergency.

At any rate, Fibber taking the advice of a numerologist has decided to change his name . . . to Ronald. This meets with a variety of reactions from the usual parade of visitors, one of whom is Throckmorton P. Gildersleeve (who will later have a radio show of his own).

(My own audio tape of this episode concludes with the note that the show had been broadcast using the facilities of the Armed Forces Radio Service.)

May 11, 1943
"Fibber Predicts Snow in May"

Fibber has purchased a barometer and has become a meteorologist. It isn't long before he is predicting the weather . . . *snow in May*! When he is met with some skepticism, he decides to check with the weather bureau. To do that, he has to use the phone, which means another encounter with Myrt. She tells him that she has heard from her brother in North Africa. Molly wants to know how Myrt knows this, given wartime censorship.

"From the way they packed them in on the boat going over there, they must be going to Sardinia," McGee comments. (Don Quinn was apparently willing to sacrifice a little geographic accuracy for the sake of a joke.)

McGee wants to call the newspaper with his snow prediction. Molly says they won't print it because the weather is a military secret. McGee thinks that's a "lot of malarkey. The weather is about as secret as a plate of fried onions."

Teeny gets a chance for a wartime message in this broadcast. Told that the purpose of McGee's barometer is to make little girls ask questions, Teeny has a question all ready: "Why does Hitler wear that ridiculous little mustache?" Her answer is a classic bit of comedy writing:

> Because a mustache is hair,
> And hare is a rabbit,
> And a rabbit has a short tail,
> And a short tale is easily told,
> And so is a bell [tolled],
> And a bell is in a belfry,
> And so are bats,
> And bats are what you use for baseball,
> And baseball is played on a diamond,
> And a diamond is full of grass,
> And so is a cow,
> And a cow is beef,
> And beef is better when it's hung,
> And so is Hitler.

Did you follow that? If so, try this poem by Wallace Wimple . . .

Let's all drive thirty-five or less,
And help the world clean up this mess.
Because we're short of tires, you know,
And they'll last longer driving slow.
If you turn so fast your tires squeal,
You know you're being a rubber heel.

At the end of the episode, Fibber learns he bought a display barometer with a dummy dial. He goes to sleep in humiliation, but wakes next morning to his predicted snowfall!

JUNE 22, 1943
"PLANNING A VACATION"

This show starts with a Johnson's pat on the back for retailers, as read by Harlow Wilcox: "Does it occur to you that your dealer renders you a valuable service? Never as valuable as now when wartime restrictions complicate his operation. He buys a little of this, a little more of that, things he believes you're going to need, and he puts them on his shelf until you come to buy them. He has to have a convenient location, people to wait on you, and maybe delivery service. Now if that's all he did, you still couldn't get along without him. But he does more. He exercises buying judgment on your behalf. Selects from among the goods offered those that he can recommend to you, and stand back of."

This is a brilliant message in wartime or any time. Rarely do manufacturers offer such credit to their partners in the channels of distribution.

The show is notable for the appearance at the door of a woman whom neither McGee has ever seen. She wishes them a good summer, and is looking forward to hearing them again in the fall. Finally, they ask her who she is. It turns out she is none other than Myrt, the telephone operator always heard *of* but heard *from*. It was her only in-person visit in the show's long history.

During the show, McGee refers to "Uppy" as a "triple-chinned non-flying fortress." (The "flying fortress" was the nickname given to the World War II B-17 bomber.)

While buying camping equipment, McGee nearly succumbs to the salesperson's pitch for a moose call. Fibber doesn't need one but "there won't be any more available for the duration [of the war]." Molly nixes the idea even though they come in three messages, "plaintive, urgent, and imperative."

Harlow Wilcox stops by for a visit while on his way to a war plant, where he plans to give a short talk on nutrition. The McGees are dubious about his topic of choice until he explains that his message will be "the importance to war workers of maintaining their health by eating the right kind of body-building food, primarily butter and milk and cheese products. That's group *four* of the government's nutrition program." He explains that nutrition experts have divided foods into seven groups and "to keep in fighting trim," one needs a food from each group daily. He goes on to list the various nutrients found in milk and finishes with: "Vitamins for Victory! . . . There's a great day coming, so drink your Grade 'A' [milk] today."

(Once again, Johnson's commercial time is given up in favor of a war message.)

Mayor LaTrivia (now a member of the Coast Guard) shows up next. The interchange between the Mayor and the McGees is one of their classics. The mayor starts it by mentioning one of his petty officers. Molly is off and running. *Petty? — that's* not a nice way to talk about officers. The mayor begins what will be a futile effort to explain. He said nothing derogatory, he insists. "If an officer's rank . . ."

Molly interrupts: "If an officer is rank, you should keep quiet about it. Nobody's perfect."

The mayor tries again: "If a superior officer . . ."

McGee this time: "You've got an inferiority complex, LaTrivia."

When the mayor refers to "ordinary seamen," the McGees hone in: "American sailors aren't ordinary: They're the best seamen there are!"

I could go on, but you get the picture. The mayor finally escapes back to the Coast Guard, nearly in tears, before Fibber and Molly admit they were joking. His final words are the hope that next time they meet there will be "No Hitlers, no ruins, no terrors."

(In case you missed this, it translates to "No hits, no runs, no errors.")

Jim Jordan concludes this exceptional broadcast with a "thank you" to the listeners and acknowledgment of the commitment by the Johnson Company to devote substantial air time in support of the war effort.

SEPTEMBER 28, 1943
"MOVIE MIX-UP"

This is the first show of the new season and serves the purpose of setting up the following week's broadcast. The McGees have noticed that their next-door neighbors have taken in a roomer. Fibber says the roomer is a procrastinator at a burlesque house: "She puts things off!" Molly notes that since *they* have an extra room, maybe they could rent it to some war worker: "Rooms are awful scarce," she reasons.

Fibber doesn't like the idea: his moose head is in that room!

During this show, Coast Guardsman LaTrivia has a chance for a message. He's in town to arrange for a weekly recruiting talk at the local movie theater. The topic: The Coast Guard needs more women.

McGee can't resist: "That's a kind of chronic complaint with sailors, ain't it?"

Undeterred, LaTrivia continues: The "Spars" (the Coast Guard equivalent of the WAVES and WACs) are recruiting, and a message that will become familiar is that "every woman recruited relieves a man for front line duty." McGee hopes they don't wear much jewelry because they'd be "Spars that jingle, jangle, jingle." (This is a pun on the then-popular song title, "I've Got Spurs that Jingle, Jangle, Jingle.")

Molly's good sense and patriotism ultimately prevail. The McGees will indeed get a roomer next week. (*Please see Theme section.*)

NOVEMBER 23, 1943
"BOOK ON ETIQUETTE"

Fibber is going through a stack of old books and one of them, he says, is about the mills business in the Solomon Island: "Guadalcanal Dairy." Molly corrects him by reminding him of the best-seller, *Guadalcanal Diary*. The book that becomes the skeleton on which this program is hung is on an 1877 book on etiquette. True to form, Fibber imposes his new views on etiquette on each subsequent guest.

Very little is said concerning the war. Doc Gamble refers to the wartime shortage of physicians, but that is all.

JANUARY 18, 1944
"FLOWERS FOR MOLLY"

Molly receives flowers from someone named "Ralph." McGee is jealous; Molly is charmed. In the end, it is determined that the flowers were a promotion of a local florist. Many women in town received them.

This episode is remarkable for one reason. The boy who delivers the flowers has a remarkable speech pattern.

"Who is dis da residence of?" the boy asks the lady of the house.

Molly wants to know who the package is from. The boy is suitably diligent in his confidential duties. "Dat, Lady, will forever remain a mystery with me, as I am only an individual which has been entrusted by the parcel delivery company to lay this precious 'boiden' in your pale white hands."

Fibber, naturally, doesn't like his attitude, but the boy doesn't care. "Inasmuch as I am 'soever' being inducted into the Armed Forces, you may button your kisser."

Fibber's remark, after the boy leaves, that "If it wasn't that I didn't want to maim a future second lieutenant, I would have parted his nose with a knuckle," generated protests from many in the military. This was one of two such *faux pas* uttered during the war. Years later, Jim Jordan observed wryly that every second lieutenant in the Army must have been listening. The other event involved Doc

Gamble's remark that as an Army surgeon he learned to stand "with my chest out, my stomach in and my mind closed." Yoder (RMYp.23) wrote that: "Those few officers who would be stuffy enough to complain all happened to be listening and protested."

FEBRUARY 25, 1944
"A NIGHT ON THE TOWN"

The McGees have decided to celebrate, for no particular reason, by having a party. But no one can join them because of other engagements. So, they decide to go out for dinner and dancing. Where to go? One option is the General Eisenhower Allied Victory Club. (The name had recently been changed from The Old Heidelberg Student Prince Beer Garden.)

This is the first appearance of Marlin Hurt as Beulah. He/she gets off to a good start with a pun. Her third husband died of "Gladstones."

"Don't you mean *gallstones*?" Molly asks.

"No, ma'am. He was a porter on the railroad and some luggage fell on him."

(For those of you who did not understand this joke, Beulah was referring to Gladstone bags.)

Finding a place to eat and dance is difficult. At one of these establishments, Alice Darling says the owner has had so many band members go into the Army that all he can get is old men. The place is expensive, but Fibber says they can afford it.

Molly demurs: "We can't lick War Stamps with our tongue in our cheeks."

The McGees ultimately spend a romantic evening at home.

FEBRUARY 1, 1944
"DIAMOND RING FOR TWENTY DOLLARS"

According to Harlow Wilcox, "Fibber is filled with the spirit that will win the war . . . the Spirit of 1875. Yes, he's going downtown to buy a bond for $18.75. Molly is telling a neighbor about it on the phone . . ."

"Oh, of course we've been buying bonds on a regular schedule, too, Mrs. Toops," Molly says, "but McGee suddenly got twenty dollars for selling an old camera and he was going to use it to make a down payment on a new gold-mounted Elks tooth, but I talked him into buying an extra War Bond."

FEBRUARY 8, 1944
"MAKING ICE CREAM"

Harlow Wilcox leads off: "It was very natural that *your* experience with Johnson's waxes should lead directly to war use of special wax finishes. I won't try to tell you what they all are but they include many surfaces such as wood, metal, rubber, and leather. And here again, the wax is used for protection of vital materials. You might be interested to know that even paints were developed that actually contain wax, called Johnson's Wax Fortified Paint®. During the war, these have been greatly restricted, but they will again be available for industry and institutions after the war. It's partly *your* use of Johnson's wax for floors, furniture, and woodwork that has led to this increased usefulness of Wax in War."

We learn that Teeny's brother is in the Marines and Teeny also has written a poem.

> There was an old lady, who lived in a shoe,
> With the housing situation, she was very lucky, too,
> So you can just imagine how her blood ran cold,
> When she heard some nasty gossip that the place was half-
> soled [sold].

On this show, the final NBC chimes were replaced by a vocalist singing, "Buy War Bonds."

FEBRUARY 29, 1944
"AROUND THE CAMPFIRE"

Harlow Wilcox delivers this war message: "Every now and then we all have to be reminded that this war is certainly not over and that we have to continually be reminded to fight waste and conserve our resources, and take better care of the things we have. This applies to food, fuel, electric power, to fats, paper, metal, and rubber. And it still applies to our household goods."

APRIL 25, 1944
"MCGEES GOING TO OREGON?"

This show opens on an encounter with a new mailman with a very strange way of speaking. (I am forced to try to capture it phonetically, but as with so many things on the McGee program, one *really* has to hear it to appreciate it).

McGEE: Haven't we met before somewhere, Bud?

MAILMAN: Cerny, I used to jerk sodas at Kremer's Drug Store —'member?

As it turns out, McGee *does* "remember," and wants to know why he left Kremer's?

MAILMAN: Well, Washington don't consider jerking sodas an essential insry [industry]. Delivering mail *is* an essential insry. So forthwith and without more ado, I am now a mailman in an essential insry.

After the War, he will "prolly" go back to Kremer's.

One quick war-related line regarding telephone operator Myrt's penchant for gossip is delivered by Molly: "That girl spills more beans than a Navy cook in a hurricane."

Harlow Wilcox spends the Johnson Company's middle commercial minutes talking about V-mail: "When you write to any boy or girl in the service, use V-mail, because V-mail delivery is guaranteed. It saves precious cargo space and it's the only kind of personal mail that's always sent overseas by air."

Fibber asks Wilcox the obvious: "What's V-mail got to do with Johnson's Wax®?"

Harlow has an answer ready: "Believe me, if you were a soldier in Australia and you got a letter inside of seven days, you'd really appreciate it. That's what V-mail does. It *moves*. It literally *flies*. So when you write to your friends and relatives in the service, get some V-mail stationery at your druggist, stationer, or dime store. Address it correctly and completely and you're guaranteed fast, safe delivery."

Then comes the wax tie-in: "Like Johnson's self-polishing Glo-Coat®, spelled g-l-o-c-o-a-t, every letter counts. And you make *your* letters count, too, when you use V-mail."

(A mighty small commercial tied to an important wartime message!)

There is something of a curiosity in this episode. When Doc Gamble hears that Fibber is worried about taxes, he snorts, "What taxes has he got to worry about? He makes just enough to keep his head above water." Inasmuch as there is no evidence anywhere in the history of the show that Fibber has any kind of paying job, this comment left me wondering.

This show's premise was an invitation, the McGees believed, to come to Oregon to look after a cousin's string of canneries. Doc Gamble, reading the letter of invitation, pronounced it canaries, which indeed it was. Oh, well.

MAY 30, 1944
"GETTING A FISHING LICENSE"

Harlow Wilcox starts off with a newspaper headline: "Boxes dropped overboard carry fighter supplies — It told how overseas shipments of vital supplies for planes tanks and jeeps are protected with wax so that they can be thrown overboard and carried in by wind and tide to waiting United States detachments in far places. Each spare part is first wrapped in waxed cloth or wax paper. This is then dipped in molten wax and parked with other wax-dipped packages into wooden boxes lines with more water-proof material. Such a package can actually be thrown into salt water with its contents — spare parts, surgical instruments, food — safe against corrosion or spoiling. And that's just one of many interesting uses that have been found for wax."

Wilcox concludes by thanking the U.S. housewives whose uses of wax inspired these wartime applications.

The McGees are talking about fishing today. Or at least Fibber is, especially about his annual unsuccessful quest for "Old Muley," a bass at Dugan's Lake. The term "fish story" takes on new dimensions with Fibber in charge, but first he needs to renew his fishing license, a simple task for most people, but McGee can find a way to complicate it. He's going to use his "influence" to keep from standing in line at City Hall. After a couple of hours trying to locate the guy on whom Fibber plans to use his influence, they find him — standing in line to buy a fishing license.

JUNE 13, 1944
"HANGING THE PORCH SWING"

Fibber is planning to put up the porch spring, but first he has to find the necessary tools. Most of them are borrowed, and many of them have no function in porch swing application.

After McGee has a brief, losing verbal joust with Teeny, Alice drops by. She was out the previous night with a boy she describes as a "Marine Merchant."

"Don't you mean *Merchant Marine?*" Molly inquires.

No, she didn't: "Creepers, what a salesman!"

Every visitor finds one of his or her tools among Fibber's assortment.

The final musical selection by the Kings, "She Broke My Heart in Three Places," is a reasonably clever play on words, the "places" being cities. I mention it only because one of the places mentioned in a list of ten is "Racine, Wisconsin, courtesy of S.C. Johnson."

In the episode's wrap-up while the McGees are enjoying the swing (yes, he actually managed to hang it), Molly hears a train whistle and is reminded of "all the boys that are over there . . . McGee, did you remember to write a check for that extra War Bond tomorrow?"

"All wrote out and on the hall table with my hat," he assures her. "Wish I could get a bigger one, but I'm straining the budget as it is."

"Oh, bother the budget," Molly says. "We'd better come out short at the end of the month then at the end of the war."

June 20, 1944
"Molly Tries to Cure Fibber of Fibbing"

The McGees have plans to spend the summer on a ranch. They spend most of the program using phony western accents. Molly also spends the program kicking McGee in the shins every time he stretches the truth.

The first encounter on the show is with Alice Darling. She is about to decline an offer of a date. Her reason is a marvel of sentence structure: "I don't think a girl should date a man to curry favor with him just because he's her foreman at the airplane plant. Should I?"

When Teeny shows up, she delivers an inside joke when she asks why *Mrs.* McGee is never in the room when she comes in. (Of course, any listener knows that Marian Jordan was playing both parts.)

Nothing else about the war was heard in this episode, but in this case it probably wasn't missed. The listeners were *in* the war. My recording of this program was recorded from the Armed Forces Radio Service. There were no commercials.

OCTOBER 24, 1944
"FOUR-DOLLAR DEBT"

A small classic is found at the opening of the show when Fibber is raving about an imagined mistake on his bank statement. McGee says his balance is $114. Molly says that's nothing to sneeze at, "unless you get caught in an overdraft."

A stranger turns up at the door to repay four dollars Fibber loaned him while on a bus trip six years before, and Alice comes down to check her calls. An inside joke is delivered when the names of her callers, Messrs. Needham, Brorby, and Louis are the same names on the S.C. Johnson advertising agency. Alice is explained to the stranger as a worker in an airplane factory: "She's a welder. Used to be a riveter, but she was too light. Gave her the hiccups."

Fibber adds that most of her boyfriends are servicemen.

Harlow Wilcox drops by but doesn't get to deliver a real commercial because the "guest" does all the talking. After dinner, which she describes as serving up a "middle-aged spread," Beulah reminds the McGees that she will take off Friday for Navy Day. Her brother will be in town on furlough. Beulah's brother is "a mighty fine boy. He got a medal for saving three sailors living at Pearl Harbor."

When Fibber says, "That's wonderful," Beulah responds, "the whole Navy is wonderful, Mr. McGee. They really in there pitchin' and it sho' burns my brother up when folks talk about celebratin' the end of the war when Germany give up. He say it like burnin' the goalpost at the end of the first half. He say we still got a long-time war on our hands, lickin' them Jappies, and anybody that quits fightin' or workin' now is just no-account trash." Beulah is proud of *all* the sailors: "Every time I walks down the street and I see a boy in that little ole blue uniform. I say to myself, I say, '*Love that man.*'" (This is the exit line usually reserved for use after talking to Fibber.)

In spite of Beulah's "Amos 'n' Andy" dialect, the point that braving and patriotism are not the sole property of white folks comes across loud and clear.

At the end of the broadcast, Fibber reveals that he bought more than a hundred dollars' worth of stock from his "honest" new friend *and* Fibber had never *been* on a bus between Boston and Albany. Fortunately, the gullible Fibber was also forgetful.

He forgot to sign the check for the stocks.

October 31, 1944
"Duck Hunting"

McGee is going duck hunting with Doc Gamble. Molly thought shotgun shells were "frozen" (i.e. the government would not allow sales), but Fibber managed to find some.

Alice Darling drops in and is invited to go along on the hunt. She begs off, saying that this is her night to write letters to the servicemen. The girls at the airplane plant have formed a club to write letters to "all the soldiers, sailors, and marines we know. We call it the 'Gee, I hope he'll answer it club.' Alice tells the boys about local goings-on, including what's playing at the movies. This is a poor excuse to note that *Heavenly Days* is playing at the Bijou. She pretends not to know that the McGees were the stars of the movie.

Fibber thinks the club is a good idea: "The only thing a soldier likes better than mail is female," he says.

Alice responds with the club motto: "Write to a serviceman. One little letter can change his cares to a caress."

The show continues in a "secret" swamp duck blind which turns out not to be so secret. When the ducks show up, a hundred guns start blasting.

The Jordans' service message at the end of the show is an encouragement to Canadians to participate in their Victory Bond drive. The message will be repeated virtually verbatim on May 1, 1945.

December 19, 1944
"Christmas Presents in the Hall Closet"

Although they don't know it yet, this will be the McGees' last Christmas during the war.

Fibber can't stand the suspense of waiting to find out what Molly has gotten him for Christmas. Most of the show is spent with Fibber "accidentally" opening most of the wrappings on most of the presents.

Alice Darling comes downstairs with a new hairstyle that is the rage in Paris. "It's called 'Hair [Herr] Hitler' because it's more trouble than it's worth," she explains. Alice has asked all of her many boyfriends not to buy her Christmas presents this year. They should put any spare money in War Bonds.

Fibber likes the idea: "Use the boy's dough to back up the doughboys," he says approvingly. Unfortunately, Alice's patriotism loses a bit of its shine when she admits that she expects the boys to give the War Bonds to her!

A conversation follows with Beulah about her "one and only" (or "few and far between") Ira. Ira has been an insurance man but may have to give that up because of a "greeting card" he just received. It was from the President of the United States and the first word was "Greetings." That's the way every draft notice began. Ira is shortsighted, she explains: "He can't identify his best friend at the other end of a taffy pull."

Not to worry, says Fibber: "He'll be alright as long as he can see well enough to pull a sergeant's leg."

Through a series of crafty maneuvers, McGee succeeds in identifying every one of his presents, just in time for Teeny and her little friends to arrive for their annual musical and vocal rendition of Clement Moore's "A Visit from St. Nicholas" ("Twas the Night Before Christmas"). It is a true delight!

Jim Jordan has a final message: "Ladies and gentlemen, two thousand years ago, a star shone over Bethlehem to light the way to peace and good will on earth. Tonight that star is reflected in the windows of millions of your homes." (Another reminder to the reader that flags with stars were hung in windows to indicate a person or persons in the military or fatal victims of the war.)

"So our Christmas wish to you," Marian says, "is that the men and women who have gone out to fulfill the promise of that symbol may soon return — mission accomplished."

Good night, all.

January 2, 1945
"Diamond Stick Pin"

It's the beginning of a new calendar year. Molly's Aunt Sarah has sent the McGees a present. This is a surprise to Fibber who regularly resents the fact that Aunt Sarah tends to keep her considerable wealth to herself. The "mail woman," (as McGee calls her), or "Bagette" (as McGee also calls her) arrives bearing the gift. She asks the recipient for some form of identification, using a ration book as an example. The package holds a ten-carrot diamond stick pin! Alice drops downstairs to borrow some V-mail stationery. The fact that the McGees are temporarily out of it allows Alice to make a small pitch for its use: "V-mail gets where it's going so much faster than ordinary mail."

Molly asks, "Why do they call it V-mail anyway?" (As if she doesn't know).

Alice believes that "it's because you can write voluminously and it gets to various villages all over the world with such 'wonderful velocity.'"

McGee admits that he likes to use V-mail because he feels like he's putting one over on the United States Post Office. A regular letter costs eight cents (!), but V-mail goes anywhere for *three* cents. "That way," Fibber says, "You can lick a stamp and stick out your tongue at the government at the same time."

Molly is quick to correct the impression that her husband doesn't like the government. (That would have been a very unusual event unless the subject was taxes.)

This week's surprise ending is the appraisal of the "diamond" by one of Harlow Wilcox's jeweler relatives. It's *glass*.

Jim Jordan ends the program with the following message: "Ladies and gentlemen, there are millions of servicemen overseas who are hungry for news, simple, gossipy news from home. Send them letters by V-mail. A lot of them and often."

"V-mail flies overseas," Marion adds; "it doesn't clog up the vital supply lines — but, most importantly, V-mail means faster and more frequent letters to our men and women overseas."

"Yes," concurs Jim; "a guy with his feet in the mud, dodging high explosives and gnawing on emergency rations shouldn't be bothered with sister's measles, late laundry, and family feuds."

Marian has the last word: "Write cheerfully. Write often. Write V-mail. *Right?*"

Good night, all.

JANUARY 9, 1945
"WILD MUSHROOMS"

Alice Darling tells the McGees that Sergeant Carling called. He is in the camouflage corps. McGee remembers when he used to stand out on the lawn disguised as a tree, until Fibber started to carve "Fibber Loves Molly" on his stomach. The sergeant is sending Alice a boomerang so they figure he's in Australia. Fibber gets in a quick jab when Alice can't remember the name of the birds that think they're alone when they stick their heads in the sand. McGee says they're called "isolationists" (a pejorative term used for those who opposed involvement in the war).

McGee has picked some wild mushrooms and everyone who hears about it believes he has picked *toadstools. N*obody wants to eat them, especially Doc Gamble, who *does* agree to stay for dinner just to be available when McGee eats the "mushrooms." Unbeknownst to the doctor, McGee had acquired some real mushrooms at the store — and ate them all himself, leading Doc Gamble to observe that "more people die from a fork in the mouth than a knife in the back."

JANUARY 16, 1945
"NO HOT WATER"

Fibber is in the barber chair when the episode opens. The barber, in an accent that is undeterminable as to origin, is telling him a story: "So I'm writing President Roosevelt a letter, see, and in it I'm saying to him 'Dear Mr. President: Look, kid, I got a great idea . . . the Army is needing plenty ladies for nursing, also we got t'owsands guys who are too small in the eyesight to draft or maybe they got seven toes on one feet or something. So I'm saying, Why not take the rejected and make them into guys for giving sick people the pills?" The barber admits there has been no response to his idea, but he's not upset; the president is probably just busy as *he* is.

Before McGee leaves, he asks the price of a shampoo. "Nick" (a great name for a barber, incidentally) quotes him the "ceiling" price of seventy-five cents. The ceiling price is posted on the wall because no one could read it on the ceiling. After threatening to report the barber to the O.P.A., McGee storms home to shampoo his own hair. (This should be easy, since he "worked himself into a lather on his way home!")

Back at home, there is no hot water. Alice and Beulah have emptied the heater. Just when McGee's about to get enough hot water for a proper shampoo, Doc Gamble drops in asking if he can take a quick shower — he'd been up all night. Fibber gives in and never *does* save the seventy-five cents he would have paid the barber.

April 10, 1945
"The Paperboy"

This episode deals with McGee's irritation with the paperboy. The newspaper, it seems, is routinely being delivered in such a way that it is impossible to find. McGee is especially irate on this day since he claims to have given the *Wistful Vista Gazette* a "scoop" the same morning.

The McGees encounter with Mrs. Carstairs results in a minor class warfare skirmish as she makes it clear that she doesn't wish to mingle with those not on the Social Register. Molly wants to know how "Carsty" is getting along with her old clothes. Just before she takes offense, Carsty realizes that Molly is referring to the collection for war victims.

It is clear that the war in Europe is over, and the writers are already anticipating the needs of the people who survived it.

At the *Gazette* office to complain about the missing paper, the McGees meet Doc Gamble. McGee offers that while at the paper, he would give them an editorial idea or two. The doctor is interested: "Let's go sit under the oaks, Dunbarton, and discuss your idea." (The Dunbarton Oaks Conference, in Washington D.C., drew up a preliminary draft for American participation in the United Nations.)

Fibber takes the opportunity to share his idea for permanent peace in the world: "Look, Germany starts all the wars. I'd take Germany and call it Switzerland, see? That's a peaceful name. And I'd take Switzerland and name it Germany. And the next time Germany wanted to start a war, she'd look around and see how small she was sittin' up there on top of the Alps and she'd change her mind."

Not surprisingly, the audience groaned.

After a program full of bluster, Fibber learns that he had failed to renew his subscription, and because of the war, a renewal would be considered a new subscription. And no new subscriptions were being accepted.

APRIL 17, 1945
"THE BANK STATEMENT AND TRAGIC NEWS"

Another tough wartime assignment for the stars and writers: Just five days before the broadcast, they learned of the unexpected death of President Roosevelt. The show deals with a bank statement which Fibber believes to be in error. The show was obviously not significantly altered, but the death of the leader of the country was soberly acknowledged at the end of the broadcast.

Harlow Wilcox continues to link a commercial with a wartime message: Johnson's Wax® "is a marvelous way to stop unnecessary traveling because with a home bright and sparkling you just hate to leave it." (This is, admittedly a rather weak link.)

At the conclusion of the broadcast, Jim Jordan says, "Ladies and gentlemen, the traditional sentiment of people from Missouri has always been 'Show me.'"

"So let us all show our new president, Mr. Harry Truman of Missouri, that he has our complete loyalty and support in the difficult task of winning this war and leading this nation to peace and security," Marian implores.

May 1, 1945
"Briefcase Bronson"

Before the show, this announcement was made: "The National Broadcasting Company reminds its listeners that regular programs will be interrupted for the broadcast of any new developments. Today, the Hamburg radio announced the death of Adolf Hitler. This report from the enemy has had no official confirmation from Allied sources. Should any developments occur on this or any other major story, you will be kept informed by NBC." This report came just two weeks after the McGees' broadcast wishing President Harry Truman well following the death of President Franklin Roosevelt.

The show opens in the post office where Fibber is looking at the "Wanted" posters. He claims that "hasn't seen so many hot mugs since the barber shop burned." (Remember when barbers prepared lather in a mug?)

McGee has studied the poster offering a reward for one "Briefcase Bronson." Fibber, of course, plans to claim that reward, especially when he learns that the criminal is at large in the vicinity of Wistful Vista.

Teeny drops by to borrow some salt to sprinkle on her Victory garden, where she's growing peanuts. Then Beulah swears "on a stack of ration books" that tonight's pot roast is tough.

At the broadcast's conclusion, there is another serious message from the Jordans. This time it is directed to Canadian listeners.

JIM: We want to wish you a complete and overwhelming success with your eighth Victory Loan Drive.

MARIAN: The citizens of the United States have a great admiration and respect not only for the fighting qualities but for the loyalty and determination of their Canadian neighbors.

JIM: We know that you'll guarantee the future security and economic welfare of yourselves and your returning servicemen by buying Canadian Victory Bonds to the utmost of your ability. Good luck.

Good night, all.

MAY 29, 1945
"NO-GO LAWN MOWER"

The lawn mower refuses to start but McGee is not dismayed: *he* can fix *any* engine! "It's nothing any red-blooded American boy couldn't do," he says for probably the hundredth time on these broadcasts.

A slight reference to the war is the note by Molly that "Geese don't need any priority for flying" when Mrs. Carstairs says her gardener accused her of being part goose because she went south every winter.

Less than a month has passed since V-E Day and without Hitler and his henchmen to talk about, reference to the war seems to be on the decline.

JUNE 5, 1945
"CLEANING THE HALL CLOSET"

Mrs. Carstairs is coming to tea and Molly wants to clean out the famous Hall Closet, just in case "Carsty" opens the closet door.

Although the connection of the following to the war is tenuous at best, I'll offer it anyway. Fibber is talking to Alice about some of his "almost-inventions." Silkworms, he points out, eat mulberry leaves and produce silk. Just think what they could produce if you fed them leaves from a rubber plant.

"*Jeepers*," says Alice; "*girdles!*"

Molly reminds Fibber they are out of sugar. Rationing must have been relaxed as McGee calls the grocer to send some over. Beulah appears long enough to deliver her standard exit line: "*Love that man!*"

Mrs. Carstairs *does* come to tea and, unfortunately, tries to leave later by the back door, releasing the contents of the Hall Closet put there by Fibber. No war-related messages appear to have been in the closet, however.

JUNE 19, 1945
"DEAL WITH MR. CARSTAIRS"

Fibber is waiting for a call from *Mister* Carstairs, the millionaire. He is working on some kind of deal which he won't reveal. He *will*, however, talk to Alice Darling about his plans to stabilize the U.S. currency: "The American dollar is worth different amounts in different places. I'd fix it so it would be worth a dollar fifteen all over the world. The fifteen cents would take care of taxes leaving everybody a buck clear."

Molly adds that her spouse also had a scheme to base U.S. currency on lead instead of gold.

That's right, Fibber says; "Every time the Government got in trouble, Washington would have to get the lead out!" (Judging by the response, his line was a real audience pleaser.)

When Carstairs calls Fibber, he wants to play hard to get. Molly says she'll tell him McGee went to London to see Churchill. He'll be back in fifteen minutes. They don't talk because Fibber pretends to be a busy signal.

Harlow Wilcox, as he has before, uses the middle Johnson's commercial time for a message about War Bonds. This he does under the guise of explaining a speech he is going to give to the Chamber of Commerce: "Victory in Europe is just a seventh inning stretch and we've got to get in there and pitch to get our men home from bases in the Pacific. I can emphasize the fact that every Bond they buy during this War Loan is a Japanese obituary and that it's no extravagance when our country has money to burn — Tokyo." Fibber wants to know if Harlow is "gonna say when you buy a War Bond, you're not doing anybody a favor but yourself."

Molly adds: "Or about how every extra bond you buy is another tape to hold down inflation."

Wilcox agrees: "It can't be said too often that War Bonds buy weapons and the best investment in the World right now is the common stock of an American rifle." (Don Quinn even works a play on words into this serious message, making it, I believe, even more effective).

When the McGee/Carstairs transaction finally transpires (in some rather contrived secrecy), it turns out that Fibber is buying a War Bond, which Carstairs describes as "the best investment in the World." Carstairs is chairman of the local bond committee. McGee then talks to himself (and the listeners): "What a deal. What a deal. A hundred bucks for seventy five and guaranteed, too! By the government. Smartest investment ever made. How about *you*, folks?"

At the end of this program, a citation from the Catholic War Veterans is read by their national chairman: "To the beloved Fibber McGee and Molly of America's millions in recognition of their successful efforts to lighten the burdens of American people in a time of great ordeal through understanding and clean comedy and in acknowledgment of their accomplishment portraying the American home through gentle humor in true dignity as a great source of national strength."

MUSIC OF THE WAR

Fibber McGee and Molly was a program with music at the beginning, during, and at the end. Billy Mills and his Orchestra, along with the vocal quartet, The King's Men, provided these interludes. By no means was all of the music patriotic in nature. That would have been overkill. But a good deal of it was.

1941

DECEMBER 9   (Pearl Harbor Day) — "My Country, 'Tis of Thee"

DECEMBER 16   "National Emblem March"

DECEMBER 21   "He's A-1 in the Army and He's A-1 in My Heart"

DECEMBER 30   "Of Thee I Sing"

1942

FEBRUARY 3   "The White Cliffs of Dover"

MARCH 3   "United States Field Military March"

MARCH 10   "Army Air Corps March"

MARCH 24   "The War Stamp Stomp"

MARCH 31   "Military Medley"

APRIL 7   "The Village Blacksmith" (turned into an
                        appeal to save scrap metal)

APRIL 14   "Keeping Our Big Mouth Shut"

MAY 12   "America is Calling"

JUNE 9   "The Bombardier Song"

JUNE 23   "The Blacksmith Song"

SEPTEMBER 29	"Praise the Lord and Pass the Ammunition"
OCTOBER 6	"This Is the Army" "It's Fun to be Free"
NOVEMBER 17	"This Is the Army, Mr. Jones"
DECEMBER 8	"New Sun in the Sky"

1943

JANUARY 5	"Hitch Old Dobbin to the Shay Again"
JANUARY 19	"Would You Rather be a Colonial with an Eagle on your Shoulder (or a Private with a Chicken on Your Knee)"
JANUARY 26	"Free for All"
FEBRUARY 2	"It's Fun to be Free"
FEBRUARY 23	"This is the Army, Mr. Jones"
MARCH 2	"Rosie the Riveter"
MARCH 16	"Ve Don't Like It"
MARCH 23	"Sky Anchors Away"
APRIL 20	"Song of the Merchant Marine"
MAY 18	"Coming In On a Wing and a Prayer"
MAY 25	"You'll Never Know"
JUNE 1	"Riding Herd on a Cloud"
OCTOBER 5	"Fun to Be Free" "Thank Your Lucky Stars"

NOVEMBER 2	"Riding Herd on a Cloud"
DECEMBER 7	"This is the Army, Mr. Jones" "American Patrol" "American Medley"

1944

MARCH 28	"You Can't Say No to a Soldier"
MAY 2	"Of Thee I Sing"
JUNE 6	(D-Day; the entire show consisted of musical numbers) "Song of the Merchant Marine" "U.S. Field Artillery March" "The Time is Now" "Semper Paratus" "This is the Army, Mr. Jones" "This is Worth Fighting For" "National Emblem March" "Song of the Bombardier" "American Patrol" "Armed Forces Medley" "Army Hymn"
NOVEMBER 14	"I'll Walk Alone"
NOVEMBER 28	"This Little Bond Went to War"

1945

MAY 22	"This Little Bond Went to War"
JUNE 19	"Buy a Bond"

AFTER THE WAR

References to the War did not end on V-J Day. Fibber, Molly, Wilcox, and the cast continued with both patriotic messages and war-related humor. I have included just a few examples.

Movie recommendation: *The Best Years of Our Lives* (1946), an excellent character study set in post-war America.

OCTOBER 10, 1945
"LATRIVIA RETURNS"

The McGee team did not discontinue their patriotic efforts when the war was over. In 1945, when Mayor LaTrivia (Gale Gordon) returned from the Coast Guard, he related that he had done his own laundry for three years. Molly confided that "Himself [Fibber], here, tried to get into the Air Force, but they required 20/20 vision." Fibber admitted that he "couldn't see a twenty-foot wall twenty feet away." (This was not the only time that Fibber joining the military for World War *II* was mentioned. There were frequent mentions of his service in the *First* World War, in which Jim Jordan *did* serve briefly).

The mayor had received a communication concerning the establishment of an interfaith chapel at the Coast Guard Academy in New London, Connecticut. The Coast Guard was founded in 1790 and still had, at the time of this broadcast, no chapel for religious worship. The McGees supported to build one. As Molly put it, "Any group that has been on their toes as long as the Coast Guard, deserves a decent place to get down on their knees." The mayor was about to respond when he was asked about seeing any action in the war, the discussion evolved into the usual encounter over the McGees' intentional misunderstanding of a phrase, in this case "Crow's Nest."

October 9, 1945
"Buying a Used Car"

The war is over and the McGees are hoping to celebrate by buying a car. Of course there are no *new* cars, so they are looking for a *used* automobile. Various guests offer advice. Teeny suggests buying a convertible with the top down: "No Ceiling." (This joke only worked because during the war there were "ceilings" on many prices).

When the McGees visit a used car lot they find a little green sedan that strikes their fancy. They also find Harlow Wilcox polishing cars — just because he enjoys using his product. He's even paying the owner to let *him* do the polishing.

As the merriment continues, the McGees become increasingly adamant about a green sedan. The salesman says it "lacks the necessary equipment for delivery," and is equally adamant about *not* selling the car.

Mayor LaTrivia (fresh from the Coast Guard) arrives just in time for one of the patented exchanges with the McGees. This time it is war related. Asked how it feels to be a civilian again, the mayor says, "If I ever set foot on a deck again, it will be because I walked through a pinochle game. And when I smell powder again, it will be on the swan-like neck of some lovely woman — some lovely *civilian* woman — on a dance floor which I have not scrubbed five times that day myself."

So far so good. But it can't last. LaTrivia says his rank was chief gunner's mate.

Molly wants to know: "Who was the gunner?"

"What gunner?" the mayor asks unsuspectingly.

"The gunner that you were the mate of," McGee asks:

"I was *not* the mate of a gunner," LaTrivia says with emphasis, "I, myself, was the gunner's mate."

"Yeah, but *what* gunner's mate?"

"*Any* gunner's mate."

"Now, that's a kind of a haphazard system. If a gunner can pick any mate he wants . . ."

"But he *can't!*"

"Yes, but you said . . ."

"Look, in the Navy, the word 'mate' means a subordinate officer, having no rank, but taking precedence over enlisted men."

"I thought you enlisted your*self*."

"I *did*."

"And if you were a mate, you took precedence over *yourself*."

As LaTrivia goes begins his frustrated bluster, Fibber observes that he sees why the mayor never rose to the rank of admiral: "You're too easy confused." The mayor then sets out to prove that he is not confused. His explanation: "I joined the Coast Guard as an apprentice seaman. Then I was made a first class seaman. Then I was promoted to gunner's mate third class."

"You skipped the first *two classes*?"

"I did *not* skip the first two classes. Second class and first class come *after* third class."

"Don't be silly, when *I* was in school . . ."

"This has nothing to do with school. A petty officer in the Navy . . ."

"*Aha*," McGee interrupts (the McGees have jumped on the term *petty* officer before). "Just because you're a little irritated LaTrivia, that don't give you the right to disparage the officers of our Navy. Some of them may be petty, but by George . . ."

This is the final straw. Before he finishes a full-fledged, tongue-twisted, verbal explosion, LaTrivia pauses and says, "Ah, it's *good* to be home again."

(These encounters between the McGees and the Mayor rank, I believe, right up there with the Abbott and Costello "Who's on First?" routine.)

The car salesman is intent on discouraging the McGees from buying the green sedan. Because it seems to be unavailable, they *really* want it. And they *buy* it for $300 and pay cash.

Then an important discovery is made: the car has no motor! It was the last car off the assembly line after Pearl Harbor.

There was a serious message from the Jordans at the episode's conclusion.

MARIAN: Ladies and gentlemen, the real test of patriotism comes after the bands have stopped playing and the guns have stopped shooting.

JIM: The guns have stopped shooting folks, but our guys are still in there pitching until they are returned to civilian life. It's to them we owe victory and it's to them we owe the recreational care and maintenance of morale until they *do* get home.

MARIAN: The agency which takes care of this is the National War Fund, and when you are called on to subscribe, give generously. We gave our boys a warm hand when they left. Let's not give them the cold shoulder now.

Good night, all.

OCTOBER 30, 1945
"MCGEE THE SCULPTOR"

Fibber has entered a sculpting contest. First prize is a hundred bucks and McGee could "use a hundred bucks like Hermann Göring could use a fast plane to Patagonia." He has borrowed a "smock" from a nearby garage so that he can be properly attired. Molly notices the wording on the back of the smock, which says, "Tires Quickly." She wonders if it is an advertisement or a character statement.

McGee says it *did* read, "Tires Quickly Repaired. It's an old pre-war smock."

This broadcast originated in the Toronto Maple Leaf Gardens where the McGees were helping in the Ninth Canadian Victory Loan Campaign.

NOVEMBER 13, 1945
"DRIVING LESSON"

Even though the war is over, the Jordans have a serious message for their listening audience:

JIM: Ladies and gentlemen, we have all been asked again to buy Victory Bonds. [Note the name change from *War* Bonds.] We don't know why anybody has to be asked.

MARIAN: Because investing three dollars to get four is really a favor to ourselves. Buying security for us and our families and preventing a ruinous inflation would seem to be simple common sense.

JIM: Of course, if you feel that the care of our wounded and the rehabilitation of our fighting men and protection of the families of those who lost their lives is important, *those* are pretty good reasons, too.

MARIAN: It might even be said that the U.S.A. holds *your* I.O.U.

DECEMBER 18, 1945
"WHITE CHRISTMAS TREE"

Fibber decides that *this* year he wants a *white* Christmas tree. One dealer offers to spray paint a green tree it for $10. McGee, though, thinks that is outrageous and doesn't know "whether to report him to the OPA or offer him half interest in the business." He decides, instead, to use a sprayer on his own.

Doc Gamble and McGee have a bit of an exchange about money. Fibber says the doctor has "more affection for a dollar than my wife has for a pound of butter [which was still being rationed at that time], and that's the love match of the year."

For Harlow Wilcox, who says he once played Shakespeare, Fibber offers: "When you play Shakespeare, that's when Othello needs a friend."

The program ends with the annual performance of a special arrangement of "Twas the Night Before Christmas," by Teeny and her little friends. Delightful, as always.

January 1, 1946

It is the first post-war New Year's Day, but the Jordans are still working hard on national interests. This was their wrap-up:

JIM: Ladies and gentlemen, when your country is at war, you naturally offer it your services, your money and, if necessary, your life. But when the War is over, it's every person's privilege; yes even duty, to think of himself again, his work, and his future.

MARIAN: The United States Merchant Marine which made such a wonderful record of work done and heroic missions accomplished offers a wonderful opportunity. It wants and needs experienced officers and men who have been to sea, men with certificates. If you're looking for a job with a great future, write or wire, Merchant Marines, Washington, D.C.

JIM: And if you've been on a well-earned holiday, we urge you to go back to your ship. You won't be the first one to go back on the water after a celebration.

(It's unusual for Jim Jordan to get the last clever line after one of these closing messages.)

Good night, all.

A FINAL WORD ON THE WORDS THAT WON THE WAR

If the reader is not convinced by now that the writers, cast, and sponsor of *Fibber McGee and Molly* were not only funny, clever and entertaining, but also fiercely patriotic, I would be terribly disappointed. It is my sincere desire to share my personal views on the magnificent job done by this team in a time of America's darkest hours. The ability to convey vital wartime information, to convince the public to share willingly (even enthusiastically) in some of the privations occasioned by rationing and shortages, to be a major part of a bond drive unequalled in the history of this or any country, and to do so in such an entertaining way that the public rated the show in the top five on radio throughout the war was nothing short of genius.

Certainly there are many examples of entertainers and their supporting the war effort — Bob Hope comes immediately to mind. But I believe, and hope the reader does too, that the efforts of the *Fibber McGee and Molly* team were unsurpassed.

EPILOGUE

THE WAR IS OVER

Studs Terkel called it *The Good War* in his best selling oral history. But isn't that an oxymoron? Can *any* war be "*good*"? When one considers the way in which America responded to the various military actions in which the country had been involved since the summer of 1945, one might say that World War II was "good" by comparison.

I have neither the inclination nor the ability to attempt any profound political or philosophical analysis concerning the "goodness" of World War II. I have, however, lived through the succeeding sixty-plus years and believe I am qualified to essay a few observations from the perspective of an interested citizen.

Korea was no fun. The term "police action" became one of derision. The people at *M*A*S*H* found plenty of humor in the conflict, but the government and the military "brass" took it on the chin plenty of times. There *was* respect for the heroic efforts of our military, but there was certainly uncertainty about what America was doing there.

And we should not forget the "Cold War."

In the late 1940s, Archibald MacLeish, is quoted by Terkel (ST, p.13): "Never in the history of the world was one people as completely dominated, intellectually, and morally, by another as the people of the United States by the people of Russia in the four years from 1946 through 1949." MacLeish went on to cite several examples, but his conclusion was especially compelling: "All this . . . took place not in a time of national weakness or decay but precisely at the moment when the United States, having experienced a tremendous triumph and fought its way to a brilliant victory in the greatest of all wars, had reached the highest point of world power ever achieved by a single state."

This, after all of their effort, must have driven the McGee team to near distraction.

There is nothing I could possibly add to an understanding of the Vietnam "conflict" except to note that American soldiers, sailors, and marines did not enjoy the overwhelming support of the general public as was the case in World War II. Such support certainly by the majority has been shown for the military serving in Iraq and Afghanistan.

Television's comedic treatment of World War II has been represented by such 1960s situation comedies as *McHale's Navy* and *Hogan's Heroes*.

On December 23, 1952, Harlow Wilcox's announcement that aluminum is going to "the defense of the nation" is the first time the Korean War is even hinted at on the program (Schulz, p.233). In the June 23, 1953, the episode "with its emphasis on cold war paranoia," was another evident reference to War issues. (Schulz, p.243)

So what about War II? Terkel's collected oral histories help us understand: "It was not like your other wars," a radio disc jockey reflected aloud. In his banality lay a wild kind of crazy truth. It was not fratricidal. It was not, most of us profoundly believed, imperialistic. Our enemy was, patently, obscene . . . It was one war that many who would have resented (your other war), supported enthusiastically. It was a "just war," if there is any such animal. In a time of nuclear weaponry [This was written in 1984], it is the language of a lunatic. But in World War Two?" (ST, p. 15). Terkel then quoted a WWII Red Cross worker, "It's a war I would still go to." (ST, p.16)

Terkel goes on, almost wistfully, "It appears that the disremembrancy of World War II is as disturbingly profound as the forgettery of the Great Depression: World War II, an event that changed the psyche as well as the face of the United States and of the World!" (ST, p.3)

FIBBER McGEE AND MOLLY ON THE AIR POST-WAR

As noted elsewhere in this book, Tom Price, in his encyclopedic work, *Fibber McGee's Closet*, has provided just about any statistic on Fibber, Molly, and the Jordans that anyone would want. And just in case you do want more, get a copy of Clair Schulz's *Fibber McGee and Molly On The Air, 1935 – 1959*.
Here are just a few statistics:

- The Hall Closet gag was used 39 times during the war alone.

- Harlow Wilcox appeared as the entertaining pitch-man 2,218 times from 1935 to 1953.

- Bill Thompson appeared on 1,555 shows, often in two or three roles.

- The inveterate Gale Gordon, in spite of a stint in the Coast Guard, appeared 348 times and, of course, had a great television and movie career.

- Arthur Q. Bryan (Doc Gamble) appeared 813 times.

From August, 1954 until March, 1956, Fibber and Molly appeared in fifteen-minute episodes. During this run of the program, most episodes featured public service announcements (PSA's) as well as commercial sponsors. Among the topics of the PSA's were: the Red Cross, CARE, Savings Bonds, hiring disabled veterans, National Guard, mail for the military, and many others.

There was no longer a live audience or any live music. Only Bill Thompson and Arthur Q. Bryan remained from the thirty-minute shows. There were various sponsors. Phil Leslie continued to write. Harlow Wilcox survived sponsor changes (Johnson's Wax® to Pet Milk to Reynolds Aluminum) and remained with Fibber and Molly until the end of the 30-minute series in 1953. John Wald replaced him, but did not become a character in the cast. For a couple of additional years, the McGees did short bits on the NBC *Monitor* series. Only the two of them appeared.

According to Price, and I certainly won't dispute him, this wonderful pair of entertainers brought their warmth and comedy to the public 11,000 times!

HOW WELL DID THE SHOW WORK?

There are various outcome measures for a radio program. Probably the most obvious is the ratings. No matter how compelling the patriotic or commercial message, it is of little value if no one is listening. People were listening to the people in Wistful Vista. Schulz (CS2 p.365) has provided ratings for the *Fibber McGee and Molly* show for the period covered in this book. The "Hooper" ratings were as follows:

1938 – 39	TIED FOR 14TH
1939 – 40	3RD
1940 – 41	4TH
1941 – 42	2ND
1943 – 44	1ST
1944 – 45	2ND
1945 – 46	1ST
1946 – 47	TIED FOR 1ST

Clearly, the show was providing something the America public needed and wanted. Sales figures of Johnson products during this period would be misleading because of wartime supply issues; however, given the company's status today as a very profitable firm with billions of dollars in sales around the world, it seems obvious that the fifteen-year association between the Jordans and the Johnsons was a success for all concerned.

The advertising agency fared quite well, too. Needham, Louis and Brorby (NLB) went through several mergers and acquisitions — a standard practice with advertising agencies. In 1986 Doyle Dane Bernbach merged with Needham-Harper World Wide and created a widely known and successful agency. Melvin Brorby, one of the founders of NLB, established a college scholarship endowment and several on the Board of the Johnson Foundation for many years. In 2002 the agency's name was listed as Doyle, Dane and Bernbach.

In the context of this book, the most important measure of success is the response of the American people.

Two charismatic industrialists, Henry J. Kaiser and Howard Hughes, became celebrities based on their fantastic production records building war weapons (by 1944 a new escort aircraft carrier every week). They deserve great credit for their genius and dedication, but as Manchester has pointed out, the production miracle was accomplished "by thousands of hard-driving executives and millions of workers, some skilled veterans and some young women (like Alice Darling), fresh from the kitchen or the bargain counter. American resources and American freedom had united them in a joint effort that Nipponese emperor worship, Mussolini's rhetoric, and Albert Speer's productive genius could not match." (WM. 361)

Fibber and Molly never stopped in their encouragement of production workers. Neither did Harlow Wilcox and Johnson's Wax®. Alice Darling was the near-perfect role model. All of this paid off.

By 1943 a third of American's vegetables were coming from twenty-million victory gardens.

- Middle aged men painted World War I helmets white and joined Civil Defense.

- Women and children collected scrap rubber, wastepaper, aluminum, tin cans, and toothpaste tubes.

- Housewives salvaged cooking grease and rolled two-and-a-half billion Red Cross bandages.

- One man even contributed the rubber mat that supported his favorite spittoon (WM, p. 370)

Something was definitely working! Most dramatic was the success of drives to sell, first Defense, then War, then Victory Bonds. As noted in the previous chapter, some 84 million children and adults purchased $185.7 billion worth of Bonds and Stamps. Jim and Marian Jordan were relentless campaigners for Bond sales, both on the show and in personal appearances. Their success was nothing short of extraordinary.

WHY DID IT WORK?

Would I have wanted Fibber McGee for my next-door neighbor during the war (or any time for that matter)? Probably not! Molly would have been okay. She was level-headed, responsible, and an all-around good person.

But the McGees would have been *interesting* neighbors — down the block! I would have had to keep an eye on my tools, but my wife and I would probably have dropped in at 79 Wistful Vista (we would have lived at 71) every Tuesday night along with the mayor, the doctor, the Old-Timer, Teeny, the Rich Lady *Du Jour*, and, of course, Harlow Wilcox. We could hardly wait to see what Fibber would be up to this week. I know we'd be welcome. Harlow Wilcox told us that at the end of each and every program.

The fact is, I *believe* the foregoing. I have listened to scores of programs (some of them repeatedly). I should know better, but I am *still* — every time — drawn into the episode as though it were *real*. I *know* it isn't. But even though one of the characters (Wilcox) delivers a commercial in the middle of the visit, and even though Billy Mills and the King's Men play and sing at the beginning, the middle, and the end. And even though the ad-libs and references to the McGee's abortive movie career, and frequent mention of their sponsor in Racine, Wisconsin, and a host of other clues to the fact that this is *not* the real world, I *still,* at age seventy-plus, can believe it *is.* Is it any wonder that the listener did? In fact, it *was* real.

Jim and Marian Jordan didn't really try to make you believe that their life was real in Wistful Vista. The fact, again, was that you *wanted* to believe it. You can't help but feel warm, comfortable, and amused. And, as a consequence, you can't *help* but listen when they tell you to buy bonds, conserve gas, support the military . . . they are your friends and neighbors. Why *not* join them in the causes about which they are so earnest? Indeed those causes seem even more compelling because the often incalcitrant Fibber has to be, but always is, convinced that what was right, *was* right.

Manchester (WM, p. 358) highlighted some of the inconsistencies associated with rationing.

- The week that cigarettes came back, every store in America was out of matches.

- When motorists who couldn't buy tires decided to resort to bicycles they might find that bicycle rationing had begun the day before.

- Why on earth did the war require restrictions on the purchase of paper, girdles, tea, diapers, bronze caskets, electric toasters, hair curlers, wigs, kitchen utensils, lawnmowers, waffle irons, egg beaters, tin soldiers, electric trains, asparagus tongs, beer, mugs, spittoons, bird cages, cameras, cocktail shakers, corn poppers, exotic leather goods, and lobster forks?

Fibber McGee and Molly never ridiculed rationing. (Well, Fibber did occasionally when it inconvenienced *him.*) Rather, they made it clear that they were living with the restrictions, more or less cheerfully. Criticism was reserved for citizens who *did* complain or try to circumvent the rules, especially via the Black Market.

The Live Audience

There is simply no comparison between a live audience and a laugh track — or nothing at all. Certainly, a laugh track tells you when you are *supposed* to laugh, but a *live* audience tells you when they, at least, don't think something's funny! The live audience was a *major* contributor to the success of this program. And, although I have no evidence of this, I suspect it was a guide to the writers and to the Jordans.

The Commercials

The Johnson commercials were, generally speaking, a remarkable contrast to some of the more egregious Madison Avenue efforts of other companies. Some examples:

- Headline: "The Great Gift to the Mothers of Men." The gift was sulfa drugs, but the advertiser was the company which produced the air conditioners who kept the scientists cool who discovered sulfa.

- A competing air-conditioner manufacturer claimed part credit for torpedoing a Japanese freighter because the periscope used by the submarine had been prepared in an air-conditioned workshop.

- Alarm clocks kept generals on time.

- A manufacturer of metal fasteners, with an illustration of a soldier in a hammock, used the pitch, "His cradle won't drop because it's furnished with clamps 30 per cent stronger than specified."

- Wartime production could be increased and everyone chewed a few sticks of Wrigley's® gum daily.

- A spectacle manufacturer tastelessly warned parents that they would need the right kind of glasses to recognize their returning sons.

- Maybe the best was the ad by an aircraft manufacturer which asked in its headline, "Who's afraid of the big Fokker-Wolf?" This one evoked a letter signed by every airman and the commanding officer at an air force base. The letter contained two words: "We are!" (WM. Pp. 347-348)

MARKET RESEARCH

Sometime in the early course of the war, William Connolly, advertising manager at S.C. Johnson and Son, decided to elicit opinions about the show from the radio audience. The company had been receiving a large volume of fan mail but, according to Connolly, "most of the letters were too complimentary to be helpful in molding the program." He wanted specific information on any weaknesses as well as those elements which contributed most to the show's popularity.

A jury of 500 women was used. Not a scientific sample, they were former winners of Electric Floor polishers in a Johnson-sponsored contest. The company had used them as "consultants" on new Johnson products. Now they were asked about the radio program. The recruitment letter asked the panelists to "be perfectly frank . . . if there are things about our show which you don't like, we want to hear them. Tell us the things you like best, and the things you like least. Then we'll do our best to make *Fibber McGee and Molly* the favorite program of the average American family."

The response averaged 100 per week as the panel was expanded beyond the original 500. The total number of responses ultimately totaled several thousand. Connolly asserted that the comments "played a definite role in the evolution of the program," but no *radical* changes resulted.

Probably the best comment on the role of the Johnson Company as "the perfect sponsor" can be found in a letter I received from

Kelly M. Semrau, Vice President of Global Public Affairs and Communication, S.C. Johnson and Son, Inc. It states: "Given the commitment to the war effort within our company, it is no surprise that we would have expected the same from the radio programs we sponsored during this time."

THE JORDANS

Jim and Marian Jordan, in their real-life personae, must be included as a major reason for success. They received excellent press coverage by doing good things. One example was their "adoption" of pilots-in-training at Lemoore Field in California. They ate with the men, served in the kitchen, and generally spread good will (ANON.5)

ALWAYS LEAVE 'EM LAUGHING

That was the motto of comedians. In preparing this book, my primary focus was on war-related messages. I tried to show how these messages could be delivered without losing the show's humor. Sometimes the message itself was humorous (Hitler tended to be the butt of jokes). Sometimes the message was delivered in the context of a humorous situation, and sometimes, especially at the end of a program, the message was strictly serious.

I am concerned now that readers unfamiliar with *Fibber McGee and Molly* may miss some of the comedic genius that made the show so popular. In the "Leave 'Em Laughing" spirit, I have decided to provide examples of several of the trademark humor *sans* wartime references.

AD-LIBS AND LAUGHTER

One facet of the program that made it so successful was the fact that all involved, but especially the Jordans, were enjoying themselves and never took themselves too seriously. Live broadcasts, which might have been daunting to some performers, were turned into opportunities for spontaneous ad-libs. Jim Jordan (as Fibber) did most of these, usually when the studio audience didn't respond as expected to a funny line. In contrast to the canned laugh tracks, which provide laughter on demand, a live audience offered instant feedback to the performers (and the writers). They took it with grace and style.

Marian, especially, laughed a lot . . . not necessarily at the planned jokes, but more often at missed cues, flubbed lines, *and* jokes that didn't work. The message was clear: "We're having fun here; why not join us?" And we *did*.

PUNS

Puns abounded in the McGees' programs. They demonstrated, if any demonstration was needed, the love that the writers had for words, their curious spellings and phonetics. Many examples could be given but when Fibber tries to hang a porch swing they offer a bouquet of puns. (June 13, 1944).

It starts with Fibber complaining about the quality of his hacksaw blades: He "could get more iron out of a can of spinach!" When Wellington drops by, he refuses to help because the last time he lent a hand, he gave Fibber his all. "In fact that is my awl!" he says indignantly. "I've been looking all over for it. . . It isn't a pleasant thing at my age to feel that one has lost his punch!" He leaves, saying that he is "looking forward to seeing Molly next . . ."

"*Week?*" she finishes.

"Yes," Wellington says wearily, "but the thought of it gives me strength."

After a typical start with Teeny she wants to know how he knew she had a porch swing. "I was walking by one night and it squealed," she replied.

When Alice wants her pliers back, Molly says, "Sure, McGee can always borrow them back in a *pinch*."

Well, you get the idea.

SIMILES

As with their puns, the writers were enamored with similes. Frankly, there are far too many to chronicle, but here are a few.

- "As much personality as an onion sandwich."

- "Getting under my skin like chiggers at a picnic."

- "Head for third base like a second base runner on a short stop's fumble."

- "As reliable as a Japanese newspaper."

Over the course of the programs there were hundreds, maybe thousands, of funny, original, pieces of such imaginative comparisons served up for our consumption.

WORD MEANINGS

Another regular feature was confusion between Fibber and Molly about word meanings. When McGee was trying to hang the porch swing (June 13, 1944), he was reminded of the time when Fred Nitney, his old vaudeville partner, came to town and the two of them sat in the swing and *remorse* about their adventures.

Molly corrects him: "You mean reminisce."

"Nope," McGee insists. "Don't mean any such thing. *Reminisce* is when you forget to do something. Like I was reminisce [in] paying the gas bill this month."

"No, that's *remiss*," Molly says, correcting him.

Fibber just laughs and says, "*Remiss* is when you take two shots at something and don't hit it either time. You're thinking of remit."

"No, no, Pet, *remit* means to pay, and you didn't."

"Then what does *remorse* mean?" asks Fibber.

"Remorse means you're sorry for something," explains Molly.

"And I am, too. I'm sorry old Fred Nitney can't drop in again one of these days and we can remorse about our adventures."

Most of these encounters ended with Mcgee being somehow, illogically correct.

EXAGGERATIONS

Quinn and Leslie must have written a million exaggerations into the show. Well, maybe that's an exaggeration. But they used them often, frequently as part of an insult. Here is one of my personal favorites. It involves Mayor LaTrivia is commenting on McGee's potential earnings as a musician: "You couldn't pick up a split Peruvian penny playing 'The 1812 Overture' while juggling three deepsea turtles blindfolded on a unicycle balancing a wheelbarrow full of pig iron on your nose and surrounded by fifty beautiful girls wearing bikini bathing suits and waving the American Flag."

TONGUE TWISTERS

Fibber frequently demonstrated his enunciation skills with a tongue twister. These were set up by a situation from which he emerged with a new nickname. Here is one, not heard on radio, but presented in *The American Legion Magazine* in an article with the byline of "Fibber McGee"; it is entitled, "The Big War and Me."

I was THE air raid warden, as a matter of fact. They laid the whole town of Wistful Vista out in squares, and made me the head of our square . . . Yes sir, Squarehead Mcgee, I was knows as around town! SQUAREHEAD McGEE, THE MOST SENSA-TIONAL SUPERVISOR OF CIVILIAN SAFETY WHO EVER SHOT OUT A STREETLIGHT WHEN THE SIREN SOUNDED, SCARING THE SOCKS OFF OF SEVERAL SILLY CITIZENS! SETTING UP A SYSTEM FOR SWITCHING OFF SIGNBOARDS AND SHOUTING SARCASTIC SAYINGS AT SKEPTICS WHOSE SHACKS SHOWED A SHINE THROUGH

SECOND STORY SHUTTERS! SLINGIN' SHOVELS OF SAND ON CIGARETTE SPARKS, AND — but that's all over now, and there's just one thing I'd like to point out — one thing I'm pretty proud of. The whole time I was in charge of the air raid warning system in our district, not a single enemy plane ever got through us! (FM)

THE MCGEES VERSUS MAYOR LATRIVIA

Virtually every time the mayor drops by 79 Wistful Vista, the McGees purposely misunderstand one of his comments, leading him on and on until he is nearly apoplectic. Eventually, he pauses, quietly says, "*McGee,*" and leaves on a note of subdued exasperation — but not without some kind of parting shot. Some of these encounters have been described earlier in the book. On June 2, 1942, Don Quinn gave the listener a twist. This time it was a double dose for the mayor. He had dropped by and refused to leave when he found out the McGees were having pot roast. He paid a price. When he told them he went by the old aphorism, "A stitch in time saves nine," McGee wanted to know "nine *what?*"

"Nine *anything,*" says the mayor, unaccountably unsuspecting of the inevitable exchange.

Molly weighs in: "Now listen if you *tore* something, Mr. Mayor, I'll get a needle and thread and fix it for you."

"No, no," the mayor explains; "it's just an old expression: 'a stitch in time saves nine.'"

"That's pretty silly," says McGee. "How can you take a stitch in time? They making clocks out of cotton or something?"

The beleaguered mayor continues: "I was merely quoting an old saw, McGee."

"*Oh,*" says Molly, "If you tore something on a saw, Mr. Mayor, it must be pretty bad. Turn around so I can see."

"I *didn't* tear anything," says the Mayor, his exasperation growing.

McGee is exasperated as well: "Then whatcha come bustin' in here for yelling for a needle and thread?"

"I *didn't* start yelling for a needle and thread," says the mayor, his voice rising.

"*I* never yell," responds Molly defensively. "It isn't ladylike, and besides. . ."

"I didn't say you *did* yell, Mrs. McGee, I merely said . . ."

"Stop arguin' with my wife!" McGee shouts.

"Now look here, McGee," the mayor begins, but he stops. "My," he says appreciatively, "something smells good."

It's the pot roast he smells, of course, and the McGees effort to drive the mayor out in a rage has failed. He stays.

When the Old-Timer then drops in, he reigns as king of confusion. He doesn't recognize the mayor. McGee tries to introduce them.

MCGEE: You know Mayor LaTrivia, Old-Timer?

OLD-TIMER: "Don't care if I do! Pleased to meet you, Sonny. Stranger in town?"

LATRIVIA: Not exactly.

MOLLY: He's the mayor, Mr. Old-Timer.

OLD TIMER: That so? 'Bout time we had a new mayor. Got an awful mess in the City Hall now. Name's LaTrivia.

LATRIVIA: *I* am LaTrivia.

OLD-TIMER: That so? Any relation?

MCGEE: Look, Old-Timer, *this* is *that* LaTrivia. He's our mayor."

OLD-TIMER: Congratulations, Sonny. Get in there and pitch. Can't do any worse than that LaTrivia.

MOLLY: Please, Mr. Old-Timer, this gentleman is Mayor LaTrivia.

OLD-TIMER:	Can't be. LaTrivia ain't a gentleman. Hey, Sonny [addressing LaTrivia], you look like a fella I went to school with.
LATRIVIA:	You don't say. I was Princeton '27 — and you?
OLD-TIMER:	Lockheed, '42. Welding School. Where you workin'?
McGEE:	We just *told* you; he's the *mayor*!
OLD-TIMER:	Glad to hear it. Whatever became of LaTrivia?
LATRIVIA:	Nothing. I'm still here.
OLD-TIMER:	Don't change the subject, young fella. I was talkin' about LaTrivia.
MOLLY:	He *is* Mr. LaTrivia.
OLD-TIMER:	Same name as the mayor, huh?
FIBBER:	Doggone it, he *is* the mayor!
OLD-TIMER:	Is *that* so? Small world, ain't it? Hey, kids, sign this petition for me, will ya'?
MOLLY:	Certainly. Let me take that pencil, Mr. Mayor.
OLD-TIMER:	Sign at the bottom there, daughter [*His standard nickname for Molly*]. That's it. You, too, Johnnie [*His standard nickname for McGee*]. And you, Sonny (*addressing LaTrivia*); what was the name?
LATRIVIA:	(*in his most sonorous voice*) LaTrivia.
OLD-TIMER:	Name's familiar. We met before some place?

MOLLY: You just met him here two minutes ago!

OLD-TIMER: *I did?* (*chuckles*) Time sure drags, don't it?

McGEE: You don't know the half of it. It's been so long
           since I ate I think all my swallows have gone
           back to Capistrano [*he wants his pot roast*].

OLD-TIMER: That's pretty good, Johnny. But that ain't the
           way *I* heared it! Way I heared it . . . (pauses).
           Hey, did you sign this petition, Sonny?

LaTRIVIA: Yes, I did.

OLD-TIMER: Much obliged, kids. (*He starts to leave.*)

LaTRIVIA: Just a minute. That petition we just signed — I
           didn't read it very carefully.

OLD-TIMER: Oh, we're gonna impeach the mayor, Johnnie.
           Fella named LaTrivia.

LaTRIVIA: (*exploding*) But I am LaTrivia.

OLD-TIMER: Well now, don't worry about it. Common
           name. Met three fellas named LaTrivia in the
           last five minutes. So long, kids. Glad to have
           met you Mr. uh, Mr. uh . . ."

LaTRIVIA: (apoplectic) LaTrivia.

OLD-TIMER: Crimeny! *Another* one?! (*He leaves*).

What wonderful nonsense!

McGee versus Doc Gamble

Fibber McGee and Doc Gamble exchanged verbal insults on virtually every program. The audience knew they weren't serious and occasionally they put down their gloves long enough to demonstrate their mutual regard. The exchanges were priceless. Here's an example, also from the porch swing episode (June 13, 1944.)

McGee has several of the doctor's tools and Gamble arrives just as Fibber and Molly are discussing this.

"You ever hear the old saying, Doc, eavesdroppers never hear anything good about their selves?" McGee asks.

"Allowing for your lousy grammar, Smudge Pot," Doc Gamble answers, "yes I have. Anybody who would eavesdrop on your conversation would be stupid enough to look in the back of a telephone book to see how it came out.

Learning what McGee is up to, Gamble thinks it's a good thing: "Get a little of that tallow away from his belt buckle."

McGee responds brilliantly: "Look who's talking about a tallow tummy. You got a bay window that the Dionne Family [the famous Canadian quintuplets] could watch a parade from. You look like you had been ringed five times in a horseshoe game and put your shirt on over it."

"I'm the professional type, My Boy," Gamble responds, somewhat incongruously, "My occupation is sedentary."

McGee is irate: "Why don't you *hire* a sedentary, you cheapskate? 'Fraid she'd steal your nine cents' worth of postage stamps?"

Molly explains that the doctor didn't mean 'secretary,' "meaning that he sets down a lot."

Doc Gamble concurs: "Exactly."

"He couldn't sit down exactly anywhere if his life was at stake. He comes in on a wing and a chair [This was a takeoff on the popular World War II song, "Coming in on a Wing and a Prayer").

Gamble thinks that's "Not bad; not very good, either." Eventually, the doctor agrees to help hang the swing but not before being tricked into opening the famous Hall Closet.

McGee versus "Uppy" and "Carsty"

Some of the funniest lines *never* to come out of Fibber McGee's mouth were occasioned by visits from Abigail Uppington, and later Millicent Carstairs. The two were virtual twins. In McGee's opinion, they were over-rich, overweight, and over-ripe. In their *absence*, he often *expressed* these views to Molly. In their *presence*, one of them would offer a straight line such as, "My husband is very fond of antiques," *or* "Don't you feel that traveling is broadening?" Just before Fibber could deliver a response, and knowing what to expect, Molly would deliver a quick, stern warning: "*McGee!*"

What he *might* have said the listeners imagined. It never failed to draw a big laugh. Again, anticipation of the familiar worked very well.

A Final Word

On March 23, 1943, Harlow Wilcox made this statement:

> It's a strange and wonderful thing that in times of great national emergency some born national leader always arises to lead his people to victory. In England there's Churchill, in America there's Roosevelt, in Russia there's Stalin, in China there's Chiang Kai-shek, and in Wistful Vista during the Red Cross Drive, there's — well, wouldn't you just know it — *Fibber McGee!*

Well, Harlow, you left out some important names: In England there was Clementine Hazier (Churchill), in America there was Eleanor Roosevelt, in China there was Soong Mei-Ling (Chang), in Russia there was Ekaterina Svanidze (Stalin). In Wistful Vista, there was, of course, Molly Driscoll.

Each of these famous couples contributed mightily to the Allied Victory but, indisputably, Fibber McGee and Molly won World War II.

REFERENCES AND BIBLIOGRAPHY

(Note: Some data are missing from the references that follow because of the quality of the only copies available)

ANON.1. "Fibber McGee Tells His Life Story," Periodical, Source Unknown.

ANON.2. "Johnson's Wax Headliner in Radio Awards," *Advertising Age.* December 6, 1937.

ANON.3. "Words At War for Wax," *Newsweek*, July 31 (Year Unknown).

ANON.4. "Radio Jury is Johnson's Index to Fans' Tast," Author, date, source unknown.

ANON.5. "Parents by Proxy," *Movie-Radio Guide*, December 12, 1940.

CJR. Charles J. Rolo, *Radio Goes to War*, Faber and Faber, London, 1952.

CS. Charles Schaden, *Speaking of Radio*, Nostalgia Digest Press, Morton Grove, IL, 2003.

CS.2. Clair Schulz, *Fibber McGee and Molly On The Air, 1935-1959*, BearManor Media, Albany, GA, 2008.

CS.3. Charles Slocum, "Fibber McGee and Molly," Source unknown.

CS.4.   Charles Siepman, *Radio in Wartime*, Oxford University Press, New York, 1942.

D.   John Dunning, *Two O'Clock Eastern War Time*, Scribner, New York, 2001.

EPS.   Erik Bernouw, *The Sponsor*, Oxford University Press, Oxford, 1978.

EWB.   Erik Bernouw, *The Golden Web*, Oxford University Press, Oxford, 1968.

FB.   Frank Buxton and Bill Owen, *The Big Broadcast*, Viking Press, 1972, New York.

FB.1.   Frank Bresee and Bob Lynes, *Radio's Golden Years.* Privately published, Hollywood, 1998.

FM.   Fibber McGee, "The Big War and Me," *The American Legion Magazine*, Vol. 40, No. 11, November 1946.

GE.   Gerald Eskanazi, "I Hid Under the Sheets," University of Missouri Press, Columbia, 2005.

GH.   Gerd Horten, *Radio Goes to War*, University of California Press, San Francisco, 2002.

GN.   Gerald Nachman, *Raised on Radio*, Pantheon Press, New York, 1998.

HB.   Howard Blue, *Words At War*, Scarecrow Press, Lanham, MD, 2002.

HJ.   Jim Harmon, *The Great Radio Comedians,* Doubleday, New York, 1970.

IS.   Irving Settle, *A Pictorial History of Radio*, Citadel Press, 1960.

JD.   John Dunning, *On the Air: The Encyclopedia of Old-Time Radio*, Oxford University Press, Oxford, 1998.

JD.1.   John Dunning, *Tune In Yesterday*, Prentice Hall, Englewood Cliffs, NJ, 1976.

JDF.   Jerry Della Femina, *From Those Wonderful Folks Who Gave You Pearl Harbor*, Simon and Schuster, New York, 1970.

JGDS.   Jack Gaven, *There's Laughter In the Air*, Greenberg Publishers, New York, 1945.

JH.   Julian Hale, *Radio Power*, Temple University Press, Philadelphia, 1975.

JJJ.   Jim Jordan, Jr., "My Mom and Dad," Periodical, source unknown.

JY.   Jordan R. Young, *The Laugh Crafters*, Past Times Publishing, Beverly Hills, CA, 1995.

K.   Christopher Sterling and John Kitross, *Stay Tuned*, Wadsworth Publishing, Belmont, CA, 1978.

KH.   Edward M. Kerby and Jack W. Harris, *Star-Spangled Radio*, Ziff-Davis Publishing, Chicago, 1944.

LCS.   Lawrence C. Soley, *Radio Warfare*, Praeger, New York, 1989.

LM.   Leonard Maltin, *The Great American Broadcast*, Penguin Books, New York, 1997.

LT.   Lawrence W. Lichty and Malach, Topping, *American Broadcasting*, Hastings House, New York, 1975.

LW.   Larry Walters, "Fibber and Molly: All American Team," *Advertising and Selling*, May 1945.

MD.   Marvin Dickman, "Franklin D. and Molly," *Nostalgia Digest*, Book 34, Chapter 3; summer 2008.

MH.   Michelle Himes, *Radio Voice*, Temple University Press, Philadelphia, 1997.

MD.1. J. Fred MacDonald, *Don't Touch That Dial*, Nelson-Hall, Chicago, 1979.

MH.   Michele Himes, *Radio Voices*, Temple University Press, Philadelphia, 1997.

MS.   Mickey Smith, *Pharmacy and Medicine On The Air*, Scarecrow Press, Metuchen, NJ, 1986.

NM.   Ned Wedgeley, *The Advertising and Business Side of Radio*, Prentice-Hall, New York, 1948.

PT.   Tom Price, *Fibber McGee's Closet*, Privately published, 1987.

RF.   Ross Firestone, *The Big Radio Comedy Program*, Contemporary Books, Chicago, 1974.

RL.   Ron Lackman. *Remember Radio*, Putnam and Sons, New York, 1970.

RMY.   Robert M. Yoder, "The McGees of Wistful Vista, *Saturday Evening Post*, April 9 and 16, 1949.

RS.   Raymond Swing, *In the Name of Sanity*, Harper, New York, 1946.

RS2.   Robert E. Summers, *America's Weapons of Psychological Warfare*, H.W. Wilson Co., New York, 1951.

SHD. Sherman H. Dreyer, *Radio in Wartime*, Greenberg Publisher, New York, 1942.

SJD. Susan J. Douglas, *Listening In*, Times Books, New York, 1999.

SK. Steve Kremer and Mickey Smith, "Fibber McGee and Kremer's Drugstore," *Pharmacy in History*, Vol. 50, #3, 2008.

SLP. Susan L. Peters, "Fibber, Molly and My Pop," *Mature Years*, Fall 1990.

SO. Charles Stumpf and Ben Ohmart, *The Great Gildersleeve*, BearManor Media, Albany, Georgia, 2002.

SP. Charles Stumpf and Tom Price, *Heavenly Days! The World of Yesterday*, Waynesville, NC, 1987.

ST. Studs Terkel. *The Good War*, Pantheon, New York, 1984.

VT. Vincent Terrace, *Radio's Golden* Years, Barnes Publishing, San Diego, 1981.

WM. William Manchester, *The Glory and the Dream*, Little Brown and Company, Boston, 1973.

Index

It would be a foolish waste of the reader's time to list here every appearance of the stars, writers, and sponsor within the preceding pages. I have, therefore, tried to guide the reader mostly by topics.

LaVergne, TN USA
04 May 2010
181466LV00004B/32/P